About Pfeiffer

Pfeiffer serves the professional development and hands-on resource needs of training and human resource practitioners and gives them products to do their jobs better. We deliver proven ideas and solutions from experts in HR development and HR management, and we offer effective and customizable tools to improve workplace performance. From novice to seasoned professional, Pfeiffer is the source you can trust to make yourself and your organization more successful.

Essential Knowledge Pfeiffer produces insightful, practical, and comprehensive materials on topics that matter the most to training and HR professionals. Our Essential Knowledge resources translate the expertise of seasoned professionals into practical, how-to guidance on critical workplace issues and problems. These resources are supported by case studies, worksheets, and job aids and are frequently supplemented with CD-ROMs, websites, and other means of making the content easier to read, understand, and use.

Essential Tools Pfeiffer's Essential Tools resources save time and expense by offering proven, ready-to-use materials—including exercises, activities, games, instruments, and assessments—for use during a training or team-learning event. These resources are frequently offered in looseleaf or CD-ROM format to facilitate copying and customization of the material.

Pfeiffer also recognizes the remarkable power of new technologies in expanding the reach and effectiveness of training. While e-hype has often created whizbang solutions in search of a problem, we are dedicated to bringing convenience and enhancements to proven training solutions. All our e-tools comply with rigorous functionality standards. The most appropriate technology wrapped around essential content yields the perfect solution for today's on-the-go trainers and human resource professionals.

D1605459

www.pfeiffer.com

Essential resources for training and HR professionals

To my daughters, Sarah and Laura, and my granddaughter, Chloe

101

Activities for Teaching Creativity and Problem Solving

Arthur VanGundy, Ph.D.

3/10

Pfeiffer

A Wiley Imprint

www.pfeiffer.com

Printed in the United States of America

ISBN: 0-7879-7402-1

Library of Congress Cataloging-in-Publication Data
VanGundy, Arthur B.
    101 activities for teaching creativity and problem solving / Arthur B. VanGundy.
        p. cm.
    Includes bibliographical references.
    ISBN 0-7879-7402-1 (alk. paper)
  1. Creative ability in business.   2. Creative ability—Study and teaching.   3. Creative thinking—Study and teaching.   4. Problem solving—Study and teaching.   5. Organizational effectiveness.   I. Title: One hundred one activities for teaching creativity and problem solving.   II. Title: One hundred and one activities for teaching creativity and problem solving.   III. Title.
    HD53.V357   2004
    658.3′1244—dc22   2004015676

Acquiring Editor: Martin Delahoussaye

Director of Development: Kathleen Dolan Davies

Editor: Rebecca Taff

Senior Production Editor: Dawn Kilgore

Manufacturing Supervisor: Bill Matherly

Printed in the United States of America

Printing   10 9 8 7 6 5 4 3 2

About This Book

Why is this topic important?

We live in a world of turbulent change. New data. New people. New technology. New problems. We are bombarded every day with something new. Realities shift faster than we can deal with them. In this turbulent world, traditional problem-solving methods no longer are effective in all situations. Routine, analytical approaches—the ideal of the Industrial Age—rarely work now. Instead, we must look for new ways to deal with change—creative solutions we can customize to fit any situation. Above all, we need new solution options, rather than relying on "the tried-and-true." The more solution options we have, the greater the odds that one will achieve our goals. Conventional brainstorming is not sufficient. Groups need exposure to diverse idea generation approaches and training in how to apply them.

What can you achieve with this book?

More organizations than ever now offer training in how to use idea generation methods. This should be a priority, since it obviously is more beneficial over time to train employees how to apply skills themselves, rather than a single spoon-feeding of the steps needed to implement one or more idea generation activities. It is better if employees also can learn how to use some of these methods and incorporate them into their problem-solving activities. Every training session that can teach employees how to apply even rudimentary skills obviously can be valuable in the long run. Thus, a unique aspect of this book is its duality in providing step-by-step guides to 101 idea generation methods while simultaneously providing participants with training in how to use them. As is fairly well known, practicing a new skill within a relevant domain can enhance significantly participant learning and applied behaviors. That is, the training is more likely to "take" if it uses challenges faced by the participants. As a result, many training sessions also can serve as idea generation events that deal with specific organizational challenges—the perfect "value-added" component!

How is this book organized?

This book is divided into three parts: (1) Getting Started, (2) Individual and Group Activities, and (3) Group Only Activities. The first section discusses the broad-reaching importance of idea generation, and the organization of idea generation activities (Chapter 1); major creative thinking principles (Chapter 2); and the general nature of problems, problem solving, creativity, and a guide for selecting activities appropriate for different situations (Chapter 3). Part II includes activities originally designed for individuals, but re-engineered for group use. Finally, Part III presents original group activities based on either brainstorming or "brainwriting" (silent, written idea generation within a group) procedures. The same format is used for each exercise. Major headings include: Background, Objectives, Participants, Materials, Supplies, and Equipment, Handouts, Time, Related Activities, Procedure, Debrief/Discussion, and Variations (if applicable). Because all of the activities are geared toward group idea generation, the Objectives and Participants sections will contain identical information. Many of the activities also will have identical information for Materials, Supplies, and Equipment, although there are exceptions.

Contents

Contents

Acknowledgments

I would like to thank the four Pfeiffer personnel who were instrumental to the development of this book. First, I would like to thank Laura Reizman for her help in working with all of the details involved in marketing this book, as well as other administrative tasks. Next, my gratitude to Kathleen Dolan Davies in handling all of the production aspects with great skill and, especially, patience. Special thanks go to Dawn Kilgore for once again helping with final production elements. Finally, I cannot thank and praise enough acquisitions editor Martin Delahoussaye. He played a pivotal role in working with me to "birth" this project during its initial conceptualization and then in working out the overall structure and format. All of these people, who work in a relatively high-stress business, were an absolute delight to work with. Thank you all.

Getting Started

Chapter 1

Creativity and Problem Solving

Creativity can solve almost any problem. The creative act, the defeat of habit by originality, overcomes everything.
    —George Lois

Before applying any of the activities presented in this book, it first is important to establish some context. This chapter provides an overview of the importance of idea generation methods, a typology of the different types of activities, and information for facilitators on how to use them

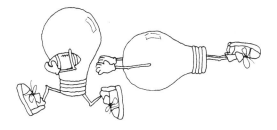

Rapidly changing environments with complex and diverse elements require flexible and innovative responses. Rigid operating systems are ineffective in such environments. Flexible systems, in contrast, are characterized by multiple solution possibilities. Creative solutions can provide flexibility by increasing our options and helping us cope and adapt. The more ideas we have, the more solution avenues will be at our disposal. New ideas can open up new worlds, new insights, and new ways of doing old things. Creativity, in short, can help us reinvent ourselves and our organizations.

Some management theorists advocate "reinventing the organization." To start over, organizations must test assumptions about their processes and procedures and devise new ways of doing things. In effect, there must be a "defeat of habit," as advertising executive George Lois notes in the quote at the beginning of this chapter. These new beginnings, however, require new ideas and new ways of looking at things—in effect, creative perspectives.

Why Use Creativity Techniques?

Organizations need creative perspectives and solutions to conceive new product, service, and process ideas, marketing strategies, and ways of allocating and using resources. *Creativity* is the magic word that can turn around an organization, company, division, or department.

Many organizations, such as 3M, Frito-Lay, and Texas Instruments, have introduced systematic creativity activities into their training and production processes with outstanding results. *Frito-Lay, for instance, reports documented cost savings over a four-year period of almost $600 million due to their creativity training programs* (Morrison, 1997). Although all may not achieve such spectacular outcomes, we can improve our current products, programs, services, and processes more dramatically than we ever imagined.

There is nothing mysterious about creativity; it's just a matter of applying the right attitude and technology in a climate receptive to creative thinking and new ideas. The technology of creativity techniques can multiply and magnify human brainpower in organizations.

Unfortunately, much of this brainpower typically is underused and underappreciated. We often take our most important and useful resources for granted. Whether because of familiarity or simply lack of awareness, we fail to harness creative minds. Or when we do use this brainpower, we lack the techniques to leverage the mind's full potential whether working alone or in groups.

Generating Creative Ideas

Many of us don't have the resources or abilities to generate the creative ideas we need. This is especially true in the business world with its complex, ever-changing environments. Competitive pressures require faster delivery of new products and services. In short, businesses are pushed to innovate before the competition does. Failure to do so can yield even fewer creative responses—and less financial profit. The need to innovate is not limited to the corporate world, however. Service, government, and nonprofit organizations also can experience similar pressures to cope with changes in markets served or the regulations imposed on them.

Organizations cannot count on internal "creatives" or customer input to solve all their problems; even traditional group idea generation has its weaknesses. *Brainstorming, as practiced in many organizations, is about as effective as consulting a crystal ball.* Even experienced brainstorming groups find that the well runs dry after interacting with the same people year after year.

Most individuals and groups in organizations occasionally need a brainpower boost to achieve "home run" or breakthrough ideas. And they need a number of methods in their idea toolkits. The more methods they can employ, the greater the odds of producing a hot idea. This need is where organizational training can help.

Creativity Training in Organizations

In recent years, organizations have turned to formal creativity initiatives to help fill their "idea pipelines." These pipelines are the conduits they use to maintain competitive advantage or achieve objectives through a constant infusion of new ideas. Many product-based organizations such as 3M and Procter & Gamble even try to generate an increasing proportion of their revenues through regular introduction of new products. Service and nonprofit or government organizations can do the same with their outputs, such as new ways to improve customer service or solicit donations. *Fresh ideas clearly are the engines that drive organizational innovation.*

There are a number of ways in which organizations can become idea generation fountains. Formal and informal in-house idea generation sessions probably are most common. Outside consultants often are brought in to facilitate planned, formal sessions. Or some organizations designate employees responsible for the generation and dissemination of new ideas. Other organizations use in-house idea generation most of the time, but periodically invite outside resources to help facilitate off-site brainstorming retreats. Of course, combinations of all of these also are possible.

Due to difficult financial environments, more organizations are looking to internal trainers to lead such sessions. *Once these trainers have received the appropriate training, they can deliver at least two services. The first is the design and facilitation of idea generation sessions for selected groups of employees.* These sessions can be scheduled several times a year or as needed. Thus, regular sessions might be held for issues of strategic importance—for instance, creating a new product line, service, or strategy to achieve a mission or vision statement. Similar sessions might be held whenever diverse input is needed for occasional tactical challenges.

The second service is training in how to use idea generation methods. Many of the activities in this book can be used without the assistance of a trained and skilled facilitator. The step-by-step presentations of the activities can be implemented by most groups with a little study and practice. Of course, *the ideal situation would be first to provide training in select activities, monitor and provide feedback when groups use them, and then encourage groups to apply them on their own,* remaining available for consultations as needed.

A Typology of Idea Generation Activities

Before looking at the activities, however, you might want to understand more about how they work. This knowledge should make them easier to use and easier to teach others to use, and also increase your understanding about creative thinking in general. If you don't want this information and want to begin using the activities, move on to Chapter 4 (or chapters following it).

It is important, however, to understand the distinction between individual and group activities. This is because the difference can be misleading with respect to which activities to use. In fact, for the purposes of this book, the distinction is an artificial one, based on how the activities originally were created. *Specifically, groups can use all of the individual activities, but individuals cannot use all of the group activities.*

This difference is because some of the group activities were designed originally with only groups in mind; others only for individuals. For instance, some activities involve passing idea cards or Post-it® Notes from one person to another. (You could try this as an individual, but you would probably feel a little silly!) Thus, activities that require interaction with other people must use other people. Some activities, in contrast, can be used by either individuals or groups. However, it is important to understand that *ALL of the 101 activities in this book can be used by groups and are presented for use by groups.*

Individual Activities

Individual activities can be classified in several ways. After reviewing the available activities, I settled on five (numbers for the individual activities are in brackets):

1. *Basic Idea Generation* (Chapter 4) require relatively little effort. An example would be asking a friend for an idea (Brain Borrow [2]).

2. *Related and Unrelated Stimuli* (Chapter 5) generate ideas by providing some sort of stimulus to play against. Such stimuli might be related directly to a problem or unrelated. Examples of related stimuli would be using the elements of a fund-raising campaign to solicit money for your nonprofit organization by using activities such as Bi-Wordal [22] or Combo Chatter [24]), both of which rely on words related to the problem. For the same problem, you also might play off of (free associate from) unrelated stimuli, such as unrelated pictures (for example, Picture Tickler [17]), words (PICLed Brains [16]), and objects (Tickler Things [21]), and see what ideas result.

3. *Combinations* (Chapter 6) blend or compare different problem elements and use the combinations and juxtapositions of elements to prompt ideas. Examples include Combo Chatter [24], Noun Action [28], and Parts Is Parts [30].

4. *Free Association Activities* (Chapter 7) rely on each previous idea triggering a subsequent idea to stimulate creative thinking. An example would be using the words "What if?" to help inspire ideas (What if. . . ? [49]). Or you might rely on exaggeration (Exaggerate That [39]) to help stretch thinking.

5. *Miscellaneous Activities* (Chapter 8) represent two types of activities: *backward* and *just alike only different*. Backward activities reverse some aspect of a problem to produce a different perspective and, it is hoped, new ideas. Thus, a group might reverse assumptions about a problem (Turn Around [52]) and use the reversals as stimulators. Just alike only different procedures use analogies to generate ideas. Two examples are Bionic Ideas [53] and Chain Alike [54].

Group Activities

One way to classify group activities is according to whether they are brainstorming or brainwriting methods. *Brainstorming, of course, refers to traditional verbal idea generation in a group. Brainwriting is a term coined in Germany that refers to the silent, written generation of ideas in a group setting.*

Brainstorming and Brainwriting

All things being equal, brainwriting groups generate more ideas than brainstorming groups. One reason is that when we interact verbally, we are often not as productive as we might otherwise be. We criticize ideas when we should not, we feel inhibited, we worry about what other people will think of our ideas, and we become sidetracked with various issues and hidden agendas. More important, research suggests that the superiority of brainwriting over brainstorming is due primarily to the fact that only one person can speak at a time in brainstorming groups (Diehl & Stroebe, 1991; VanGundy, 1993). Brainwriting groups, in contrast, may have four or five people generating ideas simultaneously.

If brainwriting yields more ideas than brainstorming, why even use brainstorming groups? The answer is that we are social creatures. Most of us would have trouble not talking for a long time. We clearly can satisfy more social needs in brainstorming groups. Moreover, some brainstorming activities provide a structure that offsets some disadvantages. Thus, *if a group follows a technique's procedures as written, it should be more successful than a traditional brainstorming group with no structure.*

To test these notions, I once conducted an experiment using six different types of idea generation procedures (VanGundy, 1993). Each procedure was tested using six categories of four-person groups:

- Groups using procedure 1 generated ideas without any formal instructions.
- Groups using procedure 2 generated ideas but were instructed to follow brainstorming rules and defer judgment (as were all subsequent groups).
- Groups using procedure 3 generated ideas using one brainstorming technique (PICLed Brains [16]).
- Groups using procedure 4 generated ideas using a brainwriting procedure in which the group members did not see one another's ideas.
- Groups using procedure 5 generated ideas using a brainwriting procedure in which the participants did see each other's ideas (Brain Purge [82]).
- Groups using procedure 6 generated ideas using combinations of brainstorming and brainwriting activities. In addition, each group using procedure 6 contained two skilled idea generation facilitators.

All the groups had 45 minutes to generate new snack food product ideas (which were evaluated later by a food products company). When ideas were counted, the groups using procedures 1 through 5 collectively generated about 1,400 ideas, and the groups using procedure 6 generated about 1,200 ideas. In fact, groups using procedure 6 generated more than ten times as many ideas as groups using procedure 1!

The results also suggested that *groups using procedure 5 (brainwriting while seeing one another's ideas) generated almost four times as many ideas as groups using brainstorming without instructions.* There clearly are advantages to both using brainstorming and brainwriting procedures (as well as using skilled facilitators).

Related Versus Unrelated Stimuli

Another way to classify group activities is according to whether the stimuli used are related or unrelated to the problem. An example of a related stimulus would be using different parts of a coffee mug to suggest ways to improve it. Most combination activities are based on this principle. Thus, you might combine the handle with the base to spark an idea. In this case, you might think of an integrated handle and base cup warmer. You could attach different cups and the coffee would keep warm even while the cup is in your hand.

An example of unrelated stimuli would be using different parts of a coffee mug to suggest ways to improve a product such as a flashlight or to improve customer service. For instance, the heat of a coffee mug might suggest adding a heated function to a flashlight to serve as a handwarmer, and a mug holding a liquid might prompt the idea of a flashlight with a small tube of water for emergencies. Or a coffee mug might suggest the idea of rewarding loyal customers with designer coffee mugs or to develop a customer service focus on "holding" onto "hot" customers by identifying them and devoting resources to retaining them. In general, unrelated stimuli are more likely to produce novel ideas than stimuli related to the problem.

Organization of Group Activities in This Book

The group approaches in this book have been organized according to whether they primarily use brainstorming or brainwriting and whether they use related or unrelated stimuli. One chapter is devoted to each combination below:

- Brainstorming with Related Stimuli (Chapter 9)
- Brainstorming with Unrelated Stimuli (Chapter 10)
- Brainwriting with Related Stimuli (Chapter 11)
- Brainwriting with Unrelated Stimuli (Chapter 12)

The different combinations possible are shown below:

	Stimuli	
Brainstorming	Related	Unrelated
Brainwriting	Related	Unrelated

This organization of the activities is more a matter of convenience than anything else. However, a few guidelines may help you decide which ones to use:

- Use brainwriting activities (Chapters 11 and 12) if: (1) there are conflicts or major status differences among members of a group or (2) there is relatively little time, group members are inexperienced at brainstorming, and no experienced facilitator is available.
- All things being equal, use both brainstorming and brainwriting activities to offset the weaknesses of each.
- If you want to generate unique ideas and the group is relatively inexperienced, use activities with unrelated stimuli (Chapters 10 and 12).
- When selecting group activities, remember that any of the individual activities also will be appropriate for groups.

Facilitator Guidelines for Working with Group Activities

Before learning about group activities, you need to know a little about how to work with groups to generate ideas. Here are some points to keep in mind:

- *Use groups of about five people.* Research has consistently shown that this is the optimal size for problem-solving groups. Four will often work well in trained groups or groups with a skilled facilitator. In a pinch, groups of six or seven will work under the same conditions.
- *Make sure all groups understand the basic ground rule of deferring judgment.* Try to create a fun environment. Encourage playfulness and humor. Research shows that groups

characterized by laughter and humor tend to generate more ideas than their less humorous and playful counterparts.

- *Use as many activities as you can in the time available.* Different activities can spark different ideas depending on the personalities and experiences of the group members. What works in one group may fizzle in another. I can still remember a group member telling me that a certain technique wasn't any good and that I should stop using it. Later that day, a member of another group remarked to me that the same technique was one of the best he ever had used. Go figure.

- Above all, when using the activities or facilitating ideation sessions, always instruct participants to follow one basic rule:

DEFER ALL JUDGMENT WHEN GENERATING IDEAS.

This rule is essential for generating ideas and you should encourage them to reinforce this rule as they interact with each other. Emphasize that the more ideas they list, the greater the odds that one will resolve their problem. They won't produce many ideas if they spend time criticizing and evaluating them. They should save evaluation for later, after they have listed all the ideas they can. You even might have participants repeat the following phrase aloud five times in a row:

No evaluation with generation!

No evaluation with generation!

No evaluation with generation!

No evaluation with generation!

NO EVALUATION WITH GENERATION!

Chapter 2

Six Key Principles for Encouraging Creativity

When in doubt, make a fool of yourself. There is a microscopically thin line between being brilliantly creative and acting like the most gigantic idiot on earth. So what the hell, leap.
   —Cynthia Heimel, writer and columnist

The activities in this book will help generate lots of ideas. There's no question about that. Idea generation methods can't do it all, however. They are just tools to help express our innate creative potential. To produce a lot of hot ideas, you need the proper frame of mind and a variety of stimuli to energize your creative brainpower. You can use this chapter for background information for yourself or trainees or you can just skip ahead to Chapter 4 if you're ready to generate ideas or provide training on how to do so.

To use and maintain this frame of mind, you need to understand a few basic creative thinking principles. These principles make up the attitudinal and psychological foundation of all idea generation approaches. You will understand your problems better if you can think more creatively, and you will generate higher-quality ideas when you apply the principles of creative thinking. However, really good creative thinking is neither simple nor easy. Therefore, the more you know about thinking creatively, the easier it will be.

Our minds are reservoirs of ideas. What we know is the sum total of all we have experienced and learned. The ideas are in there; all we have to do is get them out. However, we'll never tap all the ideas inside without the proper mental attitude and approach. There's no way we can recall everything. Moreover, we'll never think of certain ideas unless we rely on different sources of stimulation. *Our minds are free association tools as much as they are databases of ideas.*

Fortunately, we don't have to recall everything to think creatively. All we have to do is combine our innate creativity with stimulation sources and creative thinking principles. Our knowledge and experience then will help generate the associations that lead to ideas.

In this chapter we look at a few major principles of creative thinking. If you apply them when problem solving, there is no guarantee that workable solutions will result. You will, however, increase the odds that you'll be able to think of more and higher-quality ideas.

11

We will look at six major creative thinking principles in this chapter:

1. Separate idea generation from evaluation.
2. Test assumptions.
3. Avoid patterned thinking.
4. Create new perspectives.
5. Minimize negative thinking.
6. Take prudent risks.

1. Separate Idea Generation from Evaluation

If you don't remember anything else, remember this: *when you generate ideas, separate generation from evaluation. This is the most important creative thinking principle.* You'll never achieve your full creative potential until you apply this principle every time you generate ideas. The reason is simple: creative problem solving requires both divergent and convergent thinking. Idea generation is divergent; you want to get as many ideas as possible. Idea evaluation is convergent—you want to narrow down the pool of ideas and select the best ones. If you try to do both activities at once, you won't do either one well.

Effective problem solvers have learned to separate these two activities; that is, first they generate ideas and then they evaluate them. Most "average" problem solvers use a sequential approach instead: generate-evaluate–generate-evaluate-generate, and so forth. These problem solvers commingle generation and evaluation. They rarely move on to think about another idea until they have analyzed the previous idea in all possible ways. The result is a limited number of overanalyzed ideas.

For many people, such mixing may seem natural. They may use this method frequently because it is what they have always done. There is one thing wrong with this system, however: it is the worst way to generate ideas! Commingling generation and evaluation usually yields few ideas. It also creates a negative climate not conducive to creative thinking.

Before beginning any idea generation session—whether alone or in a group—remember that *the best way to get ideas is to defer judgment.* Save the analysis and critical thinking for later, after all possible ideas have been generated. Then and only then will it be time to evaluate the ideas.

2. Test Assumptions

Testing assumptions is probably the second most important creative thinking principle, because it is the basis for all creative perceptions. We see only what we think we see. Whenever we look at something, we make assumptions about reality. Optical illusions, one form of creative perception, depend on this phenomenon.

Most psychology students, for instance, are familiar with the picture that combines an old woman and a young woman (see Figure 2.1). Which of the two women we see depends on how we look at the picture. How we look at the picture depends on the assumptions we make

Figure 2.1 Wife and Mother-in-Law.

about the stimulus elements in the picture (that is, the lines and their relationship to one another). If we assume one configuration of lines, we see the old woman; if we assume another configuration, we see the young woman.

This picture was brought to the attention of psychologists by Edwin G. Boring in 1930. Created by cartoonist W.E. Hill, it originally was published in *Puck,* November 6, 1915, as "My Wife and My Mother-in-Law." It is a classic.

In one sense, optical illusions cause us to see one thing when something else may also be present. In a similar manner, people often have different responses when confronted with the same stimulus. One person may look at a flower and feel happy because it reminds them of a loving relationship; someone else, however, may look at the same flower and feel sad because it reminds them of the recent death of a loved one. Both people in this example perceive the flower, but they also "see" the qualities of either happiness or sadness. To know why we see these qualities, we must test assumptions.

The same principle holds true when using idea generation activities. They present stimuli that elicit certain responses. Our particular response will depend on the assumptions we make about a particular stimulus. *The more stimuli we use, the greater the potential idea pool.* When these stimuli and different individual reactions are used in a group, the potential quantity and quality of ideas is increased. More stimuli and more people yield more assumptions, which in turn yield more ideas. More ideas give us more options and more chances to resolve our problems.

Everyday Assumptions

We can't be effective problem solvers unless we know how to test assumptions. Unfortunately, most of us aren't very good at this. Every day we act before thinking through what we are doing or the possible consequences. In fact, we make so many daily decisions that it is impossible to test all the potential assumptions.

For instance, the simple act of talking with someone else involves many assumptions. We must assume that the other person actually heard what we said and understood us, that the person's nonverbal reactions indicate what we think they indicate, and that we can figure out any hidden meanings or purposes.

Breakthrough Solutions

Another reason testing assumptions is important is that it can yield perceptual breakthroughs. Testing assumptions can help us shift perspectives and view problems in a new light. As the philosopher Marcel Proust once said, "The real voyage of discovery consists not in seeking new lands, but in seeking with new eyes." The result often is a breakthrough solution or, at the least, a new problem definition. There is an old joke that illustrates this point nicely:

Two men were camping in the wilderness when they were awakened one morning by a large bear rummaging through their food supply. The bear noticed the men and started lumbering toward them.

The men still were in their sleeping bags and didn't have time to put on their boots, so they picked up their boots and began running away from the bear. The terrain was very rough, however, and they couldn't make much progress. The bear was gaining on them.

Suddenly, one of the men sat down and began pulling on his boots. His friend couldn't believe what he was seeing and said, "Are you nuts? Can't you see that the bear is almost here? Let's go!"

The man on the ground continued putting on his boots. As he did this, he looked up at the other man and said, "Well, Charlie, the way I look at it, I don't have to outrun the bear—I only have to outrun you!"

And so, another problem is resolved by testing assumptions. In this case, both men originally assumed the problem was how to outrun the bear. When one of the men tested this assumption, a creative solution popped out. This single act provided that man with one critical extra option. His spontaneous creative thinking enabled him to gain an edge over his "competitor."

How to Test Assumptions

In most organizations, this may all sound familiar. Sometimes all it takes is one extra option to give us an edge over our competitors or to resolve a difficult-to-solve problem. In addition to using the activities in this book, you can get that competitive edge or solve that problem by testing problem assumptions. Of course, you can't test assumptions about every problem. You can test assumptions, however, about problems of strategic importance or problems with potentially serious consequences. The lesson, then, is: be selective.

So how do you test assumptions? Albert Einstein provides one answer: "The important thing is to never stop questioning." *Ask a lot of questions about whatever problem you're trying to resolve. The more questions you ask, the better you will understand your problems.*

One way to enhance the questioning process is to use the basic journalism "five w" questions of who, what, where, when, and why. These questions can help us seek data more efficiently. For instance, you might ask the following questions: Who is the competition? Who are the customers? What does our organization do? What is our mission? Where can we make improvements? Where can we get data about our competition? When should we enter a new market? When are our customers most likely to buy our products? Why do people buy our products? Why do we want to enter a new market?

Ask lots of questions and you'll understand your organization and its environment better. If you have a better understanding, you'll get more creative insights on how to improve it. It's as simple as that.

3. Avoid Patterned Thinking

Try this little exercise: Fold your arms the way you normally would cross them. Note which hands are on top of your arms. For instance, my left arm lies under my right hand. Now quickly reverse this position (in my case, my right arm should lie under my left hand). You'll probably notice that the second position is more difficult. It's not "natural."

Here's another, similar exercise: Interlock your fingers in the way most comfortable for you. Either your right or left index finger should be on top. Reverse your fingers so the opposite finger is on top. Not so easy, is it? We all have certain patterns of behaving and thinking which impede our creative thinking.

Habit-Bound Thinking

What you just experienced is habit-bound behavior. We all have a comfortable, secure way of doing things, and there's nothing wrong with that. A little security can't hurt. A problem occurs, however, whenever we try to break out of a rut. *The very thought of doing something different can be terrifying. Yet, creative thinking frequently requires we do just that.* As Charles Kettering, inventor of the electric automobile starter, once noted, "We'll never get the view from the bottom of a rut."

Try these activities with yourself or others to illustrate habit-bound thinking: First, repeat the word "joke" three times. Now, quickly, what is the white of an egg called?

Here's another: What word is formed by adding one letter to the following? _ANY. Very good! Now, what word is formed by adding one letter to the following? _ENY.

Most people who respond to the first exercise say "yolk." Of course, this is incorrect. By repeating the word "joke," we establish a pattern involving the "oak" sound. To solve the problem, however, we have to break away from the pattern and focus on the correct answer: albumen.

The most common response to the first word in the second exercise is the word "many" (a few independent thinkers may say "zany" and mess up the demonstration). The "many" response then establishes a pattern with the sound of just one word and makes it more difficult to think of the second word, "deny."

Breaking Out of a Rut

All these activities illustrate how difficult it can be to do something differently. We become so accustomed to doing things a certain way that we may lose the ability to break away.

So what can we do? Perhaps the most important thing is to increase our awareness of how everyone is a victim of patterned thinking. Once we do this, we'll be more aware of when we are caught in a rut. Beyond simple awareness, however, we also can break away with some practice.

Familiarity is the handmaiden of habit. We sometimes become so familiar with things that we aren't even aware of it. For instance, try to draw the face of your watch in detail without looking at it. (Many people add numbers that don't even exist.) Or the next time you drive to work, notice something you've never seen before. After a few mornings of this activity, you'll be surprised at all you see. To break out of patterns, we must make a conscious effort. First become more aware of your habit-bound thinking; then deliberately practice changing it.

4. Create New Perspectives

> *When I have arranged a bouquet for the purpose of painting it, I always turn to the side I did not plan.*
> —*Pierre Auguste Renoir*

When the impressionist painter Renoir made this statement, he suggested the importance of developing creative perspectives. It could be argued that *there can be no creative product without a creative perspective.* To produce something new, we must see something new. What we see may be some previously overlooked element of a problem or a solution from combining two previously unjoined problem elements or ideas.

Two Insightful Thinkers

Perhaps the most well-known historical example of a sudden insight involves Archimedes, who jumped out of his bathtub and ran naked through the streets, shouting, "Eureka! Eureka!" This rather odd behavior followed his discovery of the principle of displacement. While taking a bath, he noticed how his body weight displaced an equal amount of water. This led him to an insight, or new perspective on how to determine whether a crown was solid gold.

A more contemporary example is Art Fry, inventor of Post-it® Notes. He combined his need for a piece of paper that would stay put when he marked his church hymns with a scrap of paper that used a "failed" glue developed by Spencer Silver, one of his colleagues at 3M. Both Archimedes and Art Fry produced a more creative perspective when they combined two previously unconnected problem elements.

Keeping Sight of the Big Picture

Not everyone can make creative connections easily. We sometimes get so close to a problem that we lose ourselves in it—something like the old expression, "We can't see the forest for the trees." In one respect, becoming deeply involved with a problem automatically increases our understanding of it. This is good. We must understand problems to deal with them.

Too much understanding, however, can be harmful because it causes us to narrow our focus and lose a broader perspective. This is bad. *Too much detailed problem awareness causes us to lose sight of the big picture. The solution: create new perspectives.*

Each activity in this book will help you produce new perspectives and see problems with new eyes. Idea generation activities do this by facilitating free association, combining problem elements, promoting interaction with other people, or eliciting responses to various stimuli. In each case, the outcome is the same: new ways of thinking about a problem. Over time, most people find that the more they use a variety of activities, the easier it becomes to create new perspectives.

5. Minimize Negative Thinking

Unless you are an exceptional person, you are a natural critic. From an early age we have learned to analyze and criticize anything new. Now that we are adults, being critical is second nature. We are experts at it.

What is your typical first reaction when someone proposes a new idea? Do you usually say something like "That's fantastic," "That's a great idea," or "That's really interesting"? Probably not.

Although there may be a few exceptions, *most of us come preprogrammed with the "automatic no" response.* Through training and conditioning in school and at home, we have learned to criticize first and think later. It's almost as if we have learned that it is better to reject something new outright than even to consider its potential value as a solution.

An Exercise in Negative Thinking
To illustrate this automatic no tendency, here's a little exercise to do by yourself or use with a group: Take five minutes and write down every negative response you can think of to a new idea. When finished, compare your list with the following one. Chances are there are a lot of similarities, if not direct duplications.

- Our problem is different.
- We tried that once before.
- We don't have enough time.
- We don't have enough help.
- Our system is too small for this.
- We've always done it this way.
- Our present method is time-tested and reliable.
- It's impractical.
- It's ahead of its time.
- It's behind the times.
- We're not ready for it yet.
- We've had too much of this lately.
- We can't teach an old dog new tricks.
- Our young, progressive group doesn't need it.
- It will require a heavy investment.
- It will never pay for itself.
- If no investment is required, how do we expect it to work?
- It's too radical.
- It's almost the same as what we're doing now.
- It looks good on paper, but it won't work.

- It violates professional standards.
- The board won't like it.
- It's outside my scope of responsibility.
- It conflicts with policy.
- The present method is working. Why rock the boat?

You probably could think of many more examples with very little effort. Now, what would happen if you tried to make a list of positive responses? Try it. Take five minutes and write down every positive response you can think of to a new idea. Most likely, this second list will be shorter than the first. It's much more difficult to think of positive responses.

Develop Balanced Responses

To break out of the negative thinking groove, try to develop more balanced responses to new ideas. There are a number of ways to do this. Here are three:

1. *Try viewing ideas as raw material;* that is, initial ideas are the fragile creatures we often transform into more workable solutions. So be gentle. Support and cradle all new ideas—they frequently can be modified or can help stimulate improved versions.

2. *Every time you hear a new idea, train yourself to think or say, "What's good about it?* What is at least one positive feature of that idea?" If you can think of one positive aspect, then you will benefit from what may initially have appeared useless. Moreover, the positive feature may stimulate a better idea.

3. *Use a balanced response to evaluating new ideas.* Say (or think) what you like about the idea, what you find interesting about it, and then what you dislike. This might help prevent the negative climate in individuals and groups that often accompanies responses to ideas.

6. Take Prudent Risks

A failure is an opportunity to start over again, but more intelligently.
   —Henry Ford

You can't be a creative thinker unless you are a failure. No one ever truly succeeds without failing first. For instance, novelist John Creasey supposedly got 743 rejection slips before he published 562 books. Sports fans know that Babe Ruth struck out 1,330 times—a pretty poor record. Fortunately, he also hit 714 home runs. And R.H. Macy failed seven times before his New York store caught on.

Creative thinking involves a certain amount of risk taking. Many people fear risks, however, because risks can lead to failure. And who wants to be branded a failure? Yet *we must take risks to have any chance to succeed.* An old quotation describes this philosophy perfectly:

To laugh is to risk appearing the fool.

To place our ideas, our dreams, before a crowd is to risk their loss.

To live is to risk dying.

To hope is to risk despair. To try is to risk failure.

The person who risks nothing, does nothing, has nothing, and is nothing.

Only a person who risks is free.

    —Anonymous

Not all risks are equal. Some risks are more serious than others. For instance, the potential risks of idea generation are much less serious than the risks of implementation. Every time we think of or suggest an idea, we take a risk. Because we can't survive without new ideas, we must constantly take such risks.

The likely negative consequences of suggesting a "stupid" idea, however, pale in comparison with the risks of implementing an idea. Introducing a product, process, or service that later fails will cost an organization much more than any embarrassment someone might experience from suggesting a so-called stupid idea. Lose face and the organization goes on to play another day; lose too much market share or customer base and the game soon may be over.

Viewed this way, risk taking isn't so bad. Because idea generation activities involve risks of generation and not implementation, be willing to suggest whatever ideas pop up. Remember, ideas are the raw material of solutions and not the final product. Initial ideas have the potential to spark more practical solutions. They don't all have to be winners. Adopt this philosophy and you'll remove a lot of pressure when generating ideas.

A Summary of Creativity Principles

1. Separate idea generation from evaluation.
2. Test assumptions.
3. Avoid patterned thinking.
4. Create new perspectives.
5. Minimize negative thinking
6. Take prudent risks.

A Training Exercise Opportunity

If time is available, you may want to present and discuss these principles with training participants. After describing each, ask small groups to brainstorm examples of each principle and how to overcome any obstacles that might be involved. For instance, suppose a group has discussed an example of how assumptions were or were not tested to avoid an error. If they don't suggest it, you might offer the importance of asking a lot of questions to uncover assumptions, with a special emphasis on the "Why" question. That is, asking "Why?" can force people to think of something they otherwise might have overlooked.

Chapter 3

Linking Problems, Solutions, and Activities

Before generating ideas, it is important to understand more about problems. It is not essential, but the material that follows could provide better insight into the types of situations in which idea generation activities are applied. You also might want to use it for general problem-solving training or as background information for training in idea generation activities.

Defining Problems

There are a number of different perspectives on the definition and nature of problems, as well as different types of problems. Here is a brief overview of some of the classic ones.

Problems as Goals

One general definition describes a problem in terms of some difficult obstacle or goal. According to this definition, anything difficult to overcome is a problem. Although this definition is descriptive, it is not precise enough for most purposes. Most challenging situations present more than a goal to overcome and, instead, involve a series of processes to apply and evaluate.

Deviation from the Standard

Kepner and Tregoe's (1981) classic definition of a problem is "a deviation from an expected standard of performance." This definition is more descriptive for general use. If you need to determine the cause of a problem, then this is an excellent definition. Day-to-day idea generation, however, is not especially concerned with problem causes. Although determining causes may be important as part of the overall creative problem-solving process, such determinations are not useful for pure idea generation.

Kepner and Tregoe's definition is essentially convergent in that problem solvers attempt to converge on a cause by eliminating various alternative explanations. Idea generation, in contrast, is more divergent—problem solvers attempt to generate many different alternatives. In the case of idea generation, however, alternatives are solutions and not

21

explanations. Because the idea generation activities in this book are divergent, Kepner and Tregoe's definition doesn't fit.

A Gap Between the Real and the Ideal

MacCrimmon and Taylor (1976) propose another definition that is more appropriate for our purposes and has remained a standard over the years. *They define a problem as a gap between a current and a desired state of affairs—that is, a gap between where you are and where you would like to be.* An example might be when you are dissatisfied with the brand position of one of your products and wish the product were more competitive. If you perceive things that way, you have a problem. If you are unaware of your competitive position or there is nothing you can do about it, however, then perhaps you don't have a problem. The same would apply to any other type of organization as well. It's all relative.

Tackling the Challenge

Most problems also involve some uncertainty and present a challenge. They can be trouble, right here in River City. You want to do something about them, but you don't know exactly what.

The type of problem you face will determine how to resolve it. For instance, if your car runs out of gas, you have a problem. The solution in this case is relatively simple: put in more gas. Any other solution would be a waste of time (unless gas was not available). You don't need to spend a lot of energy and effort being creative unnecessarily.

Organizations continually are faced with similar challenges at all levels involving perceptions of gaps between current and desired situations. Upper management typically must provide leadership on how to move the organization to achieve its vision and negotiate relationships with external constituencies; middle management must continually help allocate desired resources efficiently and effectively (desired goals); and lower management must help employees understand why they are being asked to close gaps (that is, help other organizational members deal with their seemingly unending challenges).

However, as shown by the gasoline example, not all organizational challenges require creativity. There are and always will be routine procedures designed to tackle the majority of problems. *The secret is to know when you need to be creative and when to fall back on routine procedures.* To do this, it is important to figure out what type of problem or challenge faces you.

What Type of Problem Do You Have?

Most problems can be categorized according to how much structure they possess. For instance, if your problem is well-structured, you would have a clear idea of how to solve it. You would know your current state, the desired state, and how to close the gap. The previous problem, running out of gas, is clearly a well-structured problem. In a manufacturing organization, the work days lost to injuries would be another example IF you know how many days are lost for a time period, how many days should be lost (a realistic goal), and how to reduce that gap. *If you don't know with certainty how to reduce this gap, then the problem would be more "fuzzy" or ill-structured.*

Ill-structured problems provide relatively little guidance or structure on how to solve them. An example would be a problem of generating new product ideas. In this case, there are many possible options but no clear-cut way to proceed (that is, no way that will guarantee a new product home run). Or a nonprofit organization might have an ill-structured problem of how to recruit more volunteers.

The type of problem will determine the approach to use. In general, you should hope that all of your problems are well-structured. According to Nobel Prize winner Herbert Simon, *the goal of all problem solving is to make problems well-structured.* Such problems are the easiest to solve, because you can use a routine response. Fuzzy problems with less structure require creative responses. For these problems, you must devise custom-made responses that require more time and effort. This book provides activities to help with problems that aren't well-structured.

Problem Solving

If you accept a problem as a gap between a current and a desired state, then *problem solving can be defined as the process of making something into what you want it to be.* That is, when you solve a problem, you transform "what is" into "what should be." This means you have to figure out how to do something different. You have to change the status quo into another status. How you do this is the trick.

The more ideas you generate, the closer you will come to transforming an existing problem state into a desired one. For instance, suppose you currently possess a 12 percent market share of a product line and your objective is to capture a 15 percent share. If so, you will need options to reduce the 3 percent gap. Every idea you generate increases the overall probability of reducing this gap and achieving your goal. The more ideas you can spew out, the easier it will be to resolve your problem. Thus, the more activities you have at your disposal, the easier it will be to do problem solving.

Creativity and Serendipity

> *There is only one way in which a person acquires a new idea: by the combination or association of two or more ideas he already has into a new juxtaposition in such a manner as to discover a relationship among them of which he was not previously aware.*
>
> —Francis A. Cartier

Many people don't understand the importance of having a variety of activities in their "problem solving kits." It is true, as Francis Cartier notes, that new ideas result from combining previous ideas. However, the process involved in producing new insights is not so simple. *New ideas can be generated by combining ideas discovered by chance or by searching more systematically.*

Serendipitous Discoveries

There is nothing wrong with serendipity, of course. The world today would not be the same without it. The history of science, for example, is full of stories about how new ideas came about through chance. Take rooster sperm . . . please. It may seem odd, but rooster sperm illustrates the importance of the ability to recognize a creative idea when it presents itself. Rooster sperm has been responsible indirectly for providing sight to many people, but the creative "insight" involved might never have been discovered had it not been for a series of accidental happenings.

It all started in a laboratory outside London, England, right after World War II. Scientists were experimenting with fructose as a fowl sperm preservative. Their supply of fructose was kept in a cold room the scientists shared with another laboratory located about five miles away. One day, one of the scientists entered the supply room to retrieve a bottle of fructose, picked up a bottle without a label, and used the contents inside. Eureka! The contents of the bottle successfully preserved the sperm.

It turned out that the bottle with no label actually belonged to the other lab, and the bottle contained glycerin, not fructose. Thus, serendipity played a role in solving a scientific problem. But wait. There's more! The sequel to this story is that, years later, a scientist working on organ transplants remembered the rooster experiments and the preservative powers of glycerin. His problem involved preserving human corneas for transplantation. Glycerin provided just what he needed. As a result, more people can see, thanks to that bottle with the missing label.

Searching for Solutions

The fowl sperm story illustrates more than the need for patience to allow creative solutions to emerge. Patience is important, as is the need to capitalize on chance events. *A trained, knowledgeable mind is required to recognize when combinations of events or elements suggest something new.* However, today's fast-changing, environment doesn't provide the luxury of waiting for serendipity, even for the most skilled minds. Rather, organizations need a way to search systematically for solutions. That's where this book can help in training minds to think more creatively and to generate ideas as well.

If you and the people you train or work with become familiar with the activities in this book, you'll always have a powerful resource at your disposal. With the variety of activities described, you should never run out of ideas. And, most importantly, you should never have to rely on serendipity for all of your best ideas.

A Few of My Favorite Activities

It is difficult to say that any one technique is better than another. Each of us may respond differently to any given approach. What works well for you may fizzle for me. Your mood and any number of other factors may also influence your reaction. Obviously, the same holds true for any training participants.

I do, however, have my own particular favorites, which are presented in the following "Top Ten" lists. In many cases, it was almost impossible to choose among the various activities. This was especially true for the group activities. (Remember that all the individual methods can be used by groups but not all the group methods can be used by individuals.)

Although I've provided a brief rationale statement for each activity, it may not work for you or your particular training objective or problem challenge. Experience and the selection guide at the end of this chapter will be your best resources. The activities are presented in no particular order.

Top Ten Individual Activities

1. Combo Chatter [24] (Combines two related stimuli in a way that provokes ideas much as unrelated stimuli.)

2. Picture Tickler [17] (Uses unrelated pictures to generate ideas. Many people respond well to visual stimuli, especially stimuli unrelated to a problem.)

3. I Like It Like That [55] (Analogies have been used for years to resolve especially difficult problems, have been researched by academicians favorably, and help users create novel perspectives.)

4. What if. . . ? [49] (This simple "sentence trigger" helps push us to explore the limits of our imagined possibilities and reduces restrictions imposed by conventional assumptions.)

5. PICLed Brains [16] (Based on 476 words unrelated to a problem. The number and variety of stimuli seem to help trigger free associations naturally. So it will be especially useful for those who can free-associate easily but also for those who cannot.)

6. Turn Around [52] (One of my all-time favorites due to its ability to force us to consider even the most basic assumptions that may be blocking us and to use them to provoke ideas.)

7. Exaggerate That [39] (A cousin to Turn Around [52], this activity provides another way to easily surface unwarranted assumptions and transform them into ideas.)

8. Tickler Things [21] (This relative of Picture Tickler [17] and PICLed Brains [16] provides participants with unrelated, tangible objects they can touch, see, and use as idea triggers.)

9. Get Crazy [5] (The ideas we normally might label as "crazy"—such as the telephone originally was—often are the ones that force us to expand our perspectives and then look for something practical out of the initially absurd. The deliberate search for "crazy" ideas often can move us in new directions.)

10. Preppy Thoughts [32] (One great thing about this activity is that it helps spark visual thinking by placing random prepositions between a problem statement's verb and objective, thus providing a unique combination of multiple idea stimuli.)

Top Ten Group Activities

1. What's the Problem? [70] (When other activities fail in their ability to spark unique ideas, this activity can be a savior, although the setup for the stimuli involve a little more effort. Its most powerful feature is the ease with which it can eliminate preconceived notions and spark novelty.)

2. Drawing Room [59] (Three positive features are the use of unrelated stimuli, the number of stimuli, and the requirement for people to walk around a room and look at various drawings. Research shows that movement can facilitate creative thinking.)

3. The Name Game [97] (Although it is somewhat more complex and time-consuming than many activities, it's game-like format and focus on transforming supposedly improbable ideas into workable ones makes this exercise a potential winner.)

4. Brain Purge [82] (If you need a lot of ideas in a short time and can depend on the

Linking Problems, Solutions, and Activities

group members as your primary source of stimuli, this pure brainwriting activity is for you.)

5. Museum Madness [86] (This cousin of Drawing Room [59] shares some advantages—multiple stimuli and walking around—and differs primarily in that participants browse among the written ideas of others instead of their pictures of possible solutions.)

6. Brainsketching [94] (If you have little time but like the more time-consuming Drawing Room [59] activity, this is an excellent substitute. Ideas are generated using pictures drawn by the participants, but instead of people circulating among the drawings as done in [59], this activity works by circulating the pictures among group members only.)

7. Balloon, Balloon, Balloon [92] (Need an energizer and want to generate ideas at the same time? Then this activity is for you. It also encourages novelty by using unrelated stimuli. This activity exemplifies the "fun factor" that often is vital to novel thinking.)

8. Brain Splitter [73] (Requires a little more time than some activities, but attempts to synthesize both left- and right-brained types of ideas to produce workable solutions. It also involves some physical movement with the participants as well as creates a relatively fun environment.)

9. Grab Bag Forced Association [75] (A variation of Tickler Things [21], this activity is slightly more structured, introduces random selection of the stimuli, but provides the same benefits of relying on tangible, unrelated stimulus objects.)

10. Pass the Hat [63] (Provides an interesting and usually productive blend of stimuli from problem attributes as well as from the ideas of others. The use of "silly" hats to pass around the stimuli also introduces the "fun factor" for creative climates.)

A Guide for Selecting Activities

The activities in the Top Ten lists will help you get many ideas for a broad spectrum of challenges. However, you may want more help than these lists provide. For instance, you might have specific needs for new product ideas or for ways to handle various people problems. You might want an activity that doesn't require much time but has the potential to generate a fairly large number of ideas. Or you may want an activity that can help energize a session while generating ideas as well. To help, I've put together a technique selection guide to help you make more informed choices about different activities.

This guide reflects my subjective choices based on my knowledge of and experience in using the activities over twenty-five years. Once you experiment with different activities, you may want to develop your own guide, or at least make your own judgments about which ones work best for you and people you facilitate or train.

The activities in Chapters 4 through 12 are described in the selection guide in twelve different ways:

- *Individual vs. group*: Indicates if an activity originally was developed for use by either or if a group method originally designed for groups also can be used by individuals.

As noted previously, ALL of the individual activities can be used by groups, but not all of the group activities can be used by individuals. If all or most of your training or idea generation involves groups, then this distinction is not relevant. Any of the activities will suffice with respect to this distinction. However, the individual-only activities obviously can serve a training role in helping individuals learn how to apply the activities as individuals.

- *Brainstorming vs. brainwriting:* Classifies each activity as using verbal idea generation only, written only, or a combination of both. As discussed previously, brainstorming activities involve verbal idea generation while brainwriting involves the silent, written generation of ideas in a group. A few of the activities classified as both will appear within a chapter on either brainwriting or brainstorming. The classification, however, is based on the primary emphasis being on either brainwriting or brainstorming. For instance, Brainsketching [94] requires participants to draw pictures as individuals and then pass them around the group. The pictures then are used as stimuli for participants to use in brainstorming ideas.

  Some research suggests that brainwriting—regardless of the stimulus source—may outperform brainstorming. Thus, unrelated brainwriting activities have the highest theoretical potential to produce hot ideas. Note that the operative word is "theoretical." The best may represent all categories, depending on the user and the problem.

- *Top ten activity:* Indicates activities included in my top ten lists for individual or group activities.

- *Related activities in this book:* Lists other activities generally related to the activity described. The criteria for inclusion were relatively specific. Broader criteria would have meant a much larger number of other activities and the result would not be that helpful. For instance, an activity that involves participants drawing something and passing it to other group members would be related to other activities that include drawing. However, it would not be considered as related to activities that involve passing words to other group members.

- *Suggested uses:* The two primary uses of all activities in this book are idea generation and training in how to use idea generation procedures. Thus, the primary objectives of each activity reflect these uses and are very clear-cut.

  The 101 activities also have specific applications suited to different types of organizational problems. They are not, however, as clear-cut as the two primary objectives involving idea generation. As a result, this probably is the most subjective element of the classification scheme used to guide activity selection.

  There is little research available to guide these decisions. My general recommendations are based more on intuition and experience than on any scientific criteria, so take that into account when using the guide for specific topics. The uses listed are for problems involving: Strategy, New Products/Processes/Services, Advertising/Marketing, and Human Resources (see the legend in the selection guide). This is not to say you should limit your choices to the recommended activities or that you should not consider other types of problems. Again, experience will be your best guide.

- *Estimated time requirements:* Suggests the minimum amount of time required for an activity. The number of groups and number of participants in groups will affect these estimates. In the selection guide, activities with a single or double asterisk indicate prior participant activity (*) or prior preparation for facilitators (**). For instance, Idea Shopping [14] requires participants to visit a store before attending an activity. A double asterisk, in contrast, denotes that facilitators will need to make preparations beyond what normally might be expected. An example would be Greeting Cards [96], in which facilitators must gather and organize materials for making greeting cards or Balloon, Balloon, Balloon [92], which involves purchasing balloons, inserting slips of paper, and blowing them up (of course, you also could enlist the aid of the participants in this instance).

- *Stimuli (related vs. unrelated):* As discussed previously, all of the activities are based on stimuli related to a problem, unrelated, or a combination of both. A rule of thumb is that unrelated stimuli often will yield more unique ideas than related stimuli will. However, this guideline can be affected by the creativity of the participants and factors related to a group's creative climate (that is, the perception of free and open expression of ideas).

- *Potential for idea quantity:* Subjectively estimates the probability an activity will result in a relatively large quantity of ideas within the available time. There are a significant number of research studies on the ability of different methods to generate ideas. Brainwriting methods, in particular, have the greatest potential for idea quantity. Time also can be a factor because the more time available, the greater the number of ideas that can be generated, up to a point. Responses are based on low, medium, and high probabilities of occurrence.

- *Potential for novel ideas:* Subjectively estimates the probability that ideas produced will possess statistical infrequency within the problem-solving domain (for example, ideas for customer service). The less expected an idea is for a domain, the greater the potential novelty. The research on idea novelty is less clear on what types of activities are likely to spark novelty. In general, novel ideas are more likely when unrelated stimuli are used. Responses for this category are based on low, medium, and high probabilities.

- *Difficulty of use:* Uses low, medium, and high estimates of how complicated an activity is to implement. Difficulty can be affected by the number of steps involved, tasks unfamiliar to participants, and the trainer's overall familiarity and experience in using an activity.

- *Group energy level required:* Group energy typically is lowest right after lunch and near the end of the day. All the activities are rated with respect to how much energy must be invested to complete the activities. Thus, high-energy activities might be reserved for earlier in the day. On the other hand, if an activity involves physical movement (for example, Balloon, Balloon, Balloon [92]), then the activity might help increase a group's overall energy level and work well in early or late afternoon.

- *Potential for creating a fun environment ("Fun Factor"):* Subjectively estimates the likelihood that an activity will provoke mirth and humor, which should affect both the quantity and novelty of ideas. Some research indicates that groups with high "positive affect" tend to be more creative than groups lower in positive affect. Perception of a positive, open climate can do much to bring out creative ideas. High, medium, and low also are used to rate activities on this factor.

How to Evaluate and Select Ideas in a Group

Once groups begin using the activities and generating ideas, they will need some way to process the ideas and select the best ones. There are a number of ways to do this, such as assigning a committee to narrow down the number of ideas or having participants vote on ideas by ballot or raising hands.

One method that works well in a training environment involves using Post-it® Notes, colored sticking dots, and flip charts and masking tape. The following procedure can be used after most of the activities in this book in which participants have written down ideas on Post-it Notes. It assumes that there is more than one group, but it can be modified easily for just one group. To do so, delete the stage where each group shares its best ideas with the other groups.

1. Prior to an evaluation session:
   a. Place two flip charts on stands by each table, if they are not already there.
   b. Make three signs using 8.5" x 11" paper and write lengthwise in capital letters on each sign. On one sign, write, "BEST IDEAS," on the second, "OTHER IDEAS," and on the third, "NEW IDEAS."
   c. Tape each sign to a separate wall in the meeting room. Place each sign in the middle of the wall and about six feet from the floor. For the wall designated as, "NEW IDEAS," tape two sheets of flip chart paper directly below the sign.
   d. Place on each table (for each participant) three sheets of approximately twenty sticking dots representing green, blue, and orange colors (or other colors that are different in hue (for example, orange and red might be similar in hue while green and orange would be different).

2. Tell the participants to use the flip chart on the left for ideas. (As a reminder, for most of the brainstorming activities, participants will suggest each idea verbally, write it down on a Post-it, and then pass it forward to be placed on the flip chart by a facilitator (or placed by the writer). For brainwriting activities, participants will write down all of their ideas on the Post-its without speaking and then post them on the left flip chart.

3. Emphasize that there should be only one idea on each note. If this is not the case, direct the participants to make any corrections now.

4. After all ideas for an activity have been placed on the left flip chart, have the members of each group select their best three to five ideas for that activity. Tell them to leave those ideas on the left flip chart and transfer the others to the right flip chart.

5. Instruct them to label, in capital letters, the top of the left flip chart "BEST IDEAS" and the top of the right flip chart "OTHER IDEAS." (This later designation denotes that all ideas have potential to be modified or stimulate other ideas. Therefore, there is no such thing as, "WORST IDEAS.")

6. Ask one person from each group to share his or her best ideas verbally with the large group.

7. Encourage any of the participants, including those in other groups, to use each idea verbalized as a stimulus to think of an improvement or new idea. If anyone does think of an improvement or new idea, have the person write it down on a Post-it Note.

8. After all the groups have reported, instruct each group to tape their designated sheets of flip-chart paper on the "BEST IDEAS" and "OTHER IDEAS" walls.

9. Tell all participants to place any new ideas generated from the idea sharing on a sheet of flip-chart paper on the "NEW IDEAS" wall. If the sharing sparked any new ideas, whoever thought of the idea should write it on a note and place it on the appropriate wall.

10. Have the groups repeat steps 4 through 9 until all activities have been completed and all ideas separated and place on the designated walls.

11. Instruct the participants to pick up a sheet of green dots and vote for their favorite ideas on any three of the walls with posted ideas. This way, all of the ideas can be considered. (If time is short, you might have them focus just on the "best" ideas.)

12. Tell them they can use the number of green dots that represent 5 percent of the total number of ideas. Thus, if there are 200 total ideas, they could use ten green dots. Note that they should place the dots in a way so as to not obscure the view of the idea.

13. Caution them to vote for the ideas they think are best and to try not to be influenced by how many dots an idea already has received.

14. As an option, tell them that they may not place more than two (or whatever number seems appropriate to you) dots on a single idea.

15. When all of the green dots have been placed, tell the participants to vote on the best of the "green ideas" by using the blue dots and vote with approximately 5 percent of the total of "green ideas" receiving dots. Thus, if there were thirty participants and they used their green dots to vote for eighty ideas, you would tell them that they may use four blue dots to vote for the best "green ideas."

16. Ask the participants if they are satisfied with the outcome or if they would like to discuss the votes or vote a third time. If they are satisfied, you can end the session; if they want to discuss the votes, conduct a discussion and decide whether to terminate or continue the evaluation process.

Before you begin training using any of the activities in this book, you might want to consider an idea generation warm-up exercise. It can help break the ice and prepare the participants to engage in some freewheeling thinking.

Getting Ready: Different Uses Warm-Up Exercise

Here's an exercise to help individuals and groups stretch their thinking muscles:

1. Divide participants into small groups of four to seven people. Tell them they have five minutes to think of different uses for a coffee mug. Encourage them to think of as many uses as they can and write them on a flip chart, chalkboard, or whiteboard.

2. Call time and ask each group to report how many ideas they generated.

3. Have each group try to think of at least five more ideas within four minutes.

4. Tell them to go over their lists and see if their ideas fall into categories. For instance, do some of their ideas involve uses for holding foods and nonfoods? Did any ideas involve giving mugs away as presents or awards for different events? Or did they think of building things with them (such as a coffee cup castle).

5. Note that their ideas—just as most ideas do—should fall into several categories. Tell them to describe the categories represented by their ideas and then use these categories to think of more ideas. For instance, sample categories for using coffee mugs might include holding liquid foods, solid foods, nonfood items, building things, weighing down things, supporting things, pounding things, as defensive weapons, et cetera.

6. Tell the groups the following:

   "We often use categories to stimulate ideas because they can help stretch our thinking. Unfortunately, many of us use only a limited number of categories, or we use rather conventional categories. If you really stretched your thinking, however, you might have broken away from conventional categories. You might have thought of some offbeat uses that involved crushing or otherwise altering the cups. For instance, you could remove the cup handles and use them as handles for kitchen cupboards, or you could crush the cups and use the remains for automobile tire traction on ice."

7. Have the groups share any unusual categories they might have thought of.

8. If there is time, you might want to share the following true story involving a creative use for a coffee cup that that might not occur frequently:

   Teresa Smith, manager of a Taco Mayo in Oklahoma City, was depositing the store's evening receipts in a bank's night depository. A man ran up and grabbed the restaurant's money bag from her purse. She poured a cup of hot coffee on him and then hit him on the head with the cup. The man turned and ran with the money, but also with an injured head. Perhaps he'll think twice now before he robs a coffee-mug-toting woman!

This exercise may have helped the participants think of many more ideas than they thought they could. The categories helped target their thinking and allowed them to search for ideas more systematically. All it took was a different way to conduct their idea search. The activities in the following chapters do the same thing. They help draw out more ideas than if thinking unaided. And although a group will produce more ideas than an individual, idea generation activities even will help groups surpass their collective brain power.

Activity Selection Guide

	Individual	Group	Brainstorming	Brainwriting	Top Ten Activity (Grp.)	Related Activities	Uses	Time	Stimuli	Quantity	Novelty	Difficulty	Energy	Fun Factora
Chapter 4: Basic Idea Generation														
1. Bend It, Shape It	X	X	X			16	NPS, PSI	30	R, UR	M	M	L	L	L
2. Brain Borrow	X	X	X			3	NPS, PSI	45	R	M	L	L	L	L
3. Copy Cat	X	X	X			2	PSI, A/M	45	UR	M	M	M	M	M
4. Dead Head Deadline	X	X	X			61	Any	30	R	M	L	L	L	L
5. Get Crazy	X	X	X		X	49	S, NPS, A/M	45	R, UR	M	H	M	H	H
6. Idea Diary	X	X	X	X		87	HR	45	R	H	L	L	L	L
7. Mental Breakdown	X	X	X			25,30,31,34	S, HR	60	R	M	L	M	M	L
8. Music Mania	X	X		X		55	A/M	30	UR	H	H	M	M	M
9. Name Change	X	X	X			50,51,52	Any	30	R	M	M	M	L	L
10. Stereotype	X	X	X			21,42,48	Any	30	UR	M	H	M	M	M
11. Switcheroo	X	X	X			6,38	Any	30	R,UR	M	M	M	L	M
12. Wake Up Call	X	X	X	X		6	Any	45*	R,UR	H	M	L	M	L
Chapter 5: Ticklers														
13. Excerpt Excitation	X	X		X		15,16,19	A/M, HR	20	UR	H	H	M	M	M
14. Idea Shopping	X	X	X	X		6,21	NPS, A/M	30*	UR	H	H	M	M	H
15. A Likely Story	X	X	X	X		6,20,40	S, PSI	90	UR	H	H	H	M	H
16. PICLed Brains	X	X	X		X	13,19,20	Any	45	UR	M	H	M	M	M
17. Picture Tickler	X	X	X	X	X	18,26,37,59	Any	30	UR	H	H	L	M	H
18. Rorschach Revisionist	X	X	X			17,26,37,59,62	S, HR	30	UR	M	H	L	M	H
19. Say What?	X	X	X			13,16,20	S, A/M, HR	30	UR	M	H	M	M	H
20. Text Tickler	X	X		X		15,16,19	S	30	UR	H	H	L	M	L
21. Tickler Things	X	X	X		X	14,75	NPS	30	UR	M	H	L	M	H
Chapter 6: Combinations														
22. Bi-Wordal	X	X	X			24,25,30,34,35	NPS	30	R	M	M	L	L	L
23. Circle of Opportunity	X	X	X			24,25,30,34,35	Any	30	R,UR	M	M	L	L	M
24. Combo Chatter	X	X	X		X	25,30,34,35	NPS, PSI	30	R	M	H	L	L	M
25. Ideas in a Box	X	X	X			23,24,25,30,34,35	PSI	30	R	M	M	L	L	L
26. Ideatoons	X	X	X			17,18,37,59,62	Any	45	UR	M	M	H	M	M

	Individual	Group	Brainstorming	Brainwriting	Top Ten Activity (Grp.)	Related Activities	Uses	Time	Stimuli	Quantity	Novelty	Difficulty	Energy	Fun Factor
Chapter 6: Combinations (continued)														
27. Mad Scientist	X	X	X			23,24,25	PSI	45	R,UR	M	M	L	M	H
28. Noun Action	X	X	X			22,24	Any	20	R	M	L	L	L	L
29. Noun Hounds	X	X	X			31	Any	30	UR	M	H	M	M	H
30. Parts Is Parts	X	X	X			24,25,27	NPS, PSI	60	R	M	M	H	M	L
31. Parts Purge	X	X	X			29	PSI	45	R,UR	M	M	M	M	M
32. Preppy Thoughts	X	X	X			22,24	PSI	30	R,UR	M	H	L	M	M
33. SAMM I Am	X	X	X			25	PSI	60	R	M	M	H	H	L
34. 666	X	X	X			22,23,25,27,34	PSI	45	R	M	M	L	H	H
35. Word Diamond	X	X	X		X	22,23,24,25,	Any	20	R	M	L	L	L	L
Chapter 7: Free Association														
36. Brain Mapping	X	X	X			41,43,46	S, PSI, A/M, HR	30	R	M	L	L	L	L
37. Doodles	X	X	X			17,18,26,59,62	S. A/M, HR	45	UR	M	H	M	H	H
38. Essence of the Problem	X	X	X		X	9,11,70	S, PSI, A/M, HR	30	UR	M	H	M	M	M
39. Exaggerate That	X	X	X		X	50,51,52	S, PSI, A/M, HR	30	R	M	M	M	M	M
40. Fairy Tale Time	X	X	X			15,47,80	A/M, HR	60	UR	M	H	M	M	H
41. Idea Links	X	X	X			29,46	PSI	20	UR	M	M	L	L	M
42. Imaginary Mentor	X	X	X			10,48,80	A/M, HR	45	R,UR	M	H	M	L	M
43. Lotus Blossom	X	X	X			36,37	S, NPS, PSI	30	R	M	M	M	L	L
44. Say Cheese	X	X	X			42	A/M	30	UR	M	M	L	M	H
45. Sense-making	X	X	X			44	Any	30	UR	M	M	M	L	M
46. Skybridging	X	X	X			36,41	S	20	R	M	L	L	L	L
47. Tabloid Tales	X	X	X			15,40	A/M, HR	30	UR	M	H	H	M	H
48. We Have Met the Problem . . .	X	X	X			10,42,49	S	30	R	M	H	M	M	H
49. What if. . . ?	X	X	X			5,42,48	S, NPS, A/M	30	UR	M	H	M	M	H
Chapter 8: Grab Bag														
Backward Activities														
50. Law Breaker	X	X	X			39,51,52	Any	30	R	M	H	M	M	M

	Individual	Group	Brainstorming	Brainwriting	Top Ten Activity (Grp.)	Related Activities	Uses	Time	Stimuli	Quantity	Novelty	Difficulty	Energy	Fun Factora
51. Problem Reversals	X	X	X			39,50,52	Any	30	R	M	H	L	M	M
52. Turn Around	X	X	X		X	39,50,51	Any	30	R	M	H	L	M	M
Just Alike Only Different Activities														
53. Bionic Ideas	X	X	X			54,55	Any	45	UR	M	H	H	M	H
54. Chain Alike	X	X	X			53,55	NPS, PSI	60	R,UR	M	H	H	M	M
55. I Like it Like That	X	X	X		X	53,54	Any	45	UR	M	H	M	M	H
56. What is it?	X	X	X			38,52	S	45	R	M	M	H	M	L
Chapter 9: Brainstorming with Related Stimuli														
57. Be #1	X	X	X			40,46	Any	30	R	M	L	L	L	M
58. Blender		X	X	X		74	Any	30	R	H	M	M	L	M
59. Drawing Room		X	X	X		17,18,26, 37,59,62,94	Any	30	UR	H	H	M	H	H
60. Get Real!!		X	X			5,39,50	Any	30	R	M	M	L	M	H
61. Idea Showers		X	X			5,41,49,64	Any	30	R	M	L	L	L	L
62. Modular Brainstorming		X	X			17,18,26,37,59	Any	40	R	M	M	M	M	H
63. Pass the Hat		X	X	X		82,85	Any	30	R	H	M	L	L	M
64. Phillips 66		X	X			61	Any	45	R	M	L	L	L	L
65. Play by Play		X	X			17,33,44	PSI	75*	R	M	H	H	H	H
66. Rice Storm		X	X	X		58,61,82,84,85	Any	60	R	H	L	M	M	M
67. Spin the Bottle		X	X			26,58,61,84,85	Any	30	R	M	L	L	L	H
68. Story Boards		X	X			25,30,33	Any	45	R	M	L	H	M	M
69. That's the Ticket!		X	X			63,85	Any	20	R	M	L	L	L	L
70. What's the Problem?		X	X	X		38	Any	45	R	H	H	M	L	M
Chapter 10: Brainstorming with Unrelated Stimuli														
71. Battle of the Sexes		X	X			17, 20	Any	45	UR	M	H	M	M	H
72. Best of . . .	X	X	X			20	Any	45*	UR	M	H	M	M	H
73. Brain Splitter		X	X		X	5,58,74	Any	45	R	M	H	M	H	H
74. Force-Fit Game		X	X			58,73	Any	45	R,UR	M	H	M	M	M
75. Grab Bag Forced Association		X		X		14,21	Any	30	UR	M	H	M	M	M
76. It's Not My Job		X	X			55,77	Any	30	UR	M	H	L	M	M
77. Rolestorming		X	X	X		76	Any	60*	UR	H	M	M	M	H
78. Roll Call		X	X			20,58,74	Any	45	UR	M	H	M	M	H
79. Sculptures		X	X			21,86	Any	45	UR	M	M	H	H	H
80. Super Heroes		X	X			40,42,77	Any	75	UR	M	H	H	H	H

Chapter 11: Brainwriting with Related Stimuli

	Individual	Group	Brainstorming	Brainwriting	Top Ten Activity (Grp.)	Related Activities	Uses	Time	Stimuli	Quantity	Novelty	Difficulty	Energy	Fun Factora
81. As Easy As 6-3-5		X			X	82,83,87,90	Any	20	R	H	L	L	L	L
82. Brain Purge	X			X	X	82,85,87,90,101	Any	20	R	H	L	L	L	L
83. Group Not	X			X		81	Any	45	R	H	L	M	M	L
84. Idea Mixer	X	X		X		81,82,83	Any	75	R	H	H	M	M	M
85. Idea Pool	X			X		81.82,84,101	Any	20	R	H	M	L	L	L
86. Museum Madness	X			X	X	82,84,85	Any	45	R	H	M	L	M	M
87. Organizational Brainstorms	X	X		X		83,90	Any	1 mo.**	R	H	L	H	M	L
88. Out-of-the-Blue Lightening Bolt Cloudbuster	X			X		81,82,84,85,101	Any	20	R	H	M	L	H	H
89. You're a Card, Andy!	X			X		81,82,84,85,88	Any	30	R	H	M	M	H	H
90. Your Slip Is Showing	X			X		81,83,85,86,87	Any	30	R	H	M	L	L	L

Chapter 12: Brainwriting with Unrelated Stimuli

	Individual	Group	Brainstorming	Brainwriting	Top Ten Activity (Grp.)	Related Activities	Uses	Time	Stimuli	Quantity	Novelty	Difficulty	Energy	Fun Factora
91. Altered States	X			X		81,82,84,85,86	Any	45	UR	H	H	M	M	H
92. Balloon, Balloon, Balloon	X	X	X	X		81,83,85,88	Any	45**	R,UR	M	H	M	H	H
93. Bouncing Ball	X			X		67,78,88,92	Any	30	R,UR	M	M	L	H	H
94. Brainsketching	X	X		X	X	18,59,62,82, 85,86,95	Any	45	R,UR	M	H	M	M	M
95. Doodlin' Around the Block	X			X		18,37,59,94	Any	30	UR	M	M	H	M	M
96. Greeting Cards	X			X		59,82,91,94	Any	45**	UR	H	H	M	M	H
97. The Name Game	X			X		60,82,85	Any	60	UR	H	H	H	M	H
98. Pass the Buck	X			X	X	81,84,86	Any	20	R,UR	M	M	M	M	M
99. Post It, Pardner!	X	X		X		82,83,85,86	Any	30	UR	H	H	M	M	M
100. Puzzle Pieces	X			X		62,95	Any	30	R,UR	H	H	L	L	M
101.The Shirt Off Your Back	X	X		X		82,85,86	Any	20	UR	H	M	L	H	H

LEGEND

S=Strategy, NPS=New Products/Processes/Services, PSI=Product/Process/Service Improvements, A/M=Advertising/Marketing, HR=Human Resources; *Requires participant prior activity, **Requires facilitator prior preparation; BS=Brainstorming, BW=Brainwriting, R=Related, UR=Unrelated, L=Low, M=Medium, H=High.

Individual and Group Activities

Chapter 4

Basic Idea Generation: "No-Brainers"

You have probably heard the expression "That's a real no-brainer!" In case you haven't, a no-brainer is an activity that requires little mental effort or ability. (It doesn't mean you don't need a brain!) Traditional or classical idea generation typically is considered to be a type of no-brainer in that it relies on whatever ideas we can call up without deliberate use of stimuli.

Depending on your creative thinking ability, basic idea generation activities may or may not work as well as other activities. This doesn't mean they lack the potential for yielding blockbuster ideas. All idea generation approaches have that potential. You'll just have to experiment with activities from different categories to determine the best ones for you. You also should explore the activity selection guide described in Chapter 2. (Remember, the activities in this part of the book can be used by either individuals or groups.)

NOTE: FOR ALL ACTIVITIES, REMIND PARTICIPANTS
TO DEFER JUDGMENT WHILE GENERATING IDEAS.

1

Bend It, Shape It

Background

This activity is quite basic. All you have to do is change the nature of a problem in different ways. It doesn't really matter what you change or how you change it. Just change it in any way possible. If you change something, you create a new perspective, and that perspective can lead to other new perspectives and ideas. This is basic free association.

Objectives

- To help participants generate as many creative ideas as possible
- To help participants learn how to use the activities to generate ideas

Participants

Small groups of four to seven people each

Materials, Supplies, and Equipment

- For each group: markers, two flip charts, and masking tape for posting flip-chart sheets 6+
- For each participant: one sheet each of three different colors of sticking dots (½" diameter) and one pad of 4 x 6 Post-it® Notes

Handout

- Osborn Question Check List
- Bend It, Shape It Handout

Time

30 minutes

Related Activities

- PICLed Brains [16]

Procedure

1. Distribute one Osborn Question Check List and one Bend It, Shape It Handout to each participant, review them with the participants, and answer any questions they may have.
2. Have the groups practice using the check list using a challenge of their choice or one common to all groups.
3. Encourage the participants to generate at least one idea for each of the words on the check list.
4. Ask each group to share two or three of their ideas.
5. Tell them to write down any ideas on Post-it® Notes (one idea per note) and place them on flip charts for evaluation.

Debrief/Discussion

Participants don't have to limit their ideas to those prompted by Osborn's list. Any changes will do. They can change color, shape, smell, cost, design, texture, timing, and so forth. The possible changes are limited only by their imagination.

Ask the participants to discuss whether the check list hindered idea generation in any way or if it facilitated it. Have them discuss their responses, especially why the check list hindered or facilitated their brainstorming. Also, consider having participants debrief using the following questions:

- What was most helpful about this exercise?
- What was most challenging?
- What can we apply in our work?
- How would you rate the value of this exercise to helping us with this issue?
- Will this exercise be helpful in the future for other sessions?
- What did you learn?
- What will we be able to use from this exercise?
- What ideas were generated, and which ones were most interesting?

Osborn Question Check List

Brainstorming pioneer Alex Osborn was a master at using perspective changes to suggest new ideas. He developed a list of seventy-three idea-spurring questions designed to create new perspectives. His list included such questions as:

- What other product (problem) is like this one (adapt)?
- How could I change this product (modify)?
- How could I add to this product (magnify)?
- What could I take away from this product (minify)?
- What could I use instead of this product or a portion of it (substitute)?
- How could I alter this product's composition (rearrange)?
- How could I turn this problem around (reverse)?
- What could I put together to make a new product (combine)?

Bend It, Shape It Handout

Assume that your challenge is to think of ways to improve an office stapler. Here are some samples using Osborn's Check List.

Adapt: Design a stapler that fastens without staples by pressing together sheets of paper under pressure (for example, a pair of pliers is somewhat like a stapler in that it can be used to press together things).

Modify: Use bright, metallic paint.

Magnify: Enlarge the stapler's top and make it ergonomic to fit a hand.

Minify: Design a stapler that dispenses both small and large staples.

Substitute: Make a line of staplers from different materials such as cardboard, metal, fiberglass, plastic, or polished wood.

Rearrange: Design a stapler that can staple from either end.

Reverse: Design a stapler that works by pulling up on a handle instead of pressing down.

Combine: Design a combination stapler and magnetic paper clip dispenser

2

Brain Borrow

Background

Do you sometimes feel overburdened with the responsibility for coming up with new ideas? Do you wonder how you can continue to innovate in your work or personal life? If so, you're not alone. We all occasionally experience some frustration in expressing ourselves creatively on demand. Just as we can't be all things to all people, we can't be "all ideas to all problems."

There are at least three reasons for this shortcoming. First, we are limited in how we perceive situations. We have unique perspectives that help us generate creative ideas for some problems. For other problems, however, we don't have the needed perspectives. We just can't seem to define the problem appropriately or we make untested assumptions that constrain our creative thinking.

Second, we may lack the knowledge and information needed to deal with certain problems. For instance, technical problems require specialized knowledge based on extensive formal education, training, and experience. Creativity can help only a limited amount in such situations.

Finally, we all vary in our motivations in different situations. Our individual interests dictate how motivated we will be to solve any given problem.

Thus, the issue is not whether or not we are creative. Rather, we should ask ourselves whether we can bring to a situation the perspectives and resources needed for creative solutions. If we can't, then we have a number of options. One is to use several of the activities described in this book. Another is to seek ideas from others. That is, borrow some brains. It may turn out that you don't really need a creative solution. Instead, you may just need an already-existing solution that you didn't know existed. If a problem is relatively structured and closed, an expert is often the best choice; if your problem is more open-ended, an expert may have a limited range of possible solutions. That is, if your problem has just one or only a few "correct" solutions, then an expert may be your best bet.

Objectives

- To help participants generate as many creative ideas as possible
- To help participants learn how to use the activities to generate ideas

Participants

Small groups of four to seven people each

Materials, Supplies, and Equipment

- For each group: markers, two flip charts, and masking tape for posting flip-chart sheets
- For each participant: one sheet each of three different colors of sticking dots (½″ diameter) and one pad of 4 x 6 Post-it® Notes

Time

45 minutes

Related Activities

- Copy Cat [3]

Procedure

1. Prior to a meeting, ask approximately one-half of a group to consult an expert on the problem topic. They could do this by contacting people they know as experts or get referrals from others. Local universities would be a source, as would the Internet. For instance, they could use Google.com to search for experts or written examples of their advice. Tell them to take written notes from their investigations.

2. Assemble the participants into small groups and have them compare notes with other group members. That is, have one person in each group report what he or she has learned, then have the next person do the same, and so forth (exclude any duplicate information).

3. Tell them to use this information to suggest ideas and to write down any ideas on Post-it® Notes.

4. Direct the groups to select what they think are the best three responses and take turns reporting those to the large group.

5. Have all of the groups discuss the ideas they have heard and select the top three of those.

6. Tell the groups to pick the single best response, report it to the large group, and select the best of all those reported. (To facilitate this process, you may want to have the groups place their best ideas on flip-chart sheets taped to a wall and invite the group members to vote for their favorites using colored, sticking dots—available from office supply stores.)

Debrief/Discussion

Not all the ideas from non-experts may appear practical or workable. You may want to note that ideas should be considered the raw material of solutions, in that every idea has the potential to stimulate new ideas.

Suggest that participants conduct a discussion on the benefits of using experts versus non-experts, including situations in which either or both would be most beneficial and when they might be unproductive or counterproductive. Also consider having participants debrief using the following questions:

- What was most helpful about this exercise?
- What was most challenging?
- What can we apply?
- How would you rate the value of this exercise to helping us with this issue?
- Will this exercise be helpful in the future for other sessions?
- What did you learn?
- What will we be able to use from this exercise?
- What ideas were generated, and which ones were most interesting?

Variation

- If consulting an expert is not feasible, have the participants consult several people with absolutely no knowledge of your problem and take written notes. They can be friends, co-workers, spouses, or even children. Have them do this prior to the meeting. (Such people can bring a fresh perspective to the problem. Unfettered by discipline-bound assumptions and logic, they can often see things we cannot. Not only are they more removed from the problem, but also they are more likely to avoid preconceptions. So ask them how they would solve the problem.)
- Repeat Steps 2 through 6 in the procedure above.
- If experts are available, have the groups consult them as well as non-experts and use those responses with Steps 2 through 6.

3

Copy Cat

Background

One of the first things school children learn is "do your own work." They're also told that they'll never learn anything if they copy from someone else. "Besides, the person you copy from may be wrong. So keep your eyes on your own paper!"

Although this may be good advice in school, it hasn't always held up well in the world of work. In fact, many businesses make a practice of copying other companies. Taken to the extreme, this practice can result in copyright and trademark violations as greedy people try to profit from outright ripoffs. Rolex watches, for example, frequently are copied by unscrupulous companies trying to make a quick buck with an unlicensed product.

By definition, copying someone else's idea is not a creative act. There's nothing original about an idea that is exactly the same as another. Although some people argue that a product is creative if it is new to the creator, this logic loses its appeal in the workplace.

If another organization is already marketing an idea, you lose "creativity points" if you attempt to market the same idea. The true innovator is the organization that designed, developed, and brought to market the idea. Copy an idea and you're following the leader. Moreover, research has shown that companies that market an idea first are more likely to achieve competitive advantage and an overall greater market share. (The same general principles of innovation apply also to nonprofit and government organizations.)

Does the fact that copying an idea has negative consequences mean that copying is a bad business practice? The answer is yes and no. It's bad if you copy directly without permission; it's good if you use another idea only for stimulation. Copying can help if you use only a basic concept or principle from someone else's idea. That's where the Copy Cat technique comes in.

Objectives

- To help participants generate as many creative ideas as possible
- To help participants learn how to use the activities to generate ideas

Participants

Small groups of four to seven people each

Materials, Supplies, and Equipment

- For each group: markers, two flip charts, and masking tape for posting flip-chart sheets
- For each participant: one sheet each of three different colors of sticking dots (½" diameter) and one pad of 4 x 6 Post-it® Notes

Time

45 minutes

Related Activities

- Brain Borrow [2]

Procedure

1. Have small groups borrow the basics of another idea and adapt it to their situation. Tell them to think of who is doing similar things or making similar products. There doesn't have to be a direct connection. Tell them to examine what others are doing and try to make it work for their challenge.

2. To clarify the exercise, tell them the following story:

   Kent Savage, president of Electronic Merchandising Systems, Inc., of Cincinnati, Ohio, started out in the vending machine business. He tried the conventional approach: snacks, coffee, and cold drinks. Then a few years ago, he traveled to Japan. There he saw $300 pearl necklaces and even sake offered in vending machines.

   "What an eye opener," Savage now recalls. "I realized I could break out of the mold and move into higher-priced items." And so he did. When he returned to the United States, he approached Eastman Kodak and offered to sell cameras and film in his vending machines. After two years, his vending machines now sell Kodak products in more than twenty states.

   In 1993, Savage introduced machines that sell tools on factory floors. His company now turns a sizable profit, with the machine tools expected to bring in more than $100 million over the next five years (some of which will come from exports to Japan, ironically).

Savage capitalized on his strengths and borrowed a concept from someone else. Once he had copied the basic idea, he turned the concept into a creative product suited for his business. Savage was a Copy Cat.

3. Have each group think of a story or event similar to their problem, describe it in detail, and use the descriptions as potential stimuli to copy for resolving the group problem.

4. Tell them to write down any ideas on Post-it® Notes (one idea per note) and place them on flip charts for evaluation.

Debrief/Discussion

Ask the groups to discuss the following types of questions:

- How easy was it to think of similar ideas?
- How did the similarity of another idea affect your ability to apply it to your challenge? Were more similar ideas easier or more difficult to apply?
- To what extent did your knowledge of other ideas affect your ability to apply the ideas?
- Would this technique work better with only certain types of problems? If so, what types?

Also consider having participants debrief using the following questions:

- What was most helpful about this exercise?
- What was most challenging?
- What can we apply?
- How would you rate the value of this exercise to helping us with this issue?
- Will this exercise be helpful in the future for other sessions?
- What did you learn?
- What will we be able to use from this exercise?
- What ideas were generated, and which ones were most interesting?

4

DEAD HEAD DEADLINE

Background

We live in a world of deadlines. Do it soon. Do it now. Do it yesterday. Just do it. It's an unrelenting pace with unrelenting deadlines. Tomorrows become todays, which become yesterdays—all too soon. If you don't do it now, you'll never do it. Deadlines are everywhere. You can't live with 'em; you can't live without 'em.

But you can use them to become more creative. Despite our lack of love for deadlines, they also have positive features. The most important of these is that deadlines provide motivation. And motivation can increase our idea productivity.

The use of deadlines is a simple, yet often overlooked, approach. The process involved is similar to goal setting: it gives us something to strive for and provides motivation. If we know when we have to complete a task, most of us will pace ourselves to do it. Deadlines force us to organize our thinking and move ahead.

Many of us have deadlines imposed on us. All it takes is for a boss to say, "Do such and such by tomorrow," and we'll perform. There are times, however, when we need to be creative on demand.

Objectives

- To help participants generate as many creative ideas as possible
- To help participants learn how to use the activities to generate ideas

Participants

Small groups of four to seven people each

Materials, Supplies, and Equipment

- For each group: markers, two flip charts, and masking tape for posting flip-chart sheets
- For each participant: one sheet each of three different colors of sticking dots (½" diameter) and one pad of 4 x 6 Post-it® Notes

Time

30 minutes

Related Activities

- Idea Showers [61]

Procedure

1. To stimulate idea production, impose a deadline on small groups to generate at least twenty-five ideas in 20 minutes.

2. Ask the groups to notify you if they reach their goal early. If they do, challenge them to think of five more ideas within 5 minutes and so forth until all groups have finished.

3. Tell them to write down any ideas on Post-it® Notes (one idea per note) and place them on flip charts for evaluation.

Debrief/Discussion

Whatever deadlines you impose, make sure they are realistic. Remember, however, that what is realistic is relative. It all depends on the perceiver. Thus, I might perceive a deadline of two hours as realistic, but such a time period might evoke immediate panic in someone else. If your deadline is not realistic, it won't be motivating. Ask the participants to discuss how they are affected by deadlines and in what situations they are more or less affected.

Also consider having participants debrief using the following questions:

- What was most helpful about this exercise?
- What was most challenging?
- What can we apply?
- How would you rate the value of this exercise to helping us with this issue?
- Will this exercise be helpful in the future for other sessions?
- What did you learn?
- What will we be able to use from this exercise?
- What ideas were generated, and which ones were most interesting?

5

GET CRAZY

Background

Look waaaaay down inside yourself. There are lots of hidden recesses down there, aren't there? Things known only to you and perhaps a few of your intimate friends. Things you normally don't show in polite company. That strange side only you know about. The side that views things differently.

If you look long enough, you may eventually discover the wacky you down there— the side of you that every now and then thinks of an off-the-wall idea. It's the side that makes a sudden leap of intuition, jumps to conclusions, and goes off the deep end (the side filled with clichés). You know it's in there, so admit it. Use it occasionally to your advantage. Get crazy, get zany, get ridiculous. View your problems with new eyes and use the steps that follow to help produce this same effect within the participants.

Objectives

- To help participants generate as many creative ideas as possible
- To help participants learn how to use the activities to generate ideas

Participants

Small groups of four to seven people each

Materials, Supplies, and Equipment

- For each group: markers, two flip charts, and masking tape for posting flip-chart sheets
- For each participant: one sheet each of three different colors of sticking dots (½" diameter) and one pad of 4 x 6 Post-it® Notes

Handout

- Get Crazy Handout

Time

45 minutes

Related Activities

- What If. . . ? [49]

Procedure

1. Distribute copies of the Get Crazy Handout to each participant.
2. Work through the sample exercise on the handout with the large group and answer any questions.
3. Have the participants write down the most crazy, ridiculous problem solutions they can think of. The crazier the better.
4. After about 15 to 20 minutes, tell them to forget about being crazy and zoom back to normality and get on with solving their problems and be practical.
5. Tell them to examine each of their crazy ideas to see what more practical solution it may suggest. They may not think of one for each crazy idea, but do the best they can.
6. Tell them to write down any ideas on Post-it® Notes (one idea per note) and place them on flip charts for evaluation.

Debrief/Discussion

Ask the groups to consider the following questions:

- What is a "crazy" idea? How does it differ from "normal" ideas?
- Is any idea really "crazy"?
- What effect does the type of problem have on deciding whether or not an idea is crazy?
- Would more difficult problems be more easily resolved using crazy ideas?
- What are the advantages of using crazy ideas? Disadvantages?

Also consider having participants debrief using the following questions:

- What was most helpful about this exercise?
- What was most challenging?
- What can we apply?
- How would you rate the value of this exercise to helping us with this issue?
- Will this exercise be helpful in the future for other sessions?
- What did you learn?
- What will we be able to use from this exercise?
- What ideas were generated, and which ones were most interesting?

Get Crazy Handout

Challenge: How might we get people to buy more of our product? First, get crazy and generate some ridiculous ideas such as the following:

- Threaten people with a "long vacation" if they don't buy your products.
- Pay them $1 million for every dollar they spend on your products.
- Promise them three magic wishes.
- Attach a subliminal advertising device to their televisions.
- Have your cousin Vinnie pay them a visit.
- Send your product to every home in the world as a holiday gift and invoice the home-owners.

O.K., those are pretty ridiculous. Now use each one to stimulate a more practical idea. Some examples:

- Offer free or partially funded vacations to people who place large orders.
- Develop a list of "magic wishes" with a lottery for customers to select one of the wishes; for instance, one wish might be to win one dollar every day for ten years.
- Offer discounts to people who pay with cash.
- Offer family discounts.
- Create a new product with a holiday theme.

6

IDEA DIARY

Background

Ideas are fleeting creatures. Sometimes they dart by and we capture them easily; other times they are more elusive and slip away into nothingness. Now they're here, now they're not.

The mind works in mysterious ways. We often think of ideas at the darndest times—in the shower, right before we fall asleep, right after we wake up, while driving, while talking with a friend, or even when working on an unrelated problem. Trouble arises when we can't remember these ideas. One solution to this problem is to begin an idea diary—a book or journal designed solely to record random ideas.

Objectives

- To help participants generate as many creative ideas as possible
- To help participants learn how to use the activities to generate ideas

Participants

Small groups of four to seven people each

Materials, Supplies, and Equipment

- For each group: markers, two flip charts, and masking tape for posting flip-chart sheets
- For each participant: one sheet each of three different colors of sticking dots (½" diameter) and one pad of 4 x 6 Post-it® Notes
- One small notebook and pen or pencil for each participant
- (Optional) PDA, computer, voice recorder, Internet group idea-capturing websites (for example, www.groups.yahoo.com), or other devices to record ideas

Time

45 minutes

Related Activities

- Organizational Brainstorms [87]

Procedure

1. In advance of an idea generation session, tell participants to use a small notebook or other recording medium (such as a voice recorder or PDA) and write down ideas to the challenge. Have them start this process at least one week prior to the session.

2. Stress that they should write down ideas whenever they think of them and keep their diaries easily accessible.

3. Assemble the participants into small groups of four to seven and have them compare notes. That is, have one person in each group report what he or she learned, then have the next person do the same, but exclude any duplicate information.

4. After all ideas have been reported, instruct the groups to select what they think are the best three responses and report those to the large group.

5. Have all of the groups discuss the answers they have heard and select the top three of those.

6. Tell the groups to pick the single best response, report it to the large group, and select the best of all those reported.

7. Collect all of the ideas, including those not selected during any step, organize them into priority lists, and save them for evaluation later.

Debrief/Discussion

Have the participants discuss the advantages and disadvantages of using idea diaries.

Note that one advantage is the ability to rely on mental incubation to mull over idea possibilities rather than having to think them all up at one time. Also consider having participants debrief using the following questions:

- What was most helpful about this exercise?
- What was most challenging?
- What can we apply?
- How would you rate the value of this exercise to helping us with this issue?
- Will this exercise be helpful in the future for other sessions?
- What did you learn?
- What will we be able to use from this exercise?
- What ideas were generated, and which ones were most interesting?

7

MENTAL BREAKDOWN

Background

"Chunking," in the world of information theory, has nothing to do with Chinese food. It has everything to do with managing information. Basically, chunking refers to the practice of breaking down information into smaller pieces, or chunks.

We define problems, after all, by how much information we have about them. The more information we have, the more structured the problem is. And the more structured a problem is, the easier it is to solve. Thus, the better we are at managing information, the better we should be at solving problems. Unfortunately, it's not always quite that simple.

If we have trouble solving problems, we might assume we aren't creative, knowledgeable, or motivated enough. Frequently, however, the major difficulty is perceived information overload. The information itself then becomes another problem on top of the original one.

Information scientists suggest dividing information into smaller, more manageable chunks to avoid overload. Like a computer, the human mind can process only a limited number of information bits at one time (some say the mind can process an average of seven bits simultaneously). Given this limitation, it's no wonder we can't resolve large, complex problems without making some adjustments.

One way to compensate for our techno-biological deficiencies is to list subproblems (or related problem components) and work on them in order of priority. The result is a series of related, yet smaller and more manageable, problems. Frequently, attacking a problem in this manner can lead to even more creative perspectives.

Objectives

- To help participants generate as many creative ideas as possible
- To help participants learn how to use the activities to generate ideas

Participants

Small groups of four to seven people each.

Materials, Supplies, and Equipment

- For each group: markers, two flip charts, and masking tape for posting flip-chart sheets

- For each participant: one sheet each of three different colors of sticking dots (½" diameter) and one pad of 4 x 6 Post-it® Notes

Handout

- Mental Breakdown Handout

Time

60 minutes

Related Activities

- Ideas in a Box [25]
- Parts Is Parts [30]
- Parts Purge [31]
- 666 [34]

Procedure

1. Instruct participants in small groups to write a problem challenge in question form on the flip chart.
2. Have them break down the challenge by listing every part of the problem.
3. Tell them to turn each problem into a new challenge question.
4. Ask them to select three of the new questions and generate ideas to resolve them.
5. After about 20 minutes, have the participants in each group examine the ideas to see if they might suggest any solutions to the original challenge.
6. Tell them to write down any ideas on Post-it® Notes (one idea per note) and place them on flip charts for evaluation.

Debrief/Discussion

The list of potential subproblems for most challenges is almost endless. Although it may seem obvious to subdivide a larger problem this way, the obvious often can be over-looked. This is especially true when problem solvers become overwhelmed by the enormity of the task facing them.

Ask participants the following types of questions:

- For what types of problems is this approach most likely to be effective? (for example, complex, difficult-to-understand ones) Why is this?
- When is this approach likely to be ineffective? (for example, when little time is available) Why is this?
- Why is it important to generate a relatively large number of subproblems?

Also, consider having participants debrief using the following questions:

- What was most helpful about this exercise?
- What was most challenging?
- What can we apply in our lives or to our problem?
- How would you rate the value of this exercise to helping us with this issue?
- Will this exercise be helpful in the future for other sessions?
- What did you learn?
- What will we be able to use from this exercise?
- What ideas were generated, and which ones were most interesting?

Mental Breakdown Handout

Suppose, for example, a problem challenge is: How to develop a new product marketing strategy. The amount of data for such a problem is immense. All sorts of demographics exist to confuse problem solvers. Rather than attempt to resolve this problem completely, it is much easier and more efficient to break it down into more manageable parts.

For instance, a group might generate a list of subproblems related to various marketing tactics that form a part of the larger strategy:

- How can we better define our market niche?
- How can we better define our product mix?
- How can we better promote our products?
- How can we better move existing products to existing markets?
- How can we better move new products to existing markets?
- How can we better move new products to new markets?
- How can we improve perceived customer product values?
- How can we improve packaging designs?

8

Music Mania

Music hath charms to soothe the savage beast.

James Bramston (1729)

Background

Music has a calming effect on our emotions that can help us generate ideas. Research has shown that certain types of music can affect moods and productivity.

Our brain centers associated with emotional responses are also linked to our ability to function creatively. Music has the potential to stimulate these brain centers and help us think of creative ideas. Both music and creativity involve similar processes and features such as intuition, abstract symbols, and holistic interpretations of data. Musical composition is a creative activity as well. Given this relationship between music and creativity, it makes sense that music can help stimulate new ideas.

Objectives

- To help participants generate as many creative ideas as possible
- To help participants learn how to use the activities to generate ideas

Participants

Small groups of four to seven people each

Materials, Supplies, and Equipment

- For each group: markers, two flip charts, and masking tape for posting flip-chart sheets
- For each participant: one sheet each of three different colors of sticking dots (½" diameter) and one pad of 4 x 6 Post-it® Notes
- A variety of music ranging from jazz, pop, soft rock, and classical
- Audio equipment to play the music

Handout

- (For Variation #2): Sample Ideas

Time

30 minutes

Related Activities

- I Like It Like That [55]

Procedure

1. Have each group write down a problem challenge on a flip chart.
2. Tell the participants that they are going to use music to help induce a relaxed mental state.
3. Select music that helps induce a state of relaxation and turn it on.
4. Tell the participants to get comfortable and think pleasant thoughts and let their minds drift. Give them at least 5 minutes for this activity.
5. Have the group members individually start writing ideas on the Post-it Notes, one idea per note. Tell them to avoid judging each idea and to list as many as they can for another 5 minutes.
6. Call time and ask group members to read their ideas, in turn, and then post them on a sheet of flip-chart paper for all to see. Thus, person one would read his idea and place it on the sheet of paper, person two would read her idea and post it, and so forth, until all ideas have been read and posted.
7. Ask the participants to listen to another 5 minutes of music and then repeat Steps 5 and 6.

Debrief/Discussion

If time is available, encourage the participants in each group to develop their own activities based on music and then present them to the other groups. For an interesting experiment, have the groups try all three activities above and discuss the relative merits of each.

Also consider having participants debrief using the following questions:

- What was most helpful about this exercise?
- What was most challenging?
- What can we apply?
- How would you rate the value of this exercise to helping us with this issue?
- Will this exercise be helpful in the future for other sessions?
- What did you learn?

- What will we be able to use from this exercise?
- What ideas were generated, and which ones were most interesting?

Variation #1

1. Have the groups listen to a relaxing, but lively, song all the way through.

2. Play the song again and instruct them to focus their attention on what the music is trying to say. Have them notice any changes in mood, tempo, beat, or sound level, sudden chord changes, and so on.

3. Play the song a third time, but tell them now to concentrate on general concepts suggested by the music. For instance, a sudden change in tempo may suggest surprise, a slow portion may suggest caution, and a loud part may suggest power. Have them write down these concepts as they listen and use a scribe to record them on a flip chart.

4. Tell the groups to look over all the concepts and use them to help stimulate ideas, also writing them on a flip chart.

Variation #2

1. Have the groups use the lyrics of one or several different songs as stimuli.

2. Tell them to write down on a Post-it®, as individuals, words, phrases, or complete sentences that intrigue them. For instance, someone might write down (1) "drives me wild," (2) "maybe it's the clothes she wears," (3) "you know even though the river is wide," (4) "in the middle of the night," or (5) "on the radio."

3. Post the notes on flip-chart paper and tell the groups to use the words to trigger ideas.

4. Provide them with the Sample Ideas handout.

Sample Ideas

Suppose your problem involves how to motivate employees to maintain clean office areas. The lyrics written down in Step 2 might suggest ideas such as (1) sponsoring a clean office contest and giving the winner a free rental car for the weekend, (2) holding a fun fashion contest in which participants model clothes using trash picked up in the office, (3) buying an extra-wide vacuum cleaner, (4) requiring the messiest employees to stay late to clean their offices, and (5) award the worker with the cleanest office area an MP3 music player.

9

NAME CHANGE

Background

We play name games every day. Whenever we refer to a person, object, place, or concept, we use labels known as names. The words "George," "book," "beach," and "gravity" all are names we use to communicate. Without such words, we would have trouble understanding one another. Thus, daily interactions involve a series of communication attempts using labels.

When we confront problems, we classify and identify them with labels such as "financial," "marketing," "personnel," or "quality control." These labels help us distinguish among different types of problems and provide a common basis for understanding. If I say I have a personnel problem, then you know I have a problem involving people. You may not know exactly what my problem is, but the label "personnel" helps you narrow the problem down and eliminate other types of problems as possibilities.

Although labels are essential for effective communication, they can make problem solving more difficult. One danger of labeling problems is that we may stereotype certain problems. If taken to the extreme, this tendency can restrict our ability to think of solutions.

Defining a problem with a label limits how we perceive the problem. It can create a narrow perspective even when none was intended. For instance, suppose you define a particular personnel problem as "How can we motivate employees to work harder?" Such a definition limits possible solutions for motivating employees. Although there is nothing intrinsically wrong with limiting solutions, it does decrease management's options in this case.

Objectives

- To help participants generate as many creative ideas as possible
- To help participants learn how to use the activities to generate ideas

Participants

Small groups of four to seven people each

Materials, Supplies, and Equipment

- For each group: markers, two flip charts, and masking tape for posting flip-chart sheets
- For each participant: one sheet each of three different colors of sticking dots (½" diameter) and one pad of 4 x 6 Post-it® Notes

Time

30 minutes

Related Activities

- Law Breaker [50]
- Problem Reversals [51]
- Turn Around [52]

Procedure

1. Have a group recorder write down a problem challenge on a flip chart for all to see.
2. Tell them to ask, "Why?" about their challenge, record the answer, and then use the answer to think of a new challenge statement.
3. Have them repeat Step 2 until they have generated a satisfactory challenge statement.
4. Tell them to use this statement and write down any ideas on Post-it® Notes (one idea per note) and place them on flip charts for evaluation.

Debrief/Discussion

In the example involving the motivation of employees, it might have been better to broaden the definition with a less restrictive, more positive label. For instance, the question, "Why do we want to motivate employees to work harder?" might be answered by noting, "To increase productivity." Thus, the problem might be better defined as "How can we improve employee productivity?" This switch from a motivation label to a productivity label opens up more solution alternatives and shifts the emphasis away from employees being a "problem." The situation is transformed from a motivation problem to a productivity problem.

Also consider having participants debrief using the following questions:

- What was most helpful about this exercise?
- What was most challenging?
- What can we apply?
- How would you rate the value of this exercise to helping us with this issue?

- Will this exercise be helpful in the future for other sessions?
- What did you learn?
- What will we be able to use from this exercise?
- What ideas were generated, and which ones were most interesting?

Variation

Another approach also might help avoid the limits imposed by problem labels.

1. Suggest that groups restate their challenges in a humorous way. For instance, they might restate the employee motivation problem as "how to light a fire under their tails?" or "how to squeeze blood out of a stone?"

2. Have them use these perspectives to stimulate ideas. For instance, the concept of lighting a fire might suggest an employee camping trip or a weekend retreat to discuss ways to improve productivity.

10

STEREOTYPE

Background

This exercise, as with the Brain Borrow activity [2], is based on the concept of getting a new perspective by consulting someone else. However, instead of actually talking with another person, the objective is to think as if you were someone else.

Objectives

- To help participants generate as many creative ideas as possible
- To help participants learn how to use the activities to generate ideas

Participants

Small groups of four to seven people each

Materials, Supplies, and Equipment

- For each group: markers, two flip charts, and masking tape for posting flip-chart sheets.
- For each participant: one sheet each of three different colors of sticking dots (½" diameter) and one pad of 4 x 6 Post-it® Notes

Handout

- Stereotype Handout

Time

30 minutes

Related Activities

- Tickler Things [21]
- Imaginary Mentor [42]
- We Have Met the Problem and It Is We [48]

Procedure

1. Have someone in each group write down a problem challenge on a flip chart.

2. Distribute the Stereotype Handout.

3. Instruct participants to select some occupation and think of how a stereotypical person in that position would try to resolve the challenge. Ideally, this occupation should be unrelated to the problem. Suggest that they think of how a police officer, lawyer, accountant, chemist, physician, butcher, or carpenter would resolve the problem.

4. Have them write down on the flip chart everything they know about how someone in another occupation would solve the challenge.

5. Tell them to think about kinds of solutions that person would think of and to use them to generate ideas to resolve the challenge.

6. Tell them to write down any ideas on Post-it® Notes (one idea per note) and place them on flip charts for evaluation.

Debrief/Discussion

Ask the groups to discuss what occupations might be best for what types of problems. In general, the more different an occupation is from the challenge, the more likely it is to prompt creative ideas. Also consider having participants debrief using the following questions:

- What was most helpful about this exercise?
- What was most challenging?
- What can we apply?
- How would you rate the value of this exercise to helping us with this issue?
- Will this exercise be helpful in the future for other sessions?
- What did you learn?
- What will we be able to use from this exercise?
- What ideas were generated, and which ones were most interesting?

Stereotype Handout

Suppose the challenge is to improve quality control in a manufacturing process and your group selects the occupation of carpenter. You then might write down the following notes about carpentry:

- A carpenter pounds nails on the tip with a hammer to prevent splitting wood.
- A good carpenter always "measures twice and cuts once."
- The quality of sanding determines the quality of the final finish.
- It's easier to saw wood with the grain than against it.
- Always use the right tool for the job (for instance, don't use a screwdriver as a hammer).

These descriptions then might prompt the following ideas:

- "Blunt" the impact of errors by developing a quality program that "hammers" on the theme of quality improvement.
- Require all manufacturing employees to check their output twice.
- Provide all employees with additional training in quality control activities.
- Conduct regular meetings with employees to make sure they are aligned with management's goals and philosophy.
- Make sure all employees use the latest technology to improve job quality.

11

Switcheroo

Background

Switcheroo is based on the old saying, "You can't see the forest for the trees." We sometimes get so close to our problems that we lose the perspective needed to generate creative ideas. One way to overcome this obstacle is to shift our focus to something else.

Objectives

- To help participants generate as many creative ideas as possible
- To help participants learn how to use the activities to generate ideas

Participants

Small groups of four to seven people each

Materials, Supplies, and Equipment

- For each group: markers, two flip charts, and masking tape for posting flip-chart sheets
- For each participant: one sheet each of three different colors of sticking dots (½" diameter) and one pad of 4 x 6 Post-it® Notes

Time

30 minutes

Related Activities

- Essence of the Problem [38]

Procedure

1. Have someone in each group write down a problem challenge on a flip chart.

2. Tell the group to spend 5 to 10 minutes brainstorming ideas and recording them all in writing, individually on Post-it® Notes.

3. Request that they shift their focus to another problem challenge relevant to each group and spend 5 to 10 minutes generating ideas for it. This problem should be completely different from the original one.

4. Call time and have them resume work on the original problem.

5. Tell them to write down any ideas on Post-it® Notes (one idea per note) and place them on flip charts for evaluation.

Debrief/Discussion

Switching problems in this manner will often allow us to see the original problem differently. The break from the problem provides a change in perspective. Moreover, working on the new problem often sparks ideas for the first problem. If switching to another problem doesn't help, have the groups try switching to nothing—just take a break and walk around, then return to attack the problem with new energy.

Also consider having participants debrief using the following questions:

- What was most helpful about this exercise?
- What was most challenging?
- What can we apply?
- How would you rate the value of this exercise to helping us with this issue?
- Will this exercise be helpful in the future for other sessions?
- What did you learn?
- What will we be able to use from this exercise?
- What ideas were generated, and which ones were most interesting?

12

WAKE-UP CALL

Background

Most of the activities in this book help generate ideas by actively engaging our brains. That is, we consciously use our brains to free-associate or force together stimuli to produce something new.

There is another way to bring out ideas, however—a more passive way. It actually requires little effort and involves nothing drastically different from what we do every day. All you have to do is go to sleep and then wake up. A definite "no-brainer." Going to sleep can help harness the power of our brain waves. Our brains function at varying levels of intensity depending on the time of day. Theta waves appear during sleep, whereas beta waves are predominant when we are active during the day.

Some research suggests that different brain wave patterns are related to different problem-solving actions. For instance, theta waves help generate ideas, whereas beta waves are better for analytical thinking. Theta waves are abundant just before we fall asleep and just after we wake up.

Objectives

- To help participants generate as many creative ideas as possible
- To help participants learn how to use the activities to generate ideas

Participants

Small groups of four to seven people each

Materials, Supplies, and Equipment

- For each group: markers, two flip charts, and masking tape for posting flip-chart sheets
- For each participant: one sheet each of three different colors of sticking dots (½" diameter) and one pad of 4 x 6 Post-it® Notes

Time

45 minutes (also requires one week prior preparation time)

Basic Idea Generation: "No-Brainers"

Related Activities

- Idea Diary [6]

Procedure

1. About one week before a scheduled brainstorming session, provide the following instructions for all participants to do every evening:

   - Set your alarm clock to awaken you 20 to 30 minutes earlier than usual in the morning.
   - Note what time it is when you wake up and quickly begin writing down ideas about some problem. As you list your ideas, suspend all judgment.
   - Continue writing ideas until you can't think of any more. Then note what time it is.
   - The next morning, repeat these steps, but try to spend 5 more minutes writing ideas. If you run out of ideas before the 5 minutes is up, keep writing whatever you can think of, even if the ideas seem impractical.
   - Continue this exercise for at least three more days.
   - Review all the ideas and try to transform the impractical ideas into more practical ones, writing them down in a notebook or as a word processing file.
   - Select your three best ideas.

2. Convene the meeting of the groups and tell the group members to take turns sharing one of their three best ideas from the past several days.

3. Ask the other group members to try to build on or improve this idea and to write down any new ones on Post-it® Notes, one idea per note.

4. Repeat this process until all ideas have been shared or time runs out.

5. Tell them to write down any ideas on Post-it® Notes (one idea per note) and place them on flip charts for evaluation.

Debrief/Discussion

Debrief using the following types of questions:

- In general, how well did this approach work for you as individuals?
- Were your ideas better than they normally would have been without the time up-front?
- Did you have trouble clearing your mind on first awakening?
- Was there any change in the quality of the ideas over time?

   Also, consider having participants debrief using the following questions:

- What was most helpful about this exercise?
- What was most challenging?
- What can we apply?

- How would you rate the value of this exercise to helping us with this issue?
- Will this exercise be helpful in the future for other sessions?
- What did you learn?
- What will we be able to use from this exercise?
- What ideas were generated, and which ones were most interesting?

Chapter 5

Ticklers: Related and Unrelated Stimuli

Tickler activities will tickle, tease, and tantalize ideas out of your brain. They will pull out what you know exists, but couldn't think of at the time; what you thought existed, but didn't know for sure; and sometimes what you didn't even know existed. When you use specific stimuli, ideas will pop out surprisingly fast.

Ticklers provide the stimuli needed to free-associate. A tickler is anything that stimulates an idea. You probably use many brain ticklers already. For instance, have you ever tried to think of an idea and found yourself thinking of something else instead? Say you have been distracted temporarily by a delivery truck outside. As you examine the truck, you think of things related to trucking. Suddenly the concept of transportation triggers an idea related to the problem.

Another illustration: Suppose Sally is looking for creative ways to sell a product to a really tough customer. As she considers various alternatives, she happens to glance at the clock on the wall. She absentmindedly looks at the clock and immediately focuses on the concept of time. Then she begins thinking about her customer and several ideas pop out in succession:

- Call his secretary and find out at what time he is in his best mood.
- Offer him a limited-time offer.
- Give him a watch if he buys the product.
- Send him data on how the product will help him save time.

The activities described in this chapter do essentially the same thing as the truck or the clock in these examples: they stimulate ideas. However, these activities make the process a little more systematic and help target your efforts more efficiently.

Tickler activities help generate ideas using one of three general sources of stimulation: (1) words, (2) pictures, and (3) objects. Examples of ticklers using words include: A Likely Story [15], Excerpt Excitation [13], PICLed Brains [16], and Say What? [19]. Pictures are used with Picture Tickler [17] and Rorschach Revisionist [18]. Finally, Idea Shopping [14] is an example of a tickler using objects.

When using ticklers, defer all judgment while generating ideas. The only time you even should consider judging ideas during idea generation is when you are using multiple tickler activities.

If you use more than one tickler, you might select the best ideas after using each technique. Then you could go on to the next activity and generate ideas without judging. After you have done this for several ticklers, go back and review all your ideas. Often you'll find that the ideas you review will help stimulate even more ideas.

NOTE: FOR ALL ACTIVITES, REMIND PARTICPANTS
TO DEFER JUDGMENT WHILE GENERATING IDEAS.

13

EXCERPT EXCITATION

Background

I quote others only the better to express myself.
    —Montaigne

Writers frequently use quotations to emphasize important points or to provide different perspectives on a topic. This ability to provoke new perspectives gives quotations the potential to tickle your brain and generate new ideas. As William Thackeray once said, "The two most engaging powers of an author are to make new things familiar, familiar things new."

Excerpt Excitation uses quotations to help think of ways to make familiar things new. That's an essential ingredient of creative thinking—taking what appears to be known and applying some unique twist to it. Quotations do this by forcing us to consider angles we might otherwise have overlooked.

Objectives

- To help participants generate as many creative ideas as possible
- To help participants learn how to use the activities to generate ideas

Participants

Small groups of four to seven people each

Materials, Supplies, and Equipment

- For each group: markers, two flip charts, and masking tape for posting flip-chart sheets
- For each participant: one sheet each of three different colors of sticking dots (½" diameter) and one pad of 4 x 6 Post-it® Notes
- One or more book of quotations or Internet quote websites, such as www.quotation-spage.com or www.quoteland.com

Handout

- Excerpt Excitation Handout

Time

20 minutes

Related Activities

- A Likely Story [15]
- PICLed Brains [16]
- Say What? [19]

Procedure

1. Distribute the Excerpt Excitation Handout and ask participants to review it with you and indicate to them how the ideas were derived from the quotes. Ask then if they have any questions.

2. Instruct participants to read a list of quotations from various authors covering different topics. They should review at least thirty varied quotations.

3. Have each individual select one of the quotations and think about its meaning. Have them free-associate and write down whatever idea comes to mind on Post-it® Notes to be placed on a flip chart for evaluation.

4. After about 10 minutes, tell them to select another quotation and repeat Step 2 until they have generated as many ideas as possible. Tell them to not be discouraged if not all quotations spark ideas. That's not the purpose of this exercise. If even one quotation triggers one good idea, then it was worth the effort.

5. Tell them to write down any ideas on Post-it® Notes (one idea per note) and place them on flip charts for evaluation.

Debrief/Discussion

Suggest that participants experiment and select quotations that pertain to their problem topics as well as those that do not.

Ask them to discuss why some quotes seem to work better than others.

Also consider having participants debrief using the following questions:

- What was most helpful about this exercise?
- What was most challenging?
- What can we apply?
- How would you rate the value of this exercise to helping us with this issue?
- Will this exercise be helpful in the future for other sessions?

- What did you learn?
- What will we be able to use from this exercise?
- What ideas were generated, and which ones were most interesting?

Excerpt Excitation Handout

Assume a retail store manager wishes to resolve a problem of how to reduce employee theft. She then finds two sets of quotations ("Security" and "Temptation").

Security Quotations

Probe the earth and see where your main roots run.

—Henry David Thoreau

The fly that doesn't want to be swatted is most secure when it lights on the fly swatter.

—G.C. Lichtenberg

I believe . . . that security declines as security machinery expands.

—E.B. White

Man's security comes from within himself, and the security of all men is founded upon the security of the individual.

—Manly Hall

It's an old adage that the way to be safe is never to be secure. . . . Each one of us requires the spur of insecurity to force us to do our best.

—Harold W. Dodds

Temptation Quotations

What makes resisting temptation difficult, for many people, is that they don't want to discourage it completely.

—Franklin P. Jones

All the things I really like to do are either immoral, illegal, or fattening.

—Alexander Woollcott

I find I always have to write something on a steamed mirror.

—Elaine Dundy

The only way to get rid of temptation is to yield to it. . . . I can resist everything but temptation.

　—Oscar Wilde

Don't worry about avoiding temptation—as you grow older, it starts avoiding you.

　—The Old Farmer's Almanac

To illustrate how to use quotations to generate ideas, consider the employee theft problem again. The two lists of quotations might stimulate the following kinds of ideas:

- Install weight-sensitive pressure pads in storeroom areas that would trigger alarms when stepped on during closed times (from "Probe the earth and see where your main roots run").
- Conduct intensive background checks of all current and future employees (from "The fly that doesn't want to be swatted").
- Reward employees with free trips to dude ranches when they reduce theft (from "Each one of us requires the spur of insecurity to force us to do our best").
- Assign in-house "marshals" to monitor employee behavior (from "Each one of us requires the spur of insecurity to force us to do our best").
- Attach small, easy-to-conceal alarms on valuable items so that an alarm sounds when an item is removed from a room (from "I believe . . . that security declines as security machinery expands").
- Install one-way mirrors in high-risk areas (from "I find I always have to write something on a steamed mirror").
- Use items that are often stolen as performance rewards (from "The only way to get rid of temptation is to yield to it").
- Assign big brothers and sisters to new employees to help with general orientation and to educate new workers about theft (from "Don't worry about avoiding temptation—as you grow older, it starts avoiding you").

14

IDEA SHOPPING

Background

This technique encourages participants to do something for which they may not need encouragement: hop in their cars, head for the nearest shopping mall, and shop until they drop! And some can take care of two needs at once: buy themselves something spiffy to wear or check out all the latest goods, and generate some ideas as well.

Objectives

- To help participants generate as many creative ideas as possible
- To help participants learn how to use the activities to generate ideas

Participants

Small groups of four to seven people each

Materials, Supplies, and Equipment

- For each group: markers, two flip charts, and masking tape for posting flip-chart sheets
- For each participant: one sheet each of three different colors of sticking dots (½" diameter) and one pad of 4 x 6 Post-it® Notes
- One notepad and pen or pencil for each participant to carry into a store

Handout

- Idea Shopping Handout

Time

30 minutes (also requires one week prior preparation time)

Related Activities

- Idea Diary [6]
- Tickler Things [21]

Procedure

1. Provide participants with a problem challenge at least one week prior to a training or idea generation session.

2. Prior to the session, tell participants to walk, individually, around a department or discount store and take in the sights. Tell them to check out the merchandise, watch how things are done, how people act, and so forth, writing down all of their observations.

3. Instruct them to select one item or action that catches their attention. Encourage them to examine it more closely and notice which particular attributes, characteristics, functions, concepts, or principles are represented. Remind them to write down all of their observations.

4. When the session starts, distribute the Idea Shopping Handout and discuss it with them, pointing out how the ideas were obtained.

5. Have them individually think of how their observations might help them resolve the primary challenge. Perhaps it can't help directly, but if you tell them to free-associate and see what ideas the item or action might trigger, that might help.

6. Tell them to write down on their Post-it® pads any ideas that come to mind (one idea per note).

7. Instruct them to select something else they observed, see what ideas it might stimulate, and write them on a Post-it® (one idea per note).

8. Tell them to continue this process for at least 30 minutes or until they have generated at least five ideas and placed them on flip charts for evaluation.

Debrief/Discussion

This technique has value in using unrelated stimuli (the in-store observations) and brainwriting (generating ideas in writing), both of which can help produce more, higher-quality ideas than normally might be produced. For a discussion, consider asking the following types of questions:

- What worked best and least about this exercise?
- What areas of the stores seemed to be the most useful source of stimuli?
- Did any participants have trouble using the stores for stimulation? Why or why not?

  Also, consider having participants debrief using the following questions:

- What was most helpful about this exercise?
- What was most challenging?

- What can we apply?
- How would you rate the value of this exercise to helping us with this issue?
- Will this exercise be helpful in the future for other sessions?
- What did you learn?
- What will we be able to use from this exercise?
- What ideas were generated, and which ones were most interesting?

Variation

1. After the participants have generated each idea and written it on a Post-it®, tell them to pass their ideas to the person to the right (that is, write down one idea and pass it to the right, write down the second and pass it on, and so forth).

2. Indicate that they should use each idea passed to them for possible stimulation of a new idea. If the idea passed triggers a new idea, have them write it on a new Post-it® and then pass both on to the next person to the right. (If someone can't think of a new idea based on the idea passed to him or her, tell the person not to worry and just pass on the idea to the next person.)

3. Have them continue this process until at least five ideas have gone around the group once.

Idea Shopping Handout

Tips

- Don't spend all your time in one department. Choose stimulation from a variety of areas.
- Stores are such rich sources of stimulation that they can be overwhelming. Don't try to take in too much. Instead, focus your attention as much as possible on things that interest you.

To illustrate Idea Shopping, suppose you are trying to reduce employee theft at your organization. You've tried asking the employees not to steal, but you haven't been successful. It's time to develop more creative ideas.

You head for your local Roof-Mart. After cruising the parking lot looking for a space, you finally find a spot near the garden department entrance. You begin to browse, and you spot a garden hose. Aha!

- *Idea:* Hide video cameras inside the overhead sprinklers. Connect the sprinklers to a water tank containing ammonia. If a security guard spots someone stealing something, the sprinklers automatically go off, spraying the thief's eyes with ammonia. (The thief will hate it when that happens!)

You continue browsing and notice that there are two rows of checkout stands, staggered in position to permit passage.

- *Idea:* Install two sets of motion detectors, one near the entrance of a storage room and the other inside the room. The first set serves as a silent alarm to notify you that someone is trying to enter; the second lets you know if the person enters the room.

You then walk down an aisle and see flashlights.

- *Idea:* Install airport x-ray machines at all organization exits.

After looking at the flashlights, you turn a corner and see an employee restocking shelves while standing on a ladder.

- *Idea:* Require that employees order all supplies by computer with a user ID. Employees may pick up supplies only after the computer ID has been checked and matched to the particular supplies.

15

A Likely Story

Background

Have you ever wanted to write the Great American Novel (GAN), but didn't think you could? Well, now is your chance. Even if we don't consider ourselves to be writers, we can compose brief, fantasy stories. We then can use our stories as the basis for our GANs.

Writing, like painting and sculpting, is a creative activity. All artists use a variety of stimuli to craft their creative products using free association. Some of these stimuli come from the product itself. Thus, an artist might draw a shape that stimulates another shape, which prompts a third and so forth. Creative writing works much the same way. A creative phrase, character description, or plot element might suggest other corresponding thoughts that, in turn, suggest even more. In addition, creating a story about a problem forces us to consider new information and perspectives that might have gone unnoticed.

Objectives

- To help participants generate as many creative ideas as possible
- To help participants learn how to use the activities to generate ideas

Participants

Small groups of four to seven people each

Materials, Supplies, and Equipment

- For each group: markers, two flip charts, and masking tape for posting flip-chart sheets
- For each participant: one sheet each of three different colors of sticking dots (½" diameter) and one pad of 4 x 6 Post-it® Notes

Handout

- A Likely Story Handout

Time

90 minutes

Related Activities

- Idea Diary [6]
- Text Tickler [20]
- Fairy Tale Time [40]

Procedure

1. Distribute the handout, review it with participants, and ask whether they have any questions.

2. Decide on a group challenge statement and distribute it to all participants along with the following statement:

   "Your task for this exercise is to write a brief, fictional story of fewer than 500 words (about two, typed, double-spaced pages). Your story should be related directly to the group problem. Don't worry if it doesn't make a lot of sense. Just let go of your imagination. Sometimes, humorous stories work best, but don't limit yourself. Then read over your story carefully. Scrutinize it for major themes, concepts, principles, actions, thoughts, and whatever else strikes your fancy. Make a list of these and write down any ideas suggested to resolve the challenge."

4. Distribute the handout to be used as a sample story, discuss it with the participants, and ask if there are any questions.

5. Convene the small groups and instruct members from each group to share their three best ideas, write them down on Post-it® Notes (one idea per note), place them on a flip chart, and then vote on the best ideas shared.

Debrief/Discussion

A Likely Story generates ideas using random stimulation from data generated from the story. It helps us explore our subconscious creative thoughts and use these thoughts to stimulate ideas. And the quality of writing really isn't important. What is important is to generate a variety of stimuli that might be used to trigger ideas. Consider asking the groups to discuss whether this exercise worked and why it did or did not. Note that not all groups will benefit from this exercise since it does require some creative imagination. It also is possible that someone who can't think of any ideas with one story may experience a different outcome with another story he or she writes.

Also consider having participants debrief using the following questions:

- What was most helpful about this exercise?
- What was most challenging?
- What can we apply?
- How would you rate the value of this exercise to helping us with this issue?
- Will this exercise be helpful in the future for other sessions?
- What did you learn?

- What will we be able to use from this exercise?
- What ideas were generated, and which ones were most interesting?

Variation

- Have members of each group create a story as a group and then use it to generate ideas.

A Likely Story Handout

To illustrate A Likely Story, consider the problem of helping a publisher sell more books. Here's one story, written entirely with free association. In this case, the author started by writing down the lead sentence and then going from there:

It was a day like any other day for Duke Smithers, private investigator. Eleanor Making wanted him to follow her husband for investigation of possible infidelity. Sleazy bars and cheap motels were what he knew best in these cases. One lead led to another like liquid molten lead. First a bartender sees the suspected couple and then a motel clerk denies ever seeing them. It was as if people knew how to disappear into thin air.

The thought of it made him gasp for air, and then made him parched for a drink. Yeah. A good stiff drink of cranberry juice was what he needed. He opened his desk drawer, retrieved the quart bottle of CJ (cranberry juice), and slammed it down on his desk. He untwisted the lid and thought of what he had learned so far: Mr. Making was making time with Susie Turnoverton, his former secretary who now worked as a CPA. Or was she? The more he reflected while sipping his CJ, the more he thought of how much he liked CJ. And then he passed out, a stream of red flowing from his mouth. Murdered or just resting? Who can tell?

O.K. It's a pretty stupid story. If it can help generate ideas, however, then it's a pretty smart story. To generate ideas for the problem of selling books, you could read over the story several times and think of ideas stimulated. (Another option would be to list major themes and write them down.) Here are some sample ideas:

- Hire an actor to play a fictional detective to promote a detective novel (from "private investigator").
- Start a "Frequent Purchasers" club and reward faithful customers with discounts or free books (from "infidelity").
- Sell popular paperbacks in hotels and motels (from "sleazy motels").
- Sponsor a contest with an airplane trip as the grand prize (from "disappear into thin air").
- Add a pine-scented scratch-and-sniff on the cover of a book about trees (from "gasp for air").
- Advertise health food and recipe books on bottles of fruit juice (from "cranberry juice").
- Give people a trade-in allowance on old books when buying new ones (from "Turnoverton").
- Allow people to buy books on the installment plan (from "CPA").
- Pass out book fliers with coupons in malls (from "passed out").
- Create capsules that ooze fake blood from inside murder-mystery books (from "red flowing from his mouth").

16

PICLED BRAINS

Background

We all have had our brains tickled many times while listening to others talk. Although we may not hear every word spoken, we often scan the output selectively and focus on a few key words and phrases. These words and phrases are the ones that frequently spark new ideas. Sometimes we may not be aware we are influenced by someone's words; other times, we may have an instant "Aha!" when we hear a certain word. In either case, the ideas usually flow freely.

PICLed Brains is based on the Product Improvement CheckList (PICL) (VanGundy, 1985) poster and uses a similar process to generate ideas. However, instead of relying on someone else's words, we can use random stimulus words, most of which should be unrelated to a problem.

This technique is based on the brain's ability to free-associate when presented with something new. When we first confront a new word, a stream of mental associations is triggered in our brains. Each of these mental associations has the potential to spark unique ideas, mostly because the associations are unrelated to our problems.

The Product Improvement CheckList contains stimulus words organized into four categories:

1. Try to . . . (for example, inflate it, twist it, sketch it, wipe it, tighten it)
2. Make it . . . (for example, transparent, soft, magnetic)
3. Think of . . . (for example, time bombs, escalators, oatmeal)
4. Take away or add . . . (for example, anticipation, layers, sex appeal, friction)

To generate ideas, randomly select a word from one of the four categories and see if it suggests any new ideas. Then free-associate from this word to get started. If you don't have a copy of the PICL, you can use the sample words in the handout.

Objectives

- To help participants generate as many creative ideas as possible
- To help participants learn how to use the activities to generate ideas

Participants

Small groups of four to seven people each

Materials, Supplies, and Equipment

- For each group: markers, two flip charts, and masking tape for posting flip-chart sheets
- For each participant: one sheet each of three different colors of sticking dots (½" diameter) and one pad of 4 x 6 Post-it® Notes
- (*Optional*) A dictionary or other book containing lists of words (for example, "Random House Word Menu")

Handouts

- List of Stimulus Words Handout
- PICLed Brains Handout

Time

45 minutes

Related Activities

- Excerpt Excitation [13]
- Say What? [20]
- Text Tickler [21]

Procedure

1. Distribute the List of Stimulus Words Handout (feel free to add other words or have group members add their own words).
2. Distribute the PICLed Brains Handout, one copy per person or post the words on a flip chart. Explain how to use the words and answer any questions they may have.
3. Instruct the individuals in each group to take turns picking one word unrelated to the challenge.
4. Tell them the group should use each word to free-associate and try to think of ideas to resolve the challenge. Note: if a word doesn't result in any ideas, they should select another word.
5. Tell them to write down any ideas on Post-it® Notes (one idea per note) and place them on flip charts for evaluation.

Debrief/Discussion

Some people have trouble using stimuli that are unrelated to a challenge, since they are not directly related. Ask participants to discuss why this might be. Other questions might involve why some words seem to generate more ideas than others. You also could observe that people who initially have trouble with free association often begin to loosen up and increase their ability to think of ideas over time. Observing others use the words also can facilitate learning how to free-associate from random words.

Also consider having participants debrief using the following questions:

- What was most helpful about this exercise?
- What was most challenging?
- What can we apply?
- How would you rate the value of this exercise to helping us with this issue?
- Will this exercise be helpful in the future for other sessions?
- What did you learn?
- What will we be able to use from this exercise?
- What ideas were generated, and which ones were most interesting?

List of Stimulus Words Handout

Force it	Sand it	Jiggle it	Brush it	Cushion it	Bend it
Sprinkle it	Press it	Vibrate it	Inject it	Twist it	Inflate it
Bright	Transparent	Sticky	Bounce	Spin	Pop up
Tubes	Wet	Shine	Coarse	Bubble	Zip
Balloons	Accordions	Sponges	Thermostats	Tulips	Egg shells
Mercury	Waterfalls	Syringes	Vises	Corkscrews	Gryoscopes
Funnels	Filters	Spirals	Time bombs	Bells	Waves
Mirrors	Velcro	Rhythm	Static	Turbulence	Anticipation

PICLed Brains Handout

To illustrate PICLed Brains, consider the problem of improving a common household flashlight. Here are some sample ideas:

- Make a flashlight buoyant so it floats in water if dropped accidentally (from "inflate it").

- Make the flashlight handle out of rubber so it can be twisted into different shapes as a novelty or secured to some object in order to target the light beam (from "twist it").

- Make the flashlight transparent, like a transparent telephone (from "transparent").

- Include a timer so the flashlight turns off automatically after a certain amount of time (from "time bombs").

- Design the flashlight so that it turns on whenever pressure is applied to the handle (from "anticipation").

17

PICTURE TICKLER

Background

Visual stimuli of all types can create different perceptions, thoughts, feelings, and associations. What triggers an image in one person may trigger a completely different one in someone else.

This technique is similar to PICLed Brains except the stimuli are pictures instead of words. People who have trouble free-associating from unrelated stimulus words may find it easier to free-associate with pictures. So this might be a useful technique for such people.

Objectives

- To help participants generate as many creative ideas as possible
- To help participants learn how to use the activities to generate idea

Participants

Small groups of four to seven people each

Materials, Supplies, and Equipment

- For each group: markers, two flip charts, and masking tape for posting flip-chart sheets
- For each participant: one sheet each of three different colors of sticking dots (½" diameter) and one pad of 4 x 6 Post-it® Notes
- Windmill graphic
- An assortment of color pictures from magazines and catalogs. Color pictures from such magazines as *National Geographic* work well. The best pictures are those with a variety of actions, objects, colors, textures, and other stimuli. Try to select pictures that vary in content. For instance, don't select all factory scenes or pictures of the countryside. In general, avoid pictures with people in them, especially close-ups. As a rule of thumb, have at least four magazines or catalogs for each group.

Handout

- Picture Tickler Handout

Time

30 minutes

Related Activities

- Ideatoons [26]
- Doodles [37]
- Drawing Room [59]
- Modular Brainstorming [62]

Procedure

1. Distribute the Picture Tickler Handout and have the participants look at Figure 5.1.

2. Ask the large group whether it suggests any images to them. Any specific associations? Thoughts? Feelings? If so, suggest that the visual stimuli in the picture may have affected them.

3. Ensure they understand how to use the picture to generate ideas. Answer any questions they might have.

4. Distribute the magazines and catalogs to each group.

5. Have the group members take turns selecting a picture that the large group then will describe in detail and write down descriptions of on a flip chart. Encourage them to note any relationships, concepts, and principles visible. Emphasize the importance of describing actual or implied actions or processes. Note that the purpose of this exercise is to stimulate ideas, not achieve consensus on correctness. This reminder is important because members are likely to disagree with others about the accuracy of their descriptions.

6. After all the descriptions have been recorded, tell the groups to look them over and see which ones might stimulate ideas. To help them think of ideas, have them take turns free-associating aloud and be playful with their associations. (This way they will be more likely to generate fresh perspectives. Rigidity is an enemy of creative thinking.)

7. Tell them to write down any ideas on Post-it® Notes (one idea per note) and place them on flip charts for evaluation.

Debrief/Discussion

Many people respond best to visual stimuli when generating ideas. People who tend to create mental images when generating ideas probably respond well when looking at visual stimuli. Note that one way to test whether they are visual thinkers is to ask group members to take turns observing each other's eyes while the other thinks of a creative solution to some problem. If someone looks to the left and up, he or she is probably conjuring up visual images. (This is true because the right side of the brain—which is involved with creativity—controls the left side of the body.)

Also consider having participants debrief using the following questions:

- What was most helpful about this exercise?
- What was most challenging?
- What can we apply?
- How would you rate the value of this exercise to helping us with this issue?
- Will this exercise be helpful in the future for other sessions?
- What did you learn?
- What will we be able to use from this exercise?
- What ideas were generated, and which ones were most interesting?

Picture Tickler Handout

Here's an example of how to use a picture of a windmill as a source of idea stimulation. The problem involves improving a household telephone. First, describe the picture shown in Figure 5.1.

There is a windmill. It is down by the old windmill stream (not the river, but the stream). It's where I first met you. The air is relatively calm. The wind turns the blades, which turn gears to pump water out of the fields. The faster the wind blows, the faster the blades turn. The windmill building provides protection from the elements. Many windmills are needed to pump out all the water.

Figure 5.1.   Windmill

Next, use the descriptions to spark ideas. Here are some examples:

- Put the telephone on tiny wheels to roll around on a desk (from "The wind turns the blades").
- Add an LCD panel that shows your name and welcomes you every time you pick up the phone to make a call (from "It's where I first met you").
- Make a telephone receiver that is shaped like a boat and floats in water (from "pump water out of the fields").
- Use different sound effects to notify users of incoming calls, such as driving rain, pounding surf, or hail (from "The windmill building provides protection from the elements").
- Create an inflatable telephone (from "pump out all the water").

18

RORSCHACH REVISIONIST

Background

This exercise uses what psychologists call "ambiguous stimulus materials." To keep things simple, we'll call them ASM. ASM are stimuli that have no apparent meaning. Instead, we tend to project meaning onto these stimuli based on how we interpret the world.

A psychologist, for instance, might use Rorschach inkblots to determine whether a client has an aggressive personality. The client presumably will project aggressive tendencies in response to seeing the inkblots. Another person with a different personality might describe feelings of tranquility in response to the same inkblot.

Rorschach Revisionist is based on the principle of standard inkblot tests. However, instead of using inkblots to assess one's personality, they are used as sources of stimulation to generate ideas. Thus, instead of projecting personality, participants project their ideas and thinking perspectives.

Objectives

- To help participants generate as many creative ideas as possible
- To help participants learn how to use the activities to generate ideas

Participants

Small groups of four to seven people each

Materials, Supplies, and Equipment

- For each group: markers, two flip charts, and masking tape for posting flip-chart sheets
- For each participant: one sheet each of three different colors of sticking dots (½" diameter) and one pad of 4 x 6 Post-it® Notes.
- One or two bottles of washable, black liquid ink for each table
- One sheet of 8.5" x 11" paper for each participant

Handout

- Rorschach Revisionist Handout

Time

30 minutes

Related Activities

- Picture Tickler [17]
- Ideatoons [26]
- Doodles [37]
- Drawing Room [59]
- Modular Brainstorming [62]

Procedure

1. Distribute the handout showing a sample inkblot exercise. Discuss how the stimuli were collected and then used to generate ideas. Ask if they have any questions.

2. Instruct each participant to make an inkblot by folding the 8.5" x 11" paper in half on the 8.5-inch side (as opposed to lengthwise) so that each half is roughly 5.5 inches long and unfolds like a book.

3. Tell them to place a large (about 1.5 inches in diameter) drop of ink on one-half of their folded paper and then fold it over (as if closing a book) onto the side without any ink. Tell them to press down hard so that the ink is smeared around on the paper. The result is their personal inkblot.

4. Ask the participants to study their personal inkblots and encourage them not to fixate on the first image they see or they may have trouble seeing other images. Have them turn the inkblot upside down and sideways and look at it straight down and from an angle. Then suggest that they squint at it and rotate it to create different perspectives.

5. Ask each individual to share his or her inkblot with the other group members and describe what he or she sees in as much detail as possible. They may see many different images in each inkblot, so encourage them to share all of the images.

6. Caution them about limiting themselves to generating ideas prompted directly from the inkblot stimuli. For example, if they see nothing but animals in an inkblot, they shouldn't feel obligated to use only animals as stimuli. Instead, tell them to let their intuition take over and concentrate on the inkblots and let the free associations flow. Then write down whatever ideas come to mind. For example, from animals they might free-associate to zoos and then to amusement parks and so on.

7. Ask the group members to use the descriptions of each inkblot as stimuli to gener-

ate ideas, write them down on Post-it® Notes (one idea per note), and place the notes on a flip chart for evaluation.

Debrief/Discussion

This can be a fun exercise since it produces diverse stimuli as well as perceptions as to what those stimuli represent. Ask the group members to discuss how easy or difficult it was for them to see images within the inkblots and to use them as idea triggers.

Also consider having participants debrief using the following questions:

- What was most helpful about this exercise?
- What was most challenging?
- What can we apply?
- How would you rate the value of this exercise to helping us with this issue?
- Will this exercise be helpful in the future for other sessions?
- What did you learn?
- What will we be able to use from this exercise?
- What ideas were generated, and which ones were most interesting?

Variations

- Suggest that other group members note what they see in the other inkblots and use their descriptions to help trigger ideas.
- Use different colored inks and ask the group members to discuss whether that made any difference in their experiences in creating stimuli or thinking of ideas.

Rorschach Revisionist Handout

Refer to the inkblot shown in Figure 5.2 to stimulate ideas for improving a telephone. First, describe the inkblot, for example:

- A jet aircraft with swept-back wings
- Siamese twins on a teeter-totter in the large part on the top of the inkblot
- A spider
- A frog holding a modern sculpture
- An Amazon beetle
- A moon-landing craft
- A mirror image of stalagmites
- The remains of a spider dropped from a twenty-story building
- Two alligators with conjoined twins on their backs
- A Vulcan tree root

Figure 5.2.   Inkblot

Next, use the descriptions and any intuitive reactions to generate ideas:

- A children's telephone in the shape of a airplane fighter (or frog, spider, beetle, space-ship, or alligator)
- A teeter-totter type of telephone in which the phone base goes down when the receiver is lifted (and vice versa)
- A telephone designed as a copy of a modern sculpture
- A telephone that "walks" across the table toward you when it rings
- A stainless steel telephone
- An alligator telephone that cradles the receiver in its mouth
- A "piggyback" telephone that contains a detachable cellular phone and a computer database of names and addresses
- A telephone that comes apart as a puzzle

19

SAY WHAT?

Background

Idea generation should be like a rolling stone that gathers no moss. We should be able to free-associate so fast we don't have time to judge our ideas. This is especially true in groups, in which people in glass houses shouldn't throw stones. If we criticize others' ideas, we should criticize our own.

Figures of speech liven up what we read and hear. They give substance to our communications and can convey intended meanings more clearly. They also can become tiresome if used repetitively or improperly, as illustrated in the previous paragraph (that is, "a rolling stone . . ." and "people in glass houses . . . ").

We all use clichés, proverbs, and maxims as part of our everyday speech. However, if we want to use them to resolve our problems, we must use them systematically. That is where this exercise comes in handy.

Objectives

- To help participants generate as many creative ideas as possible
- To help participants learn how to use the activities to generate ideas

Participants

Small groups of four to seven people each

Materials, Supplies, and Equipment

- For each group: markers, two flip charts, and masking tape for posting flip-chart sheets
- For each participant: one sheet each of three different colors of sticking dots (½" diameter) and one pad of 4 x 6 Post-it® Notes.

Handouts

- Clichés, Proverbs, and Maxims Handout
- Say What? Handout

Ticklers: Related and Unrelated Stimuli

Time

30 minutes

Related Activities

- Picture Tickler [17]
- Ideatoons [26]
- Doodles [37]
- Drawing Room [59]
- Modular Brainstorming [62]

Procedure

1. Distribute the Clichés, Proverbs, and Maxims Handout.
2. Distribute the Say What? Handout and discuss it with the participants, answering questions they might have.
3. After discussing a challenge to work on, instruct the groups to review the list of Clichés, Proverbs, and Maxims and have each person select one that looks interesting.
4. Tell the individuals to write down what they think is the intended meaning behind the maxim or cliché they chose and to use as much detail as they can with their descriptions.
5. Have the individuals in each group share their descriptions, in turn, with the other group members.
6. Tell them to use the descriptions to brainstorm ideas as a group, write down ideas on Post-it® Notes (one idea per note), and place them on a flip chart for evaluation.

Debrief/Discussion

This is an exercise in which the specific selections can determine the outcome. That is, some selections might result in a higher quantity and quality of ideas than others. Some people might be able to use the phrases more easily than others to trigger ideas, or some may find this approach better than when using another technique using single words, such as the PICLed Brains [16] approach.

Also consider having participants debrief using the following questions:

- What was most helpful about this exercise?
- What was most challenging?
- What can we apply?
- How would you rate the value of this exercise to helping us with this issue?
- Will this exercise be helpful in the future for other sessions?

- What did you learn?
- What will we be able to use from this exercise?
- What ideas were generated, and which ones were most interesting?

Clichés, Proverbs, and Maxims Handout

- A friend in need is a friend indeed.
- A penny saved is a penny earned.
- A rolling stone gathers no moss.
- A stitch in time saves nine.
- Absence makes the heart grow fonder.
- Actions speak louder than words.
- All roads lead to Rome.
- All that glitters is not gold.
- All work and no play makes Jack a dull boy.
- An ounce of prevention is worth a pound of cure.
- Beggars can't be choosers.
- Better late than never.
- Better safe than sorry.
- Big oaks from little acorns grow.
- Don't bite off more than you can chew.
- Don't borrow from Peter to pay Paul.
- Don't burn a candle at both ends.
- Don't put all your eggs into one basket.
- Don't rock the boat.
- Early to bed and early to rise makes a man healthy, wealthy, and wise.
- Every cloud has a silver lining.
- Experience is the best teacher.
- Familiarity breeds contempt.
- Fools rush in where angels fear to tread.
- For every drop of rain that falls, a flower grows.
- Forewarned is forearmed.
- Go ahead. Make my day!
- Good fences make good neighbors.
- He who hesitates is lost.
- He who tends a fig tree will eat its fruit.
- His bark is worse than his bite.
- It never rains but it pours.

- It takes two to tango.
- It's easier to catch flies with honey than with vinegar.
- Jack of all trades, master of none.
- Keep your nose to the grindstone.
- Look before you leap.
- Loose lips sink ships.
- Misery loves company.
- Neither a borrower nor a lender be.
- Nothing ventured, nothing gained.
- Out of sight, out of mind.
- People who live in glass houses shouldn't throw stones.
- Rome wasn't built in a day.
- Seeing is believing.
- Something must be seen to be believed.
- Spare the rod and spoil the child.
- Stone walls do not a prison make.
- The early bird gets the worm.
- The grass is always greener on the other side of the fence.
- The meek shall inherit the earth.
- The pen is mightier than the sword.
- Too many cooks spoil the broth.
- Two heads are better than one.
- Two's company and three's a crowd.
- Waste not, want not.
- Where there's smoke there's fire.
- You can lead a horse to water, but you can't make him drink.
- You can't judge a book by its cover.
- You're barking up the wrong tree.

Say What? Handout

To illustrate this technique, consider the problem of how to recruit professional employees. To generate ideas, you might select two proverbs. The first is "Stone walls do not a prison make." This proverb might elicit the following free associations:

- Although you can imprison my body, you can't imprison my spirit.
- Many people create their own "mental" prisons that restrict their ability to think creatively.
- Stone walls are generally built from the bottom up in layers.
- It is much easier to go over, under, or around stone walls than through them.

These interpretations then might spark the following ideas:

- Emphasize personal and professional growth opportunities or, if they don't exist, create them (from "you can't imprison my spirit").
- Demonstrate in-house creativity sessions at professional meetings to show how much fun it is to work for your organization and how creativity is encouraged (from "Many people create their own mental prisons").
- Provide intensive orientation sessions to lay a good foundation for understanding the organization (from "Stone walls are generally built up in layers").
- Promise new executives direct access to upper management (from "Stone walls are generally built up in layers").
- Provide new executives with a personal mentor to help cut through the red tape during their first year on the job (from "It is much easier to go over, under, or around stone walls than through them").

For the second proverb, you might select "All work and no play makes Jack a dull boy." It might suggest the following thoughts:

- We all occasionally need to relax and recharge our batteries.
- We should strive to achieve balance in the amount of work and play we do.
- Dull people can be unpleasant to be around.

These interpretations might prompt the following types of ideas:

- Provide professionals with executive sabbaticals (from "We all occasionally need to relax and recharge our batteries").
- Require all employees to take a "play break" every day (from "We should strive to achieve balance in the amount of work and play we do").
- To keep people sharp, require job rotation (from "Dull people can be unpleasant to be around").

20

TEXT TICKLER

Background

Many people like to read for entertainment or to learn something new. For some people, there's nothing like curling up with a good novel. Reading helps tickle our gray matter, whether the material is Shakespeare or a clothing catalog. The more we read, the more stimulation we receive.

Sometimes, when we least expect it, a potential solution will pop out as we read. This may happen through some subconscious association or because we occasionally ponder a current problem while reading and something we read sparks an idea. Although such ideas may frequently occur by chance, we can make idea generation more predictable. That's where the Text Tickler exercise can help.

Text Tickler involves randomly selecting words from different sources and then using them to prompt ideas. It doesn't matter where you get the words, as long as you have a varied pool from which to choose.

Objectives

- To help participants generate as many creative ideas as possible
- To help participants learn how to use the activities to generate ideas

Participants

Small groups of four to seven people each

Materials, Supplies, and Equipment

- For each group: markers, two flip charts, and masking tape for posting flip-chart sheets
- For each participant: one sheet each of three different colors of sticking dots (½″ diameter) and one pad of 4 x 6 Post-it® Notes.

Handout

- Text Tickler Handout

Ticklers: Related and Unrelated Stimuli

111

Time

30 minutes

Related Activities

- A Likely Story [15]
- PICLed Brains [16]
- Say What? [19]

Procedure

1. Prior to the session, gather an assortment of old books, catalogs, magazines, newspapers, or any source of words, including dictionaries, to distribute during the session.

2. Distribute the Text Tickler Handout and discuss it with the participants, answering questions they might have.

3. At the start of the session, distribute at least one source of stimuli (a magazine or catalog) to each group member.

4. Instruct each participant to select a word or phrase from his or her word source.

5. Tell them to examine the word or phrase and use it to trigger at least one idea and write it on a Post-it® Note.

6. Have the group members pass their Post-it® Notes to the person on their right and tell them to write down any new ideas stimulated.

7. Tell the groups to repeat Steps 3 through 5 and conclude once all group members have selected and reported on a random word and generated an idea or when time is no longer available.

8. Have them place the notes on flip charts for evaluation.

Debrief/Discussion

This technique should appeal especially well to people who are good at creating visual images from reading different words. It also helps people who can free-associate easily so that one word leads to another, thus creating different perspectives.

To facilitate a discussion, try the following types of questions:

- Did some words lead to more ideas than others? If so, what were they and why?
- What types of problems might this activity work best with and why?
- Why is it important that the stimulus words be different from the problem challenge?

Also, consider having participants debrief using the following questions:

- What was most helpful about this exercise?
- What was most challenging?

- What can we apply?
- How would you rate the value of this exercise to helping us with this issue?
- Will this exercise be helpful in the future for other sessions?
- What did you learn?
- What will we be able to use from this exercise?
- What ideas were generated, and which ones were most interesting?

Text Tickler Handout

Assume you own a hotel chain and want to attract more customers. First, you need to select some random stimulus words. You are reading a newspaper while flying with several of your staff members to visit one of your hotels.

While reading movie reviews, you see the word "grumpy." This word sparks the idea of offering "Grumpy Room Service." All food orders are delivered by a grumpy delivery person as a novelty service. Or in another variation of Grumpy Room Service, give guests a free meal if any staff member treats them grumpily. Then look for another word and choose "research." This word might trigger the idea of in-room computers with easy-to-access business databases for the business traveler. Finally, you see the word "film" and think of installing picture phones in all the rooms.

21

TICKLER THINGS

Background

Everybody has things. They're all around us. Life would be boring without things. They make our world more interesting by providing us with varied stimuli.

We can see, touch, hear, taste, and smell things. Although specific things may give us pleasure or pain, all things stimulate us. They provide something to which we can react in a number of ways, depending on our personalities and previous experiences. The new perspectives things can give us are the basis for this technique, a cousin of PICLed Brains [16], Picture Tickler [17], and Text Tickler [20].

Objectives

- To help participants generate as many creative ideas as possible
- To help participants learn how to use the activities to generate ideas

Participants

Small groups of four to seven people each

Materials, Supplies, and Equipment

- For each group: markers, two flip charts, and masking tape for posting flip-chart sheets
- For each participant: one sheet each of three different colors of sticking dots (½" diameter) and one pad of 4 x 6 Post-it® Notes

Handout

- Tickler Things Handout

Time

30 minutes

Related Activities

- Idea Shopping [14]
- Grab Bag Forced Association [75]

Procedure

1. Distribute the Tickler Things Handout and discuss it with the participants, answering questions they might have.

2. Gather an assortment of objects representing varied types of things. Examples include pipe cleaners, clay, toy balls, plastic animals, light bulbs, books, radios, candles, watches, telephones, bottles, cans, et cetera. All objects should be unrelated to the problem.

3. Place at least six different objects on each table with small groups of participants.

4. Distribute the handouts to each participant and review the example.

5. Instruct each group to select an object unrelated to the problem, and ask if there are any questions.

6. Have them describe the object in some detail. Encourage them to include physical characteristics as well as how people react to the object and use it. Remind them that action descriptions are important, so they shouldn't limit themselves to single-word nouns.

7. Tell them to use their descriptions to stimulate ideas and assign someone to write down each idea on a Post-it® Note and place it on a flip chart.

8. Instruct them to repeat Steps 5 through 7 until they have generated at least twenty ideas or run out of time.

Debrief/Discussion

One positive feature of this exercise is its use of tangible objects. Thus, it is well suited for those with less ability to visualize and free-associate. The use of an actual object that can be seen and touched makes it easier for some to relate to and play off of for stimulation. If you want to lead a discussion, you could ask the groups to compare differences in using unrelated words, pictures, or objects as idea triggers.

Also consider having participants debrief using the following questions:

- What was most helpful about this exercise?
- What was most challenging?
- What can we apply?
- How would you rate the value of this exercise to helping us with this issue?
- Will this exercise be helpful in the future for other sessions?
- What did you learn?
- What will we be able to use from this exercise?
- What ideas were generated, and which ones were most interesting?

Tickler Things Handout

Assume you are an executive flying to a hotel site with several staff members. You want more ideas for attracting customers. One of your managers suggests using an airplane seat as the stimulus object. Right away, Nan (Ms. Creativity) Smith suggests recliner chairs in hotel rooms. Other staff members chime in with such ideas as stereo headsets in rooms and special beds with mattresses that can be raised and lowered.

You next challenge your staff members to use an airplane as a stimulus. Nan immediately suggests theme hotel rooms such as aeronautical or outer space rooms. Even Robert (Mr. Analytical) Jones has an idea: join with an airline to offer special discounts for people who fly the airline and stay at your hotel.

Combinations

To combine is to put together. When you put things together, you combine them in ways that may or may not be unique. It all depends on what you combine and who observes the result. That is, it's a matter of perspective.

Each combination is a stimulus that has the power to prompt any number of associations. And associations can help spark ideas. Thus, whatever we combine—whether related or unrelated to a problem—has the ability to yield creativity.

The activities in this chapter rely on the principle of combination and the stimuli and associations that result. Some activities combine things related to the problem, some combine things unrelated to the problem, and some combine related and unrelated things.

Combination activities are a little like "ticklers" (Chapter 5) in that both activities use various stimuli. The difference lies in how we respond to the stimuli. Ticklers provide direct stimulation; combinations stimulate more indirectly by joining together various elements in new ways.

NOTE: FOR ALL ACTIVITES, REMIND PARTICPANTS
TO DEFER JUDGMENT WHILE GENERATING IDEAS.

22

Bi-Wordal

Background

Take a word—any word. Now take another word and put them together. What do you get? Two words, of course! But you also get a certain meaning conveyed by those two words. Replace one of the words with another and the meaning conveyed by the combination may change dramatically. Thus, the stimulation value of any combination of words will vary depending on the words involved.

Objectives

- To help participants generate as many creative ideas as possible
- To help participants learn how to use the activities to generate ideas

Participants

Small groups of four to seven people each

Materials, Supplies, and Equipment

- For each group: markers, two flip charts, and masking tape for posting flip-chart sheets
- For each participant: one sheet each of three different colors of sticking dots (½″ diameter) and one pad of 4 x 6 Post-it® Notes
- One thesaurus for each group

Handout

- Bi-Wordal Handout

Time

30 minutes

Related Activities

- Combo Chatter [24]

101 Activities for Teaching Creativity and Problem Solving

- Ideas in a Box [25]
- Parts Is Parts [30]
- 666 [34]
- Word Diamond [35]

Procedure

1. Prior to the session, distribute to all participants one copy each of the Bi-Wordal Handout and ask them to read it.

2. Start the session by reviewing the handout and ask if there are any questions.

3. Have each group state their problem challenge so that it involves a verb and an object.

4. Tell the group members to select the verb and object, write them on a flip chart, and look up alternative meanings (synonyms) for each in a thesaurus.

5. Have them write the other meanings in a column below the verb and subject.

6. Instruct them to select one word from each column and use the combination to trigger ideas.

7. Tell them to write down any ideas on Post-it® Notes and place them on flip charts for evaluation.

Debrief/Discussion

One positive feature of this technique is that it easily can provide new perspectives simply by substituting different words in the problem challenge statement.

Although we can experience mental blocks when trying to solve problems, the blocks exist often only because of the words we have chosen to use. Thus, the difficulty is not that we can't think of creative ideas; it might be due more to how we state a problem. This technique illustrates this point rather nicely.

To further demonstrate the important role of initial problem statements, you might ask participants to trade their finished activities with each other or try to resolve the challenge of another group and see how the outcome might differ.

Also consider having participants debrief using the following questions:

- What was most helpful about this exercise?
- What was most challenging?
- What can we apply?
- How would you rate the value of this exercise to helping us with this issue?
- Will this exercise be helpful in the future for other sessions?
- What did you learn?
- What will we be able to use from this exercise?
- What ideas were generated, and which ones were most interesting?

Bi-Wordal Handout

Suppose you are an organization that wants to generate ways to increase the amount of money it donates to community service projects. This problem involves a combination of the words "increase" and "money." For most people, this particular combination would simply mean: "get more money." Pretty simple. But it doesn't help us think of many ideas.

What if we now substitute a synonym for the word "increase"? We look in a hard-bound or computer software thesaurus and look at several choices: advance, boost, jump, raise, hike, magnify, and snowball. Then we experiment with different combinations of these words with the word "money." Thus, we can generate combinations such as "boost/money," "jump/money," "hike/money," and "magnify/money."

If we can substitute synonyms for one of the words, then we also can substitute for the other. In this case, a thesaurus provides such substitutes for the word "money" as cash, currency, greenbacks, dough, wampum, and income. Next, we combine the word "increase" with these words and get such combinations as "increase/greenbacks" and "increase/wampum."

All these combinations can stimulate ideas. For instance, we could have employees volunteer their time to help with automobile emergencies and solicit donations from those they help (from "boost/money"). Or we could ask artistic employees to design and sell jewelry to raise funds (from "increase/wampum"). You get the idea.

But wait. There's more. We don't have to be limited to the words "increase" or "money" in combinations. We also could use any of the other synonyms on the lists. For instance:

Increase	Money	Advance	Cash
Boost	Currency	Jump	Greenbacks
Hike	Dough	Magnify	Wampum
	Snowball	Income	

To generate ideas on how to increase money, we select words randomly from each column, combine them, and use the new meaning to spark ideas. That's all there is to it. Here are some sample ideas:

- Sponsor a walk or run where participants contribute $5 for each mile they travel (from "hike/cash").
- Use payroll deductions for contributions (from "advance/income").
- Sponsor a carnival with shell games. People bet on the outcome. The proceeds go to charity (from "jump/currency").
- Give donors T-shirts with modified pictures of the denominations they contributed (from "magnify/greenbacks").
- Sell snow cones and doughnuts (from "snowball/dough").

23

Circle of Opportunity

Background

In one respect, all creative activity is a gamble. We invest our time, effort, and creative abilities in some problem with an unknown outcome. We can't always predict the result. Sometimes our creative efforts may even make things worse. It's a crapshoot of the mind.

All gambling involves some form of randomness. Chance makes things interesting. It determines whether we win or lose. We can't control chance, but we can try to capitalize on it and use it to our advantage. We can use randomness, for example, to help prompt ideas. In particular, random combinations of problem attributes can create associations that lead to breakthrough ideas.

The Circle of Opportunity activity, created by Michael Michalko (1991), is based on the random combination of problem attributes.

Objectives

- To help participants generate as many creative ideas as possible
- To help participants learn how to use the activities to generate ideas

Participants

Small groups of four to seven people each

Materials, Supplies, and Equipment

- For each group: a set of die, markers, two flip charts, and masking tape for posting flip-chart sheets
- For each participant: one sheet each of three different colors of sticking dots (½" diameter) and one pad of 4 x 6 Post-it® Notes

Time

30 minutes

Related Activities

- Combo Chatter [24]
- Ideas in a Box [25]
- Parts Is Parts [30]
- 666 [34]
- Word Diamond [35]
- A Likely Story [15]

Handout

- Circle of Opportunity Handout

Procedure

1. Instruct the groups to write down their challenge statement on a flip chart.
2. Distribute the Circle of Opportunity Handout, review it with the participants, and ask for any questions they might have.
3. Have them draw a circle on a flip chart about two feet in diameter, and number it like a clock, placing the numbers inside the circle.
4. Tell them to generate a list of twelve attributes that are either related or unrelated to their problem. Related attributes would describe major problem features. For instance, an airline promotional campaign might include such attributes as people, costs, travel, and airports. Unrelated attributes are common to many problems. Examples include substance, structure, color, shape, texture, sound, and politics. Tell them to write each attribute next to one of the numbers.
5. Direct them to take turns throwing one die to choose the first attribute and a pair of dice to choose the second.
6. Tell them to free-associate on each attribute individually and then on the two combined and to write down on a flip chart each association as it is verbalized.
7. Have them look for connections between their associations and their problems. Encourage them to think about what the associations remind them of, any analogies suggested, and any relationships between associations.
8. Tell them to write down any ideas on Post-it® Notes and place them on flip charts for evaluation.

Debrief/Discussion

This is an excellent exercise to use after a break or at the end of the day when people start getting tired. Its drawing requirements, visual elements, and throwing dice can help provide some needed energy—especially if group members take turns drawing or throwing the dice.

Also consider having participants debrief using the following questions:

- What was most helpful about this exercise?
- What was most challenging?
- What can we apply?
- How would you rate the value of this exercise to helping us with this issue?
- Will this exercise be helpful in the future for other sessions?
- What did you learn?
- What will we be able to use from this exercise?
- What ideas were generated, and which ones were most interesting?

Circle of Opportunity Handout

To illustrate Circle of Opportunity, consider ways to improve a briefcase. First, construct a circle as shown in Figure 6.1 with twelve different attributes.

You roll a die and get the number 5 (security); you roll both dice and get the number 10 (materials) for the second attribute. You free-associate using these attributes: plastic, hidden, bulletproof vest, case-hardened steel, alarms, motion detectors, and video cameras. These free associations might help you think of such ideas as:

- Installing hidden security pockets in a briefcase

- Constructing the briefcase out of bulletproof materials so it can be used as a shield

- Installing an alarm and motion detectors to go off whenever someone unauthorized tries to move the briefcase

You roll a die again and get the number 6 (padding) and then both dice and get the number 9 (colors).

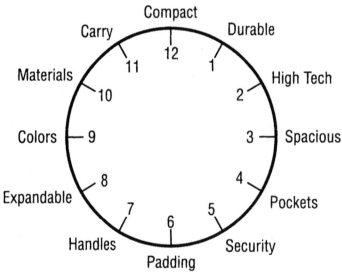

Figure 6.1.   Circle of Opportunity

Your free associations are soft, spongy, pockets, and rainbow. From these associations you think of the following ideas:

- A multicolored briefcase

- Different colors for each file of an expanding filing pocket

- A padded handle in a contrasting color

- A padded compartment in a contrasting color for use when carrying a notebook computer so you can remove the compartment when you aren't carrying the computer and save space

24

Combo Chatter

Background

This technique was originally known as Semantic Intuition when researchers at the Battelle Institute developed it in the 1970s (Schaude, 1978). "Semantic Intuition" is certainly an impressive name, but it's a little pretentious for this book. I decided to simplify things and call it Combo Chatter.

The typical new-product process involves generating ideas, selecting the best ones, developing them into workable products, and then assigning them names. Combo Chatter reverses that process somewhat: instead of generating ideas and then names for the ideas, it generates names and then the ideas. For instance, if a company wants to improve the toaster they market, they might think of a toaster made of see-through plastic and name it, "BreadView." Combo Chatter might produce the same see-through product but do it using the words "bread" and "view" in juxtaposition. Although this example applies to new product improvements, that doesn't mean it is appropriate only for new product development. It can work very well for almost any challenge.

Objectives

- To help participants generate as many creative ideas as possible
- To help participants learn how to use the activities to generate ideas

Participants

Small groups of four to seven people each

Materials, Supplies, and Equipment

- For each group: markers, two flip charts, and masking tape for posting flip-chart sheets
- For each participant: one sheet each of three different colors of sticking dots (½" diameter) and one pad of 4 x 6 Post-it® Notes.

Handout

- Combo Chatter Handout

Time

30 minutes

Related Activities

- Ideas in a Box [25]
- Parts Is Parts [30]
- 666 [34]
- Word Diamond [35]

Procedure

1. Distribute the handout, review it with the participants, and answer any questions they may have.
2. Instruct participants to generate two lists of five to six words related to their problem and write them on a flip chart. Tell them to do this as a group.
3. Have each group member take turns selecting one word from each list and have the group use the combination to stimulate ideas.
4. Direct them to write down any ideas on Post-it® Notes and place them on flip chart paper for evaluation.

Variation

- If time is available, have individual group members generate their own lists of words for the group to use as idea triggers.

Debrief/Discussion

This can be a useful technique for at least two reasons: (1) it has the potential to create many different perspectives and (2) it combines elements of both related and unrelated stimuli. That is, it uses attributes related directly to the problem and combines these attributes to create a more or less unrelated stimulus. Thus, it helps create perspective changes not possible with activities that rely on a single stimulus.

Also consider having participants debrief using the following questions:

- What was most helpful about this exercise?
- What was most challenging?
- What can we apply?
- How would you rate the value of this exercise to helping us with this issue?
- Will this exercise be helpful in the future for other sessions?
- What did you learn?
- What will we be able to use from this exercise?
- What ideas were generated, and which ones were most interesting?

101 Activities for Teaching Creativity and Problem Solving

Combo Chatter Handout

Assume a manufacturer of coffee cups wants to design a new coffee cup. They might list "things involving coffee cups" and "things involving people who drink coffee," as shown below:

Coffee Cups	**People**
Handles	Tense
Hot	Addicted
Logos	Cream and sugar
Breakable	Grind beans
Spills	Carry cups

After examining different combinations, they might generate the following types of ideas:

- Squeezable handles to relieve tension (from "handles/tense")
- Squeezable handles that inject cream or sugar (from "handles/cream and sugar")
- A combination coffee cup and bean grinder (from "handles/grind beans")
- Insulated coffee cups (from "hot/carry cups")
- Cups that break down into small pieces for easy carrying (from "breakable/carry cups")

25

Ideas in a Box

Background

Ideas in a Box—originally known as Morphological Analysis or Matrix Analysis—was developed by astronomer Fritz Zwicky (1969) to help generate scientific ideas. As with other combination activities, Ideas in a Box prompts ideas by forcing together problem attributes that lead to new ideas. Although the activity has variations, the one presented here is typical.

Objectives

- To help participants generate as many creative ideas as possible
- To help participants learn how to use the activities to generate ideas

Participants

Small groups of four to seven people each

Materials, Supplies, and Equipment

- For each group: markers, two flip charts, and masking tape for posting flip-chart sheets
- For each participant: one sheet each of three different colors of sticking dots (½" diameter) and one pad of 4 x 6 Post-it® Notes.

Handout

- Ideas in a Box Handout

Time

30 minutes

Related Activities

- Circle of Opportunity [23]

- Combo Chatter [24]
- Parts Is Parts [30]
- 666 [34]
- Word Diamond [35]

Procedure

1. Distribute the handout to participants, review it with them, and ask for any questions they might have.
2. Have each group obtain a sheet of flip-chart paper and tape it lengthwise to a wall or lay it down on a table.
3. Tell them to list major problem attributes across the top of the sheet of paper.
4. Direct them to list potential or existing subattributes for each category.
5. Have them combine one or more subattributes from each category and use the combination to suggest ideas.
6. Tell them to write down any ideas on Post-it® Notes (one idea per note) and place them on flip charts for evaluation.
7. Select another combination of subattributes and use it to generate ideas.
8. Have them continue this process until you have generated all possible ideas.

Debrief/Discussion

This exercise provides a relatively systematic way to consider different idea variations. Its emphasis on unrelated stimuli, however, may make it somewhat limiting. However, it is an excellent exercise to use for people who think in structured ways and like to analyze situations. Ideas in a Box might also work well with people who are good at free-associating from an initial stimulus word. You might test this last observation by asking participants to select one of their subattributes, take turns free-associating words, and then using these words to help trigger ideas.

Also consider having participants debrief using the following questions:

- What was most helpful about this exercise?
- What was most challenging?
- What can we apply?
- How would you rate the value of this exercise to helping us with this issue?
- Will this exercise be helpful in the future for other sessions?
- What did you learn?
- What will we be able to use from this exercise?
- What ideas were generated, and which ones were most interesting?

Ideas in a Box Handout

Suppose you are director of packaging design for Snafu Snack Food Company. Sales of your Cheesy Chunk Crackers have been slipping. Market research indicates supermarket consumers consider two criteria when buying cheese cracker products: (1) ability of the package to catch their eyes and (2) value-added or unique features.

You have been directed to redesign the current box to emphasize value-added features. Your boss gives you free rein to make changes, so you decide to use Ideas in a Box to help spark ideas. You set up a matrix as shown in Table 6.1.

Container Shapes	Container Materials
Cylindrical	Cardboard
Spherical	Plastic
Rectangular	Metal
Pyramidal	Combinations

Types of Closures	Lining Materials
Ziploc®	Wax paper
Clips	Aluminum foil
Adhesive	Regular paper
Screw cap	Cellophane

Table 6.1.   Ideas in a Box Matrix

Next, select one subattribute from each column. For instance, you might design a cylindrical package made of plastic with a screw top and an aluminum foil lining. Or you might select a spherical container made of combinations of materials with clips for closures and a cellophane lining. You get the idea. Although Ideas in a Box may not always prompt unique ideas, it will help you search systematically for possible combinations.

26

Ideatoons

Background

If you liked Ideas in a Box and are a visual thinker, then you'll like Ideatoons. Ideatoons are based on the work of architects Christopher Alexander, Sara Ishikawa, and Murray Silverstein (1977), who used a visual thinking activity known as "pattern language" to help create new building designs.

The architects developed abstract visual symbols that substituted for words. Each symbol represented a particular problem attribute. The symbols helped bring out potential relationships between attributes that, when identified, could trigger ideas. For instance, vertical arrows might point toward a curved line at the top of a page. This symbol might then suggest different ways of supporting or building an arch.

Michael Michalko (1991) adopted this visual approach and used it to describe Ideatoons—graphic problem representations. (This technique is also similar to the Symbolic Representation activity developed by VanGundy, 1983.) You don't need to be an artist to use Ideatoons—you just need the ability to draw anything remotely resembling something else.

Objectives

- To help participants generate as many creative ideas as possible
- To help participants learn how to use the activities to generate ideas

Participants

Small groups of four to seven people each

Materials, Supplies, and Equipment

- For each group: markers, two flip charts, and masking tape for posting flip-chart sheets
- For each participant: one sheet each of three different colors of sticking dots (½" diameter) and one pad of 4 x 6 Post-it® Notes..

Time

45 minutes

Related Activities

- Picture Tickler [17]
- Rorschach Revisionist [18]
- Doodles [37]
- Drawing Room [59]
- Modular Brainstorming [62]

Handout

- Ideatoons Handout

Procedure

1. Distribute the Ideatoons Handout, review it with the participants, and answer any questions they may have.

2. Tell them to divide their problem into major attributes.

3. Ask them to illustrate each attribute with an abstract, graphic symbol. Have them do this on a Post-it® Note (one illustration per note). Encourage them to focus on the general nature of their drawings and not to worry about how correct or artistic they might be.

4. Instruct them to place the completed cards, face up, on their tables and experiment with different groupings of the symbols. Caution them to avoid consciously creating any particular patterns and not to worry about having to use every note with each arrangement of symbols.

5. As they arrange and rearrange the symbols, tell them to use each combination of symbols to free-associate and see what ideas are suggested. Tell them that they don't have to limit themselves to combinations of symbols, but also may use individual ones.

6. Note that if they start to run out of ideas, they may add another Ideatoon or begin a new set.

7. Tell them to write down any ideas on Post-it® Notes (one idea per note) and place them on flip charts for evaluation.

Debrief/Discussion

This technique can be quite stimulating and fun to do in a group. It works especially well for people who free-associate well and can think symbolically. On the other hand, people who expect literal perspectives may have difficulty. Fortunately, most groups contain at least a couple of people who can help stimulate others. It is especially important that you encourage the participants to have fun. If time is available, you might ask them to discuss how easy it was for them to use the symbols.

Also consider having participants debrief using the following questions:

- What was most helpful about this exercise?
- What was most challenging?
- What can we apply?
- How would you rate the value of this exercise to helping us with this issue?
- Will this exercise be helpful in the future for other sessions?
- What did you learn?
- What will we be able to use from this exercise?
- What ideas were generated, and which ones were most interesting?

Ideatoons Handout

Suppose you are a packaging design director concerned with developing new cheese cracker box designs. First, you develop a list of problem attributes: box, package opening, closure, and package lining. Next, illustrate these attributes using graphic symbols such as the ones shown in Figure 6.2. Then experiment with different combinations of symbols to help kick start your imagination.

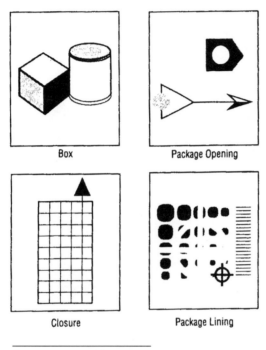

Figure 6.2.   Ideatoons

Here are some sample ideas:

- A box with two chambers: one for crackers and one for cheese spread (from the box and package opening symbols).

- A box with disposable, tear-off closures. Use each closure strip only once (from the box and closure symbols).

- Nested package linings with a vacuum in between (from the package opening and package lining symbols).

- Put a cheese cutter inside each package so consumers can stamp out pieces of cheese to conform to the shape of different crackers (from the package opening and closure).

27

Mad Scientist

Background

This technique, developed by Doug Hall (1994), is similar to Circle of Opportunity [23]. Instead of using a circle, however, Mad Scientist uses Green Die and Red Die lists of problem attributes. Attribute lists for each die are numbered 1 through 6.

The attributes for Mad Scientist differ from those used for Circle of Opportunity in two ways: (1) Mad Scientist categories are more general and (2) some of the categories may be completely unrelated to the problem. The procedure for combining attributes also is different: Circle of Opportunity combines two different attributes from the circle, whereas Mad Scientist combines two different lists of attributes.

Objectives

- To help participants generate as many creative ideas as possible
- To help participants learn how to use the activities to generate ideas

Participants

Small groups of four to seven people each

Materials, Supplies, and Equipment

- For each group: markers, one green and one red die (or any two dice of different colors), two flip charts, and masking tape for posting flip-chart sheets
- For each participant: one sheet each of three different colors of sticking dots (½" diameter) and one pad of 4 x 6 Post-it® Notes.

Handout

- Mad Scientist Handout

Time

45 minutes

Related Activities

- Circle of Opportunity [23]

Combinations

- Combo Chatter [24]
- Ideas in a Box [25]

Procedure

1. Distribute the Mad Scientist Handout, review it with the participants, and answer any questions they may have.

2. Have each group take a sheet of flip-chart paper and lay it on a table or tape it to a wall, lengthwise.

3. Read aloud the following:

   "List six general categories across the paper for the Green Die categories. Four or five categories should be related directly to the problem. The others may be unrelated or even somewhat whimsical. For each general category, list below it four or five examples, such as the briefcase materials shown in Table 6.2. Do the same thing for the Red Die categories, as shown in Table 6.2. As you can see from the table, it's O.K. to use some of the same categories as in the Green Die list."

4. Tell them to roll a green die (or designate a white die as "green") and select a category based on the number shown.

5. Tell them to roll a red die (or designate a white die as "red") and select a category based on the number shown.

6. Have them look over the lists from both categories and generate ideas by combining one word from each category (or using any of the single words as stimuli).

7. Tell them to write down any ideas on Post-it® Notes (one idea per note) and place them on flip charts for evaluation.

Debrief/Discussion

A major advantage of Mad Scientist is that it provides a greater number of stimuli than the Circle of Opportunity. Although Mad Scientist takes more time to set up, the resulting stimuli are well worth the trouble. You also may want to use this exercise when the groups need a little boost of energy. The game-like atmosphere provided from rolling dice can help spark groups in ways not possible with conventional brainstorming.

Also consider having participants debrief using the following questions:

- What was most helpful about this exercise?
- What was most challenging?
- What can we apply?
- How would you rate the value of this exercise to helping us with this issue?
- Will this exercise be helpful in the future for other sessions?
- What did you learn?
- What will we be able to use from this exercise?
- What ideas were generated, and which ones were most interesting?

Mad Scientist Handout

To illustrate Mad Scientist, the Green and Red Die lists for the problem of improving a briefcase might be set up as shown in Table 6.2.

Green Die

1	2	3	4	5	6
Places	*Materials*	*Shape*	*Weird*	*Function*	*Flavors*
Boardroom	Leather	Round	Elvis	Sprinkling	Cherry
Home	Plastic	Square	Pickles	Weight	Lemon
Office	Diamond	Sphere	Frogs	Sorting	Strawberry
Kitchen	Metal	Flat	Madonna	Flying	Chocolate

Red Die

Storage	*Time*	*Closures*	*Weird*	*Function*	*Sizes*
Pockets	Morning	Zippers	Superman	Reminders	Executive
Boxes	Afternoon	Button	Crystal	Wake Up	Compact
Shelves	Tea	Snaps	Ears	Typing	Overnight
Files	Noon	Straps	Birthday	Faxing	Regular

Table 6.2   Mad Scientist Table

To illustrate this exercise, assume that your group has been assigned the challenge of improving a briefcase. Someone in your group rolls the green die and gets a 4 ("weird") and rolls the red die and gets a 1 ("storage"). You then can use the words in these categories as stimuli by examining single words or combining different words from the two categories. Here are some sample ideas from these two categories:

- An Elvis briefcase shaped like a guitar with a picture of the "King" on the side (from "Elvis")
- A compartment with a cold pack to keep food from spoiling (from "pickles" and "pockets")
- Folding legs to turn a briefcase into a display case (from "frogs")
- A briefcase with a built-in, battery-powered compact disc player (from "Madonna" and "boxes")

28

Noun Action

Background

Words, like people, can assume many different faces. Depending on our moods, we can communicate a variety of feelings and behaviors. Yet no matter how many faces we show or how many emotions we express, we still are the same people.

In a similar way, the same basic word can communicate different meanings depending on how it is used and in what form. Nouns can become verbs and vice versa. It all depends on how you use them.

You can take advantage of this versatility of words to help generate ideas. Specifically, you can experiment with different noun and verb relationships and see what ideas emerge.

Objectives

- To help participants generate as many creative ideas as possible
- To help participants learn how to use the activities to generate ideas

Participants

Small groups of four to seven people each

Materials, Supplies, and Equipment

- For each group: markers, two flip charts, and masking tape for posting flip-chart sheets
- For each participant: one sheet each of three different colors of sticking dots (½″ diameter) and one pad of 4 x 6 Post-it® Notes.

Handout

- Noun Action Handout

Time

20 minutes

Related Activities

- Bi-Wordal [22]
- Combo Chatter [24]

Procedure

1. Distribute the handout, review it with the participants, and answer any questions they may have.
2. Have groups write down their challenges on the top of a flip chart and underline a verb and a noun (typically the objective, but it doesn't have to be). If possible have them use a different colored marker for the underline.
3. Tell them to switch the verb and noun and use the combination to suggest ideas. For instance, a challenge to improve spotty customer service might be restated as: "servicing spotty customers." This then might suggest an idea of concentrating service on infrequent customers.
4. Tell them to write down any ideas on Post-it® Notes (one idea per note) and place them on flip charts for evaluation.

Debrief/Discussion

A major limitation of this exercise is its reliance on only the verb and the noun in a problem challenge statement. It might be more advantageous to experiment with different verbs and nouns. Nevertheless, because the word combinations typically are unique juxtapositions, the potential exists for unique ideas as well. This exercise also involves relatively little time, so that is another factor in its favor.

Also consider having participants debrief using the following questions:

- What was most helpful about this exercise?
- What was most challenging?
- What can we apply?
- How would you rate the value of this exercise to helping us with this issue?
- Will this exercise be helpful in the future for other sessions?
- What did you learn?
- What will we be able to use from this exercise?
- What ideas were generated, and which ones were most interesting?

Noun Action Handout

Consider a problem of improving a telephone. In this case, the problem involves the verb "improve" and the noun "telephone." If you switch the noun and verb you get "telephoning improvements." This combination might suggest the idea of a telephone that repairs itself automatically or a special toll-free number so customers can call the manufacturer with improvement ideas.

29

Noun Hounds

Background

Bloodhounds are used to track people and animals. They search for a scent, lock onto it, and then pursue their quarry relentlessly. Hounds go from one scent to the next until they achieve their objective.

The Noun Hounds technique works in a similar manner. You start with a random noun and then go from one association to the next until you generate a sufficient number of ideas.

Noun Hounds (also called Modifier Noun Associations) originally was developed by VanGundy (1983, 1988) to generate new product ideas using a random noun and a modifier unrelated to the problem. You then free-associate from this combination to generate ideas.

Objectives

- To help participants generate as many creative ideas as possible
- To help participants learn how to use the activities to generate ideas

Participants

Small groups of four to seven people each

Materials, Supplies, and Equipment

- For each group: markers, two flip charts, and masking tape for posting flip-chart sheets
- For each participant: one sheet each of three different colors of sticking dots (½" diameter) and one pad of 4 x 6 Post-it® Notes

Handout

- Noun Hounds Handout

Time

30 minutes

Related Activities

- Parts Purge [31]

Procedure

1. Distribute the handout, review it with the participants, and answer any questions they may have.

2. Read aloud the following instructions: "Think of any noun (person, place, thing, quality, or action) and a word to modify it. These words should not be related directly to the challenge. Include some contradictory or just plain silly combinations. For instance: flying geese, glowing apples, silent springs, intelligent shrimp, falling stars, rising elephants, quivering rocks. Write down these combinations on a sheet of flip-chart paper."

3. Tell them to select one of the noun-modifier combinations and free-associate from it, writing down whatever comes to mind, with each idea leading to the next.

4. Direct them to use the noun-modifier combinations and all the associations as stimuli to generate ideas.

5. Tell them to write down any ideas on Post-it® Notes (one idea per note) and place them on flip charts for evaluation.

Debrief/Discussion

This exercise easily can provide unique perspectives by the word combinations as well as a spirit of "silliness" the combinations might provoke within a group. It will work especially well with individuals who are relatively uninhibited verbally and/or can free-associate with little concern for the "correctness" of their associations.

Also consider having participants debrief using the following questions:

- What was most helpful about this exercise?
- What was most challenging?
- What can we apply?
- How would you rate the value of this exercise to helping us with this issue?
- Will this exercise be helpful in the future for other sessions?
- What did you learn?
- What will we be able to use from this exercise?
- What ideas were generated, and which ones were most interesting?

Noun Hounds Handout

Suppose your objective is to improve a flashlight. For your modifier and noun you think of the combination "rising elephants." Next you free-associate: leaping trunks, swiveling suitcases, twisting airplanes, flapping wings. You then use these combinations to suggest the following ideas:

- A telescopic flashlight capable of holding a variable number of batteries (from "rising elephants")
- A storage compartment for small objects such as a spare bulb (from "leaping trunks")
- A hovercraft flashlight that floats above the ground or water (from "twisting airplanes")
- A flashlight with shutters for signaling (from "flapping wings")

30

Parts Is Parts

Background

Sometimes creativity is a hit-or-miss proposition. Random stimuli may or may not spark ideas. Free associations are relatively unpredictable. You really don't know how you'll respond to a particular stimulus until you encounter it. Then, once you respond, you don't know if the resulting ideas will be winners.

There's nothing necessarily wrong with this. Unpredictability keeps things interesting and makes the occasional hot idea all the more exciting. There are times, however, when you might want to generate ideas a little more systematically. That's where Parts Is Parts might help.

Parts Is Parts is based on the "Heuristic Ideation Technique (HIT)" developed by Edward Tauber (1972). It generates ideas by creating heuristics or rules of thumb. (A rule of thumb is a guideline that increases the chances of achieving a certain outcome.) Heuristics then are used to structure the idea generation process.

Tauber believes that heuristics can make idea generation more efficient and ensure that only the best idea candidates will be considered. Although HIT originally was intended for new product idea generation, it also will work for a variety of other problems.

Two heuristics help make idea generation more efficient. The first assumes that most ideas can be described using a two-word combination. For instance, the words "toaster/tart" represent a combination that might suggest a breakfast food product. The second heuristic is that some combinations will be viewed as more interesting than others. In particular, combinations that come from different categories have a greater chance of suggesting unique ideas than combinations from similar categories. As an example, the combination "ice cream/cereal" might be perceived as more interesting than the combination "vegetables/fruits."

Objectives

- To help participants generate as many creative ideas as possible
- To help participants learn how to use the activities to generate ideas

Participants

Small groups of four to seven people each

Materials, Supplies, and Equipment

- For each group: markers, two flip charts, and masking tape for posting flip-chart sheets
- For each participant: one sheet each of three different colors of sticking dots (½" diameter) and one pad of 4 x 6 Post-it® Notes

Handout

- Parts Is Parts Handout

Time

60 minutes

Related Activities

- Combo Chatter [24]
- Ideas in a Box [25]
- Mad Scientist [27]

Procedure

1. Distribute the Parts Is Parts Handout, review it with the participants, and answer any questions they may have.
2. Have participants lay a sheet of flip-chart paper on a table or tape it to a wall lengthwise.
3. Tell them to create an idea generation grid containing attributes from two problem areas as shown in Table 6.3. An example would be a grid that contains packaging formats (e.g., bag, boil-in-bag, box, pan, jar, can, tube) and different food forms (e.g., cookie, biscuit, gravy, bread, dressing, steak, juice, dips). Another example might involve ways to increase museum attendance using attributes such as performance arts (e.g., improvisation, ballet, acting) and memberships (e.g., a "frequent attender" status, backstage visits, or special discounts on products).
4. Direct them to assign numbers to each possible combination (e.g., bag/dip = 1; box/steak = 2; bag/juice = 3; tube/gravy = 4). Or, using the museum example: ballet/backstage = 1; acting/discounts = 2.
5. Tell them to examine all the combinations and eliminate any already commercialized or now being used.
6. Have them circle combinations with the greatest potential.
7. Direct the participants to create brief statements for each of the remaining combinations. Emphasize that they should include reasons.

8. Ask them to select the best combinations and transform them into marketable ideas.

9. Tell them to write down any ideas on Post-it® Notes (one idea per note) and place them on flip charts for evaluation.

Debrief/Discussion

This exercise may be a little too structured and complicated for some. Doing it as a group should help since participants can help each other. Another negative feature is that it relies on related stimuli so that many ideas may not be unique (unless there are creative participants who can make them so). On the other hand, its very structure and relatively systematic approach to combining stimuli provide it with the potential for fairly large quantities of ideas. One area in which this exercise might prove to be especially valuable would be during market research.

Also consider having participants debrief using the following questions:

- What was most helpful about this exercise?
- What was most challenging?
- What can we apply?
- How would you rate the value of this exercise to helping us with this issue?
- Will this exercise be helpful in the future for other sessions?
- What did you learn?
- What will we be able to use from this exercise?
- What ideas were generated, and which ones were most interesting?

Parts Is Parts Handout

An example of the "HIT" technique is shown **in** Table 6.3 involving the challenge of generating new food product ideas. The sample uses packing formats and food forms as the two product areas or elements. A number between 1 and 24 is used for each possible combination.

Packaging Formats

Food Forms	Aerosol	Bag	Tube	Box
Bread	1	7	13	(19)
Steak	2	8	(14)	20
Cookie	(3)	(9)	15	21
Dip	4	(10)	16	22
Juice	5	11	(17)	23
Gravy	6	12	18	24

Table 6.3.   Parts Is Parts Combinations

Combinations 7, 9, and 21 are crossed out since they represent existing products (bread in a bag, cookies in a bag, and cookies in a box). Combinations 4, 10, 11, 15, 18, and 20, however, are circled since they represent potential new product ideas. For instance, these combinations might suggest the following ideas:

- A dip in an aerosol spray that can be sprayed on bread or crackers (#4)

- Vegetable dip in a designer bag for individual dipping (#10)

- Different juices in a bag that can be drunk by squeezing, pouring, or using a straw (#11)

- Cookies in a tube—similar to potato chips in a cardboard cylinder (#15)

- Gravy in a tube, especially for children who can use it to write letters and draw pictures on their food (#18)

- Box steak lunches that can be reheated in microwavable packages (#20)

31

Parts Purge

Background

If you like to free-associate, you'll like the Parts Purge technique. It originally was developed by VanGundy (1992) as Attribute Association Chains. You can use this activity to generate ideas by listing problem attributes, free-associating from each attribute, and then using the free associations as stimuli for ideas. It's as simple as that: free-associate on problem parts and generate, generate, generate.

Objectives

- To help participants generate as many creative ideas as possible
- To help participants learn how to use the activities to generate ideas

Participants

Small groups of four to seven people each

Materials, Supplies, and Equipment

- For each group: markers, two flip charts, and masking tape for posting flip-chart sheets
- For each participant: one sheet each of three different colors of sticking dots (½" diameter) and one pad of 4 x 6 Post-it® Notes

Handout

- Parts Purge Handout

Time

45 minutes

Related Activities

- Noun Hounds [29]

Procedure

1. Distribute the Parts Purge Handout, review it with the participants, and answer any questions they may have.

2. Have each group obtain a sheet of flip-chart paper and tape it lengthwise to a wall or lay it down on a table.

3. Tell them to follow the example and list major problem attributes across the top, and then list subattributes next to each major attribute.

4. Instruct them to take turns and select one of the subattributes and write down the first word they can think of. That is, to free-associate by writing down a second word stimulated by the first, and so forth until that person has listed four or five words for each subattribute.

5. Tell them to repeat Step 4, but have another group member do the free-associating and continue doing this until all group members have been involved or no more words remain to use for free association.

6. Direct all group members to use the free associations to stimulate ideas.

7. Tell them to write down their ideas on Post-it® Notes (one idea per note) and place them on flip charts for evaluation.

Debrief/Discussion

Parts Purge uses both related and unrelated problem stimuli. This can make it a versatile activity to apply to a variety of types of problems with a variety of brainstorming personality types (that is, people who prefer one type of stimulation over another). The required free associations and reliance on all group members can help push out thinking boundaries and engage the participants more than in less structured brainstorming activities.

Also consider having participants debrief using the following questions:

- What was most helpful about this exercise?

- What was most challenging?

- What can we apply?

- How would you rate the value of this exercise to helping us with this issue?

- Will this exercise be helpful in the future for other sessions?

- What did you learn?

- What will we be able to use from this exercise?

- What ideas were generated, and which ones were most interesting?

Parts Purge Handout

Suppose you want to improve a table lamp. First, list major attributes and subattributes:

- Name: table lamp
- Parts: base, bulb, cord, shade, switch
- Shapes: round, cylindrical, pleated
- Functions: illuminates, heats, collects dust
- Material: cloth, metal, rubber

Next, free-associate using one or more of the attributes. For example:

- Table lamp: lantern, cow, tipsy, shed, fire, Chicago
- Base: acid, soda, water, bottle, drink
- Switch: spank, paddle, ping pong, table, games
- Illuminates: lights, sky, stars, rockets, gravity
- Metal: heavy, light, air, breath, oxygen

Finally, use these free associations to generate ideas to improve a table lamp:

- A lampshade with shutters to create different lighting effects (from "lantern")
- A lamp with a swivel base to allow reading light adjustments (from "tipsy")
- Lampshades with panoramic pictures of major cities (from "Chicago")
- A lamp with video games built in (from "games")
- A magnetically levitated lamp (from "gravity")
- A hovercraft lamp that can be moved easily around a large table (from "air")

32

Preppy Thoughts

Background

The activities in this chapter generate ideas by combining related or unrelated problem attributes. Although such combinations have great potential, it sometimes helps to introduce additional stimuli.

Preppy Thoughts will help provide this variety by introducing action words into combinations. The basic procedure originally was suggested by Crovitz (1970) using a technique known as Relational Algorithms. The Preppy Thoughts activity provides the same stimulation using random selections of relational words (for example, prepositions) that are inserted between a problem verb and object.

Objectives

- To help participants generate as many creative ideas as possible
- To help participants learn how to use the activities to generate ideas

Participants

Small groups of four to seven people each

Materials, Supplies, and Equipment

- For each group: markers, two flip charts, and masking tape for posting flip-chart sheets
- For each participant: one sheet each of three different colors of sticking dots (½″ diameter) and one pad of 4 x 6 Post-it® Notes

Handout

- Preppy Thoughts Handout

Time

30 minutes

Related Activities

- Bi-Wordal [22]
- Combo Chatter [24]

Procedure

1. Distribute the handout, review it with the participants, and answer any questions they may have.
2. Have someone in each group write the problem on a sheet of flip chart paper and underline the action verb and the object (for example, "How might we _reduce littering_?")
3. Tell group members to take turns selecting a relational word and inserting it between the verb and the object.
4. Have the entire group use the combination as an idea stimulus, write down any ideas on Post-it® Notes, and place them on a flip chart for evaluation.
5. Instruct the groups to repeat Steps 3 and 4 and continue this process until time is called.

Debrief/Discussion

One of the best features of this activity is its ability to create unique stimuli using related problem words. The simple juxtapositioning of a preposition between two related stimuli helps provoke associations—often visual ones—that two related words together might not produce. In this respect, Preppy Thoughts has the potential to create an experience similar to one using unrelated stimuli. After the participants have finished using this exercise, you might ask them if they experienced visual images more than they normally do with other approaches.

Also consider having participants debrief using the following questions:

- What was most helpful about this exercise?
- What was most challenging?
- What can we apply?
- How would you rate the value of this exercise to helping us with this issue?
- Will this exercise be helpful in the future for other sessions?
- What did you learn?
- What will we be able to use from this exercise?
- What ideas were generated, and which ones were most interesting?

Preppy Thoughts Handout

The relational words below are the forty-two that Crovitz suggested:

about	at	for	of	round	to
across	because	from	off	still	under
after	before	if	on	so	up
against	between	in	opposite	then	when
among	but	near	or	though	where
and	by	not	out	through	while
as	down	now	over	till	with

VanGundy (1988) added an additional nineteen prepositions:

above	behind	beyond	past	upon
along	below	during	since	within
amid	beneath	except	throughout	without
around	beside	into	toward	

As an example, consider a problem of how a restaurant could attract more customers. The action verb and object are "attract" and "customers."

Here are some possible ideas from inserting relational words between these two words:

- Have special community nights in which people are seated across from someone new in order to make new friends (from "attract/across/customers")

- Offer special low rates for meals eaten before a certain time (from "attract/before/customers")

- Place advertising fliers on cars of supermarket customers and offer them a discount in exchange for their grocery receipts (from "attract/near/customers")

- Hire a public relations firm (from "attract/about/customers")

- Add an outdoor patio (from "attract/out/customers")

- Give discounts to overweight people (from "attract/round/customers")

- Have a special room for people who like to eat on the floor (from "attract/under/customers")

- Give discounts to customers who help recruit new customers (from "attract/with/customers")

- Start an eating club with one free meal for every ten purchased (from "attract/since/customers")

- Specialize in healthy foods and offer free diet planning (from "attract/within/customers")

33

SAMM I Am

Background

With apologies to Dr. Seuss, SAMM I Am actually refers to a method known as Sequence-Attribute Modifications Matrix. It was developed by Brooks and later described by Souder and Ziegler (1977). SAMM I Am differs from other activities in that it was designed specifically for problems involving a sequence of steps (for example, various processes). Thus, it will not be useful for more general idea generation problems.

Objectives

- To help participants generate as many creative ideas as possible
- To help participants learn how to use the activities to generate ideas

Participants

Small groups of four to seven people each

Materials, Supplies, and Equipment

- For each group: markers, two flip charts, and masking tape for posting flip-chart sheets
- For each participant: one sheet each of three different colors of sticking dots (½″ diameter) and one pad of 4 x 6 Post-it® Notes

Handout

- SAMM I Am Handout

Time

60 minutes

Related Activities

- Circle of Opportunity [23]
- Ideas in a Box [25]
- Mad Scientist [27]
- 666 [34]

Procedure

1. Have each group obtain a sheet of flip-chart paper and tape it lengthwise to a wall or lay it down on a table.

2. Distribute the SAMM I Am Handout, review it with the participants, and answer any questions they may have.

3. Tell them to list the major process activities and then ways to modify any process (for example, speed up, eliminate, rearrange), as shown in the handout.

4. Have them draw a matrix with process steps listed on the left and potential modifications listed along the top.

5. Instruct them to examine each cell (the intersection of steps and modifications) and use them to suggest possible ideas/modifications for that step.

6. Tell them to write down their ideas on Post-it® Notes (one idea per note) and place them on flip charts for evaluation.

Debrief/Discussion

This technique obviously is limited in its applicability to a diversity of problems. On the other hand, that is a definite plus for any process improvement challenges. Used appropriately, this exercise has the potential to generate a variety of process improvements in a systematic way. If time is available, ask the participants to discuss in what ways, if any, this technique could be used for other types of problems such as marketing, new product development, customer service, or other organizational problems.

Also consider having participants debrief using the following questions:

- What was most helpful about this exercise?
- What was most challenging?
- What can we apply?
- How would you rate the value of this exercise to helping us with this issue?
- Will this exercise be helpful in the future for other sessions?
- What did you learn?
- What will we be able to use from this exercise?
- What ideas were generated, and which ones were most interesting?

SAMM I Am Handout

Suppose you want to improve the way restaurant customers pay their bills. Major activities and possible modifications are shown in Figure 6.3.

Process Activities	Eliminate	Substitute	Rearrange	Combine	Increase	Decrease
1. Hand bill to cashier						
2. Get out credit card						
3. Hand card to cashier						
4. Cashier processes card						
5. Cashier returns card						
6. Sign card receipt						
7. Hand receipt to cashier						
8. Cashier returns copy						

(Table header: Potential Modifications)

Figure 6.3.   SAMM I Am System Modifications

After examining the matrix, you might come up with the following ideas:

- Install electronic credit card machines at each table (much like those at many automobile service stations).

- Eliminate paper meal checks. Allow regular customers to run a tab.

- Eliminate credit card papers. Handle credit card purchases electronically for customers with PDAs. Customers link up their PDAs with those of the restaurant. The transaction is then handled electronically: the customer's bank account is debited and the restaurant's account is instantly credited.

- Give preferred customers special credit cards that look like brass plates. When customers are ready to pay their bills, they use the brass plates (restaurant credit cards).

34

666

Background

Time to gamble again! Get out those dice and help Papa get a new pair of shoes (or something like that). But don't expect to win money like the devil. In fact, don't even think of the devil. The 666 technique has nothing to do with old Beezelbub.

The 666 activity is the creation of Doug Hall (1994). It is based on principles of combination and free association and is somewhat similar to Circle of Opportunity [23] and Mad Scientist [27]. The problem elements used, however, are not organized into logical categories. As in Mad Scientist, you use dice to select elements to combine.

Objectives

- To help participants generate as many creative ideas as possible
- To help participants learn how to use the activities to generate ideas

Participants

Small groups of four to seven people each

Materials, Supplies, and Equipment

- For each group: markers, one white, one green, and one red die (or any three dice of different colors),two flip charts, and masking tape for posting flip-chart sheets
- For each participant: one sheet each of three different colors of sticking dots (½" diameter) and one pad of 4 x 6 Post-it® Notes

Handout

- 666 Handout

Time

45 minutes

Related Activities

- Bi-Wordal [22]
- Circle of Opportunity [23]
- Ideas in a Box [25]
- Mad Scientist [27]

Procedure

1. Have each group obtain a sheet of flip-chart paper and tape it lengthwise to a wall or lay it down on a table.
2. Distribute the handout, review it with the participants, and answer any questions they may have.
3. Tell them to generate three lists of six problem elements and number each element within each list. Say that these elements may or may not be related to their particular problem.
4. Instruct them to label the lists "White Die," "Green Die," and "Red Die" (or other colors corresponding to the dice used).
5. Ask each person in each group to take turns rolling each die and select the element indicated for each list.
6. Tell them to use the combinations of the three elements to spark ideas.
7. Have them write down their ideas on Post-it® Notes (one idea per note) and place them on flip charts for evaluation.

Debrief/Discussion

666 evokes an alchemy of the creative process: A "brew" of stimuli is stirred together to craft multiple ideas for resolving a challenge. The three columns of stimuli provide a fertile matrix of word combinations for group members to use as springboards for generating ideas. Seeing multiple words together this way can help participants free-associate and make unique combinations. The game aspect of rolling dice also makes this an appealing exercise.

Have the participants debrief using the following questions:

- What was most helpful about this exercise?
- What was most challenging?
- What can we apply?
- How would you rate the value of this exercise to helping us with this issue?
- Will this exercise be helpful in the future for other sessions?
- What did you learn?
- What will we be able to use from this exercise?
- What ideas were generated, and which ones were most interesting?

666 Handout

An example using the problem of inventing new types of soup is shown in Table 6.4.

White Die	**Green Die**	**Red Die**
1. Cracker Jack stuff	1. Lunch time	1. Metal cylinders
2. Secret ingredients	2. Award winning	2. Exotic nutrition
3. Astronaut parties	3. Liquid delight	3. Healthy and wealthy
4. Annual physicals	4. Children's party	4. Heated flavor
5. Security time	5. Loose goose	5. Just like Mom's
6. Syrups	6. Free radical	6. Bowl full of joy

Table 6.4.   666 Example

After you have rolled the dice, you might think of the following types of ideas:

- Gourmet soup with secret ingredients (2–3–3)
- Soup to eat after exercising (like Gatorade®) (4–5–3)
- Soup cans with pictures of famous mothers (5–1–5)
- A chicken soup can with a Sterno® container built into the bottom (6–5–4)
- Soup cans with prizes inside (1–6–4)

35

Word Diamond

Background

Hot new ideas shine and sparkle with radiant brilliance. They illuminate their surroundings and blind lesser ideas. Everyone wants a shiny, multifaceted new idea, but you can't always get what you want. Sometimes you have to settle for a so-so idea.

The Word Diamond technique won't ensure that all your ideas will sparkle. It will, however, provide you with another systematic approach to idea generation. And it's a breeze to implement.

This technique originally was developed by VanGundy (1983) as a simple combination procedure using elements of a problem statement. Thus, it is similar to Bi-Wordal [22]. Instead of using alternative word meanings, however, Word Diamond generates ideas by combining words in the problem statement in different ways.

Objectives

- To help participants generate as many creative ideas as possible
- To help participants learn how to use the activities to generate ideas

Participants

Small groups of four to seven people each

Materials, Supplies, and Equipment

- For each group: markers, two flip charts, and masking tape for posting flip-chart sheets
- For each participant: one sheet each of three different colors of sticking dots (½" diameter) and one pad of 4 x 6 Post-it® Notes

Handout

- Word Diamond Handout

Time

20 minutes

Related Activities

- Bi-Wordal [22]
- Circle of Opportunity [23]
- Ideas in a Box [25]

Procedure

1. Distribute the Word Diamond Handout, review it with the participants, and answer any questions they may have.
2. Tell the groups to state their problems so that they contain at least four major problem attributes or elements, including both nouns and verbs.
3. Have them select four major words or phrases from this statement and write them on a flip chart, arranging the words or phrases in the shape of a diamond. There should be one word at each vertex (point) of the diamond.
4. Tell them to select one of the four words or phrases, combine it with another, and write down any ideas prompted.
5. Ask them to continue selecting and combining words until they have tried generating ideas from all possible combinations.
6. Have them write down their ideas on Post-it® Notes (one idea per note) and place them on flip charts for evaluation.

Debrief/Discussion

This is yet again another exercise with the potential to create unique perspectives by the combination of related problem elements. The visual of the diamond shape helps participants create word combinations easily that may spark unique ideas. It also consumes relatively little time, so it is a time-efficient technique because the number of word combinations is limited. On the other hand, the small number of words can be a limiting factor by providing a smaller number of stimuli than other activities.

Consider having participants debrief using the following questions:

- What was most helpful about this exercise?
- What was most challenging?
- What can we apply?
- How would you rate the value of this exercise to helping us with this issue?
- Will this exercise be helpful in the future for other sessions?

- What did you learn?
- What will we be able to use from this exercise?
- What ideas were generated, and which ones were most interesting?

Word Diamond Handout

Suppose you are losing scientists to your competitors. In particular, you want to encourage more professional employees to remain in the research and development (R&D) department. First, select four words or phrases: encourage, employees, remain, and R&D. Next arrange them in the shape of a diamond, as shown in Figure 6.4.

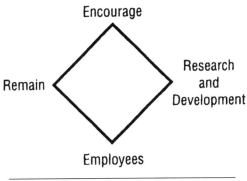

Figure 6.4.   Word Diamond Sample

Finally, use various combinations to suggest ideas:

- Give incentive rewards for employees who achieve special professional recognition (from "employees/encourage").
- Match up younger employees who are more likely to leave with older employees and form a buddy program (from "employees/encourage").
- Establish two career tracks—one managerial and one nonmanagerial—to take into account different professional growth needs (from "employees/remain").
- Develop a "Pride in R&D" public relations campaign to promote team spirit (from "R&D/employees").

Chapter 7

Free Association Activities: "Blue Skies"

Blue skies: Happy days are here again. Put on a happy face. It's time to let loose and see what happens. Be footloose and fancy-free. Go on and let go. Allow the ideas to flow and grow. Build on them. Create highways to the skies and then float back down. Light as a feather in your cap. Tip the waiter and smile, smile, smile, all the while thinking of what might be. Set your mind free and free-associate.

Everything you read in the previous paragraph is based on free association. I started with the words "blue skies" and let loose. I had no idea where my thoughts would take me. I tried to think in the general area of idea generation, but I avoided any preconceived thoughts.

The paragraph may not be logical, but it is creative, and it contains many stimuli. That's the idea. I was able to create many thoughts and perspectives from the initial stimulus of "blue skies." Each sentence in the paragraph has the potential to stimulate additional thoughts. Even the most cliché-ridden sentence has that potential.

Stimuli trigger associations, which trigger ideas. That's how the human mind works. We flit from one concept to another. Think about it. It's not that difficult. We can think of anything we want. That's a lot of power packed into one convoluted mass of gray matter. And it's ours. All we have to do is harness it.

Although it may seem paradoxical, the best way to harness our creative brainpower is to let go. Allow one thought to lead to another. Be playful. Forget all the analytical stuff. Take the time to sink into a "deep think."

The activities in this chapter are based on the principle of free association. They rely on our ability to let go and generate one idea or concept from another—to flit about in our minds. Each activity helps structure this process a little differently. As a result, each activity has the potential to create many different perspectives and types of ideas.

However, it's up to us to make the activities work. The more we let go, the more we will boost our brainpower. And the more we boost our brainpower, the more ideas we'll produce.

Before trying a free association technique, think a little about how we generate ideas. Try to get into the appropriate mind-set and think about how easy it can be to flow from one thought to the next. Then just let your mind go.

NOTE: FOR ALL ACTIVITIES, REMIND PARTICIPANTS
TO DEFER JUDGMENT WHILE GENERATING IDEAS.

36

Brain Mapping

Background

Make an outline for how to make a ham sandwich. Go ahead and try it. Finished? O.K. Your outline may look something like this:

    I. Get out ham.
   II. Get knife.
       a. Hold ham securely.
       b. Slice ham.
  III. Open package of bread.
       a. Remove two pieces.
       b. Put bread on plate.
  IV. Place slice of ham on one piece of bread.
   V. Get out mustard.
       a. Open jar
       b. Get knife.
       c. Stick knife in jar.
  VI. Spread mustard on second piece of bread.
 VII. Place second piece on top of ham slice.
VIII. Cut sandwich in two.
  IX. Eat sandwich.

Now think through your experience. You probably spent a lot of time thinking about the order of each activity. For instance, you may have started with "Open a package of bread" and then remembered you would need a ham. What to put next probably occupied most of your time and effort. Thus, outlines often force us to spend more time thinking about sequence than about content. They also disrupt our thinking because we have to alternate focusing on sequence and on content.

Outlines are based on a "left brain" process. To improve on this situation, we need a "right brain" process. We have two brain hemispheres: a logical, sequential, analytical left brain and an intuitive, holistic, creative right brain. Every time we solve a problem we use both sides of our brains. Sometimes we use the left a little more and sometimes the right.

Tony Buzan (1976) developed Brain Mapping to capitalize on the strengths of our right brains. He originally conceived of this technique as a tool to help students take notes. He soon found, however, that Brain Mapping was useful for a variety of activities, including idea generation.

Objectives

- To help participants generate as many creative ideas as possible
- To help participants learn how to use the activities to generate ideas

Participants

Small groups of four to seven people each

Materials, Supplies, and Equipment

- For each group: markers, two flip charts, and masking tape for posting flip-chart sheets
- For each participant: one sheet each of three different colors of sticking dots (½" diameter) and one pad of 4 x 6 Post-it® Notes

Handout

- Brain Mapping Handout

Time

30 minutes

Related Activities

- Idea Links [41]
- Lotus Blossom [43]
- Skybridging [46]

Procedure

1. Distribute the Brain Mapping Handout, review it with the participants, and answer any questions they may have.

2. Tell them to list, on a flip chart, all major problem elements. They should include relevant people, processes, issues, time schedules, expectations, outcomes—anything that helps them understand the challenge.

3. Instruct each group to tape three pieces of flip chart paper on a wall so that the sheets are side-by-side. If a wall is not available, have them put the paper on a table.

4. Have them select the most central, core problem element of those they listed and write it down on the center of a sheet of flip-chart paper. This element should capture their primary concern.

5. Tell them to draw a box or other more appropriate shape around this concern. For instance, if your concern is employee tardiness, you might draw a clock around the problem statement.

6. Direct them to draw a line about four inches long, extending from one side of the central shape, and write a related word on the line.

7. Say, "Depending on what you think of next, (a) draw another line extending from the central shape, or (b) draw a line related to a subtopic (or subattribute) for the first line."

8. Tell them to continue drawing lines and adding topics until they have run out of ideas.

9. Tell them to write down these ideas on Post-it® Notes (one idea per note) and place them on flip charts for evaluation.

Debrief/Discussion

Brain Mapping is an internationally popular idea generation technique for both individuals and groups. It is visually very appealing and quite functional with respect to how the human brain thinks in branches, not in rigid outline format.

Have participants debrief using the following questions:

- What was most helpful about this exercise?
- What was most challenging?
- What can we apply?
- How would you rate the value of this exercise to helping us with this issue?
- Will this exercise be helpful in the future for other sessions?
- What did you learn?
- What will we be able to use from this exercise?
- What ideas were generated, and which ones were most interesting?

Variation

- Assign two groups to brainstorm ideas on the same challenge. Have one group use Brain Mapping and the other a conventional outline form. Compare results and reactions when finished and discuss reasons for any differences. Ask group members to discuss what difference word choices might have on the outcome. How different would the results have been if other words had been used? It is possible that different words or branches would not have made any significant difference if there were a large number of words and branches. Ask the participants if they think that conclusion is valid.

Brain Mapping Handout

If you've never seen a Brain Map before, these steps may not be clear. For an example, see Figure 7.1, which shows a Brain Map on ways to improve a bed.

As you examine this Brain Map, don't expect to find all the elements placed in a logical way. For instance, I placed the ideas for awakening or helping you sleep under the "sleeping" category because that's where I thought of them. It would have made more sense to put them under the "mattress" category. But remember, it doesn't really matter how you generate ideas, just so you get them out.

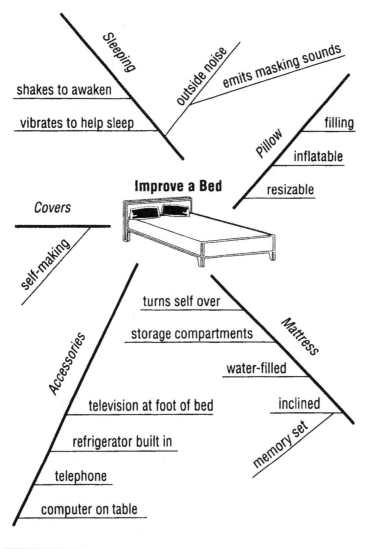

Figure 7.1.   Sample Brain Map

37

Doodles

Background

You've probably heard the expression "That's usin' the ol' noodle!" It means, of course, that you were able to apply your brainpower effectively. Well, noodle power can also help us generate ideas with doodles.

You know how to doodle, don't you? Just start scribbling on a sheet of paper and express your creative urges. Let your pen or pencil take off and draw swirls, loops, circles, boxes, arrows, spirals, or whatever feels right. You already may have practice doodling. Most of us doodle while talking on the phone or listening to a boring speech. (Did you ever notice that there seems to be a direct correlation between how boring a speech is and how elaborate your doodles are?)

Because doodles provide an outlet for creative expression, they also can help generate ideas. VanGundy (1988) designed a technique known as Symbolic Representations, which uses doodles as the basic idea generation mechanism. Although this activity is similar to Ideatoons [26], there is one major difference: the doodles are based on one or more major principles underlying the problem. This focus helps target the doodles a little more than mere random scribblings.

Objectives

- To help participants generate as many creative ideas as possible
- To help participants learn how to use the activities to generate ideas

Participants

Small groups of four to seven people each

Materials, Supplies, and Equipment

- For each group: markers, two flip charts, and masking tape for posting flip-chart sheets
- For each participant: one sheet each of three different colors of sticking dots (½" diameter) and one pad of 4 x 6 Post-it® Notes

Handout

- Doodles Handout

Time

45 minutes

Related Activities

- Picture Tickler [17]
- Rorschach Revisionist [18]
- Ideatoons [26]
- Drawing Room [59]
- Modular Brainstorming [62]

Procedure

1. Distribute the handout, review it with the participants, and answer any questions they may have.

2. Tell them to think of the major principle underlying their problem.

3. Instruct each group to tape three pieces of flip-chart paper on a wall so that the sheets are side-by-side. If a wall is not available, have them put the paper on a table.

4. Tell them that one person should draw an abstract symbol that represents this principle and not to worry if they don't have artistic abilities. Say that they just should draw whatever pops into their minds regarding the principle and to try to elaborate and provide some detail for each drawing.

5. Instruct them to have another person free-associate from this symbol and draw another.

6. Have someone different from each group then draw at least three additional symbols.

7. Tell the groups to examine all their symbols and use them as stimuli to generate ideas, writing them on Post-it® Notes to place on flip-chart paper for evaluation.

Debrief/Discussion

This can be a fun activity if participants are not hindered by a fear of ridicule for lack of natural artistic talent. You might remind them that some of the best symbols (that is, most useful for stimulating ideas) are those drawn by people without artistic talent. You also might conduct a discussion on the value of deferring judgment when producing any creative output. Too much analysis and criticism (whether internal or external) can be detrimental to creative activities. Since there obviously is no "correct" way to draw the symbols, there should be little hesitation in drawing them. Much the same can be said about preliminary ideas in the formative stage.

Also consider having the participants debrief using the following questions:

- What was most helpful about this exercise?
- What was most challenging?
- What can we apply?
- How would you rate the value of this exercise to helping us with this issue?
- Will this exercise be helpful in the future for other sessions?
- What did you learn?
- What will we be able to use from this exercise?
- What ideas were generated, and which ones were most interesting?

Variation

- Have the participants draw three or four symbols individually and then share them with the rest of the group to use as idea stimuli.

Doodles Handout

Suppose your problem is how to attract more customers to your restaurant. The major underlying principle is attraction, or how to increase or get more of something. Draw a symbol representing this principle. Next, use this symbol as a stimulus and draw another symbol and then another until you have four or five. Sample symbols are shown in Figure 7.2.

After you have examined each doodle, the following ideas might come to mind:

- Have "Dinner with a Local Celebrity" nights. After customers are seated in the restaurant between certain hours, a lottery is held and the winner gets to have dinner with a local celebrity.

- Ask customers to brainstorm ideas to increase business. Give free dinners to those who suggest the best ideas.

- Offer special "sampler" meals in malls.

- Install small video monitors on tables so customers can watch their food being prepared in the kitchen.

- Offer evening river cruises with appetizers at the restaurant, the entrée on the boat, and dessert back at the restaurant.

Figure 7.2.   Sample Doodles

38

Essence of the Problem

Background

An essence is something concentrated that retains its basic properties. It is the internal factor that gives something special characteristics. For instance, perfume is the essence of flowers, and grapes are the essence of wine. Thus, an essence is a root or source element, what we use to identify with something, or what makes something "real." Because essence is a source element, it defines what is and what can be. Essence provides potential, boundaries, and scope. It communicates meaning, which leads to understanding.

Each problem has an essence that defines what is and what can be. By examining the "what is," it is possible to explore the "what can be." That is, understanding essence makes it possible to extract potential ideas from problem statements, because all problems exist on a continuum of abstraction. Thus, the essence of a given problem is that broad concept behind it. The essence of reducing crime, for instance, might be "prevention." In this case, the "what is" could be "incidence of crime" and the "what can be" might be "reduced incidence of crime."

This activity is very similar to What's the Problem? [70] in concept, but different in execution. The basic principle of searching for an "essence" is in both. When using What's the Problem?, attention is focused on increasingly abstract levels of the original problem's verb. For instance, a problem of how to increase parking would focus on progressively more abstract ways to increase things (not just parking). When using Essence of the Problem, in contrast, attention is focused on different perceptions of the "essence" of "increase parking."

Objectives

- To help participants generate as many creative ideas as possible
- To help participants learn how to use the activities to generate ideas

Participants

Small groups of four to seven people each

Materials, Supplies, and Equipment

- For each group: markers, two flip charts, and masking tape for posting flip-chart sheets

- For each participant: one sheet each of three different colors of sticking dots (½" diameter) and one pad of 4 x 6 Post-it® Notes

Handout

- Essence of the Problem Handout

Time

30 minutes

Related Activities

- Name Change [9]
- Switcheroo [11]
- What's the Problem? [70]

Procedure

1. Distribute the Essence of the Problem Handout, review it with the participants, and answer any questions they may have.
2. Tell the group members to write down the problem challenge on a flip chart visible for all to see.
3. Ask the participants to write down, individually, on a Post-it® Note, what they think is the essence of the problem, in the form of a word or brief phrase. Tell them to focus on the objective as demonstrated in the handout.
4. Have them pass this note to the person on their right.
5. Instruct them to review the note passed to them and then write down another word or phrase on a new note, and keep it without passing it. Each group member now should have two Post-it® Notes containing "essence" words, one from the person on their left and the one they just wrote. (*Note:* There may be duplication among the group members, but this is to be expected and requires no special action.)
6. Ask the group members to take turns sharing their two words or phrases and invite the other group members to use these words as stimuli to help brainstorm ideas. Tell them not to worry if their initial ideas are not directly related to the words. Free association is welcome so that one word leads to another.
7. Have them write down their ideas on Post-it® Notes and place them on flip charts for later evaluation.

Debrief/Discussion

This is an excellent technique to help participants create new problem perspectives. Its focus on abstract levels of a problem can prompt ideas normally not possible with conventional approaches.

101 Activities for Teaching Creativity and Problem Solving

Emphasize how this technique differs from all of the others in that it is designed to remove the obstacles we often face by becoming too close to our problems—becoming too familiar, so that our very understanding of challenges works against us in resolving them. Ask group members to provide examples from their lives of similar situations and to discuss the validity of this premise.

Also consider having participants debrief using the following questions:

- What was most helpful about this exercise?
- What was most challenging?
- What can we apply?
- How would you rate the value of this exercise to helping us with this issue?
- Will this exercise be helpful in the future for other sessions?
- What did you learn?
- What will we be able to use from this exercise?
- What ideas were generated, and which ones were most interesting?

Essence of the Problem Handout

Consider the problem of reducing vandalism in factory lunchrooms. One group member believes that the essence of the problem objective is "destruction," writes it down on a note, and passes it to the person on his right. The person receiving that word then might write down "defacement." This person then has two notes containing the words "destruction" and "defacement." They read these words aloud to the other group members and the group uses them to help spark ideas. For instance, the combination, "destruction-defacement" might suggest an idea of creating a lunchroom that appears to be defaced, but is done so in an artistic way. Another idea might be to place pictures of all the workers in the lunch room with the hope they wouldn't destroy the room (from "defacement"). Or the word, "destruction" might trigger an idea to completely destroy the current lunch room and invite the workers to participate in its reconstruction. Finally, "defacement" might suggest literally taking the faces away from the lunch room and eliminating it altogether.

39

Exaggerate That

Background

Have you ever stretched the truth? Come on, now—be truthful. Most people have exaggerated something, at some time in their lives, even if it's only a slight distortion. Exaggerations not only make us feel better, they also can add excitement to our interactions. The more extreme and vivid our exaggerations, the more attention they will attract.

Each instance of truth stretching is a stimulus. And stimuli can help generate ideas. There must be the makings of an idea generation activity here somewhere! And there is. It's known as Exaggerated Objectives (Olson, 1980). With it, you generate ideas by listing problem criteria, exaggerating them in any way possible, and then using the exaggerations as stimuli to prompt ideas.

Objectives

- To help participants generate as many creative ideas as possible
- To help participants learn how to use the activities to generate ideas

Participants

Small groups of four to seven people each

Materials, Supplies, and Equipment

- For each group: markers, two flip charts, and masking tape for posting flip-chart sheets
- For each participant: one sheet each of three different colors of sticking dots (½" diameter) and one pad of 4 x 6 Post-it® Notes

Handout

- Exaggerate That Handout

Time

60 minutes

Related Activities

- Law Breaker [50]
- Problem Reversals [51]
- Turn Around [52]

Procedure

1. Distribute the handout, review it with the participants, and answer any questions they may have.
2. Tell them to list the major criteria (objectives) they would use to evaluate potential solutions to their problem challenges.
3. Instruct them to exaggerate or stretch each criterion in any way possible. Encourage them to avoid any concern with how "correct" their exaggerations are. There is no such thing as correct with this technique.
4. Have them use each exaggeration as a stimulus to spark new ideas, write them down on Post-it® Notes, and place on a flip chart for evaluation.

Debrief/Discussion

The often-used phrase of "think outside the box" applies to this technique (as well as others in this book). In this case, exaggerating criteria forces us to think about a challenge in unique ways—ways in which we might not otherwise find ourselves thinking. In fact, such thinking often is the hallmark of "natural" creative thinkers, who have the ability to distort and twist problem statements and come up with novel ideas.

Have participants debrief using the following questions:

- What was most helpful about this exercise?
- What was most challenging?
- What can we apply?
- How would you rate the value of this exercise to helping us with this issue?
- Will this exercise be helpful in the future for other sessions?
- What did you learn?
- What will we be able to use from this exercise?
- What ideas were generated, and which ones were most interesting?

Exaggerate That Handout

Suppose, for example, you want to attract more international airline passengers. You might use the setup shown in Table 7.1.

Original Criteria	Exaggerated Criteria	Possible Solutions
1. Minimal cost	1. Costs more than $1 million	1. Have a lottery for free tickets
2. Safety not compromised	2. Kills thousands of passengers	2. Offer an on-board dinner mystery theater
3. Uses current personnel	3. Uses fired personnel	3. Offer on-board career-planning seminars
4. Returns investment within one year	4. Becomes the "black hole" of unprofitable investments	4. Offer continuing education credits for training seminars

Table 7.1. Example of Exaggerate That

40

Fairy Tale Time

Background

Story telling is an ancient art dating back to when humans first communicated with words. It has provided most societies with an oral history long before written records were kept. Stories help perpetuate the foundational myths people use to teach succeeding generations about their cultures. For instance, fables, nursery rhymes, and fairy tales have been used to transmit life's lessons to countless people in a number of different cultures.

Although modern technology has diminished its importance, story telling still has the potential to help solve problems. Stories from the past can help suggest ideas for today's problems. Create a story and we create stimuli that can trigger new thoughts and concepts. The richer and more elaborate our stories, the richer and more elaborate the stimuli.

One special type of story, with great potential for sparking ideas, is the fairy tale—a story of magical events with a moral. Such stories are excellent sources of idea stimuli for all sorts of problems. Because they serve as a source of unrelated stimuli, stories do not have to be related to the problem or faithful to the original fairy tale. In fact, it sometimes is beneficial if the story is as different as possible.

Objectives

- To help participants generate as many creative ideas as possible
- To help participants learn how to use the activities to generate ideas

Participants

Small groups of four to seven people each

Materials, Supplies, and Equipment

- For each group: markers, two flip charts, and masking tape for posting flip-chart sheets
- For each participant: one sheet each of three different colors of sticking dots (½" diameter) and one pad of 4 x 6 Post-it® Notes
- Copies of common fairy tales such as "Rapunzel," "Hansel and Gretel," "Little Red Riding Hood," "Tom Thumb," "Sleeping Beauty," "Snow White," and "Rumpelstiltskin"

Handout

- Fairy Tale Time Handout

Time

60 minutes

Related Activities

- A Likely Story [15]
- Tabloid Tales [47]
- Super Heroes [80]

Procedure

1. Distribute the Fairy Tale Time Handout and copies of the fairy tales, review the exercise example with the participants, and answer any questions they may have.
2. Tell participants to select one of the fairy tales and have one person read it aloud.
3. Have them write down, on the flip chart, the story's major elements (characters, actions, dialogue, plot, morals, events).
4. Instruct them to use these elements as stimuli for triggering ideas.
5. Tell them to write down any ideas on Post-it® Notes (one idea per note) and place them on flip charts for evaluation.

Debrief/Discussion

One major advantage of this technique is that it can allow a group to really express its creativity in developing a story or playing off of a known fairy tale. The fact that most fairy tales are unrelated to most problem challenges can help produce unique perspectives. If time is available, ask the participants if they think it would be more productive to make up their own fairy tales, modify existing ones, or use existing ones without changing them. Have them discuss why any such preferences might exist.

Also consider having participants debrief using the following questions:

- What was most helpful about this exercise?
- What was most challenging?
- What can we apply?
- How would you rate the value of this exercise to helping us with this issue?
- Will this exercise be helpful in the future for other sessions?
- What did you learn?
- What will we be able to use from this exercise?
- What ideas were generated, and which ones were most interesting?

Variation

- If time is available, ask the participants to write their own fairy tales and repeat Steps 3 and 4 above.

Fairy Tale Time Handout

Suppose you're a divisional manager in a medium-size manufacturing firm. You and Jim Oversee—one of your line supervisors—are discussing ways to cut costs. Jim notes that he recently has received increasing numbers of employee theft reports. You decide this is an area in which you could cut costs significantly. You define the problem as, "How might we reduce employee theft?" To help resolve this problem, you decide to write your own version of "Cinderella"—one of the best-known fairy tales. After some thought, you compose the following story:

Cinderella (aka "Cinder"), a beautiful young maiden, is treated badly by her two stepsisters. She must do all the cooking and cleaning while they busy themselves with fancy clothes and social events. One day it is announced that the prince is holding a ball to find a wife. The wicked stepsisters are certain the prince will want to select one of them. [So far, so good. Nothing really different here. But then. . . .] Although Cinder says she would like to go, the stepsisters laugh in her face and tell her to bake a pumpkin pie instead.

The evening of the ball arrives and the stepsisters leave Cinder to bake her pie. Instead, Cinder decides to change clothes first. And then she eats some salad with dressing, while dressing. As Cinder leafs through her meal while bemoaning her fate, her Fairy Godmother (FG) appears and grants her a wish. Cinder's stepsisters never allowed her to eat her favorite vegetable, so she asks her FG to turn her into a rutabaga. FG smirks and tells Cinder that her magic wand only works with mice and pumpkins. "O.K., fine," says Cinder as she tosses her salad over her shoulder. "I suppose I shall have to be a pumpkin, then. Mice are not nice."

With a wave of her wand, FG transforms Cinder into a pumpkin. FG waves her wand again and visually challenged mice materialize to take Cinder to the ball. Off they go into the night. Their goal: the castle ball. Their plan: sneak into the castle kitchen and offer the pumpkin for dessert.

Being visually challenged, the mice can't see too well, however. Instead of going to the castle, they go to a poor farmer's cottage. The farmer's wife chases away the mice with her carving knife. (Did you ever see such a sight in your life?) Unfortunately, Mrs. Farmer slips on the mice tails and falls on her knife. The farmer rushes in to say goodbye to his dying wife and decides to make a pumpkin pie with the pumpkin the nice mice brought.

The Fairy Godmother has been watching all of this. She sees the farmer raise his dead wife's knife to carve the pumpkin. Suddenly there is a . . . POOF! The pumpkin turns into a beautiful maiden, thanks to FG. The farmer is awed by Cinder's beauty and asks her to marry him. Cinder agrees and they decide to toast each other with pumpkin punch in the punch bowl.

While he leaves the house to bury his ex-wife, Cinder picks up the dipper and

Free Association Activities: "Blue Skies"

begins to pour some punch into a cup. The dipper slips and crashes to the ground, breaking into two pieces. Cinder panics and picks up one of the pieces, turns on her left slipper, and bolts out the door with the mice in hot pursuit. The farmer hears all the commotion and returns to the cottage in time to see Cinder running away with the not-so-nice mice in pursuit and Cinder holding the remainder of the dipper. He pushes away a lock of his hair and then vows, to no one in particular: "Somehow, someday, I'll find the fair maiden with the glass dipper!"

Based on this story, here are a few sample ideas for reducing employee theft:

- Install hidden video cameras that record everything employees do (from "visually challenged mice").

- Have a subliminal audiotape that periodically reminds employees not to steal (from "stepsisters . . . tell her to bake a pumpkin pie instead").

- Use voice-recognition locks on storage areas where too many keys might exist (from "laugh in her face").

- Provide rewards to customers who report incidents of theft (from "they decide to toast each other").

- Have weekly tea or coffee breaks where managers solicit theft-reduction ideas (from "pour some punch into a cup").

- Install body temperature sensors that notify security whenever an unauthorized employee enters an "off limits" area (from "bolts out the door with the mice in hot pursuit").

- Offer a free "makeover" for employees who report shoplifting or theft (from "The pumpkin turns into a beautiful maiden").

- Recruit an employee from another division to work undercover and report on theft problems (from "sneak into the castle kitchen").

- Install locks with retina identification that works only with certain employees—an alarm sounds if anyone else tries to open the locks (from "her magic wand only works with mice and pumpkins).

- Have all employees submit to a voice stress analyzer to determine if they are telling the truth about theft (from "The farmer rushes in to say goodbye to his dying wife").

41

Idea Links

Background

We all generate ideas using free association. In fact, many of the activities in this book are based on it. We generate one idea, use it to generate another idea, use it for another, and so forth until we have generated all we can or that time allows. Unlike other free-association activities, however, Idea Links requires free association in a specific direction, beginning with the action verb and working toward the object in the challenge statement. The goal is to direct associations to end up with a link to the object.

Objectives

- To help participants generate as many creative ideas as possible
- To help participants learn how to use the activities to generate ideas

Participants

Small groups of four to seven people each

Materials, Supplies, and Equipment

- For each group: markers, two flip charts, and masking tape for posting flip-chart sheets
- For each participant: one sheet each of three different colors of sticking dots (½" diameter) and one pad of 4 x 6 Post-it® Notes

Handout

- Idea Links Handout

Time

20 minutes

Related Activities

- Noun Hounds [29]
- Skybridging [46]

Procedure

1. Distribute the Idea Links Handout, review the exercise example with the participants, and answer any questions they may have.
2. Tell each group to tape together two sheets of flip-chart paper, end to end, to a wall or other hard surface such as a table. They should tape together the ends that meet so there is one continuous sheet.
3. Have them write down their problem statement on another sheet of flip-chart paper so that it incorporates an action verb and an object.
4. Tell them to write the verb on the left side of taped-together paper and the object on the right side.
5. Instruct them to draw five, six-inch lines to the right of the first word so that the last line ends just before the object word (see the exercise handout).
6. Direct the participants to take turns free-associating a word from the verb and write it on the first line; the next person then uses this word to free-associate and write the word on the second line; and so forth.
7. Have them continue to free-associate from one word to another, writing each word on one of the lines, and make the final word link to the object.
8. Tell the groups to review all the associations and use them to trigger new ideas, writing them on Post-it® Notes and placing them on flip-chart paper for evaluation.
9. If time is available or you want to generate more ideas, have the groups repeat Steps 4 through 9.

Debrief/Discussion

Idea Links can be a fun technique as well as a creative thinking exercise. It is easy to use and can result in many ideas. It also would be ideal as a warmup exercise to loosen up participants. An interesting question to ask is whether or not participants found themselves evaluating their free associations. If done "correctly," there should be no judging about the "correctness" of a free association. Any word should qualify; the words do not need to be justified logically.

Also consider having participants debrief using the following questions:

- What was most helpful about this exercise?
- What was most challenging?
- What can we apply?
- How would you rate the value of this exercise to helping us with this issue?

- Will this exercise be helpful in the future for other sessions?
- What did you learn?
- What will we be able to use from this exercise?
- What ideas were generated, and which ones were most interesting?

Variation

- To add a little zest to this exercise, have individual participants write down their free associations by themselves as quickly as possible. Then have them take turns and write their results on the flip-chart paper for the group to use as idea triggers.

Idea Links Handout

If your problem is to improve a table fan, you might set it up as follows:

Improve _____ _____ _____ _____ _____ fan

Next, begin free associating by filling in the blanks:

Improve *increase* *speed* *car* *traffic* *congestion* fan

Finally, use the free associations to think of ideas. For instance, you might put a fan on wheels to roll around on a table (from "car") or design a fan that blows air in pulses, like a cough (from "congestion").

Here's another example:

Improve *better* *butter* *bread* *dough* *blow* fan

These words prompt ideas such as putting a chemical on the blades to blow scented air (from "butter") and making a fan with gold blades (from "dough").

Note: Although the connection between the words may not appear to be logical, that is O.K. Free association does not have to "make sense." For instance, in the example immediately above, the word "butter" follows the word "better." When I thought of butter, it was because that is what saying a word similar in sound made me think of. The connections between "butter" and "bread" and "dough" are more transparent. However, following "dough" with "blow" was based only on rhyming.

42

Imaginary Mentor

Background

Did you ever have a secret friend to whom you told all your problems? Do you have an inner voice that helps you solve problems? Are they out to get you?

If you answered yes to all three questions, you may want to obtain professional counseling! If you answered yes to the first two questions, you may want to delay treatment. Apparently, many people listen to an inner voice for guidance. For instance, General Douglas MacArthur supposedly conjured up his hero-father for advice on military strategy. The poet Milton called his inner guide "Celestial Patroness" and described how she helped him compose his writings.

I'm not suggesting that we all have a little person living inside us. Instead, I believe we all have subconscious motives, impulses, feelings, and images. All this material has tremendous potential as a vast, untapped reservoir of creativity.

The problem is that we can't always access our subconscious on demand. We have no set of commands or buttons to push to enter our subconscious minds. Instead, we have to enter them more indirectly. One way to access our subconscious thoughts is to create a personal, internal mentor.

Objectives

- To help participants generate as many creative ideas as possible
- To help participants learn how to use the activities to generate ideas

Participants

Small groups of four to seven people each

Materials, Supplies, and Equipment

- For each group: markers, two flip charts, and masking tape for posting flip-chart sheets
- For each participant: one sheet each of three different colors of sticking dots (½" diameter) and one pad of 4 x 6 Post-it® Notes

Time

45 minutes

Related Activities

- Stereotype [10]
- We Have Met the Problem and It Is We [48]
- Super Heroes [80]

Procedure

1. Instruct the participants verbally as follows:
   - Release all your tension and try to relax as much as possible.
   - Visualize a soft, glowing white light surrounding your body. Allow the light to make you feel secure and comfortable.
   - Think of your favorite place (house, mountain, forest, stream, boat).
   - Visualize yourself walking into this place. Notice all the details. Try to imagine what it looks like. Experience any sounds, textures, or smells. Absorb as much as you can.
   - Imagine your personal mentor walking toward you. Look closely at his or her face. What are you experiencing? Think of any special feelings or emotions. Include as much detail as possible.
   - Say to your mentor, "Please be my guide and help me think of new ideas. Lead me in resolving my problem."
   - Tell your mentor about your problem. Give him or her as much relevant information as you can. Try to keep your interaction realistic. Listen carefully whenever your mentor speaks to you. Don't be discouraged if ideas don't pop out suddenly. It takes time.
2. Tell them to write down any ideas on Post-it® Notes (one idea per note) and place them on flip charts for evaluation.

Debrief/Discussion

It is difficult to fathom the full potential of the human mind, especially the subconscious. We should try to appreciate its ability to help us resolve problems. Imaginary Mentor is a good start. However, some people may have difficulty being engaged by this technique. It may be too abstract or esoteric and not concrete enough for them to respond with new ideas. Try to engage the participants in a discussion about the usefulness of such visually oriented approaches and what types of people might benefit most from them.

Also consider having participants debrief using the following questions:

- What was most helpful about this exercise?
- What was most challenging?
- What can we apply?

- How would you rate the value of this exercise to helping us with this issue?
- Will this exercise be helpful in the future for other sessions?
- What did you learn?
- What will we be able to use from this exercise?
- What ideas were generated, and which ones were most interesting?

43

Lotus Blossom

Background

The lotus is a pinkish water lily. As with most flowers, lotus blossom petals are nested together. Numerous petals radiate outward from the center, in ever-widening circles. One petal leads to the next and so forth, just like free association. Perhaps there is the making of an idea generation technique here!

This technique takes advantage of visualization, free association, and a structured approach to creating idea stimuli. Yasuo Matsumura, president of Clover Management Research (Chiba City, Japan) developed the Lotus Blossom Method of generating ideas (also called the MY technique, after his Japanese initials).

Objectives

- To help participants generate as many creative ideas as possible
- To help participants learn how to use the activities to generate ideas

Participants

Small groups of four to seven people each

Materials, Supplies, and Equipment

- For each group: markers, two flip charts, and masking tape for posting flip-chart sheets
- For each participant: one sheet each of three different colors of sticking dots (½" diameter) and one pad of 4 x 6 Post-it® Notes

Handout

- Lotus Blossom Handout

Time

30 minutes

Related Activities

- Brain Mapping [36]
- Doodles [37]

Procedure

1. Distribute the Lotus Blossom Handout, review the exercise example with the participants, and answer any questions they may have.
2. Tell each group to tape together two sheets of flip-chart paper, side-to-side, to a wall or other hard surface such as a table.
3. Instruct them to replicate the drawing in Figure 7.3, starting with writing a central theme (problem) in the center of the paper, as shown in Figure 7.3.
4. Have them think of related ideas and concepts and write them in the surrounding circles, A through H.
5. Tell them to use each of these ideas as a separate central theme or problem for the surrounding lotus boxes.
6. Encourage them to try to generate eight ideas for each of these themes and write them in the surrounding boxes, 1 through 8.

Debrief/Discussion

Consider having participants debrief using the following questions:

- What was most helpful about this exercise?
- What was most challenging?
- What can we apply?
- How would you rate the value of this exercise to helping us with this issue?
- Will this exercise be helpful in the future for other sessions?
- What did you learn?
- What will we be able to use from this exercise?
- What ideas were generated, and which ones were most interesting?

Lotus Blossom Handout

Suppose your problem involves ways to improve a wristwatch. Write "Improve a wristwatch" in the center of a sheet of paper. Then write eight related concepts in surrounding circles: (a) watch hands, (b) wrist strap, (c) date, (d) time, (e) second hand, (f) battery, (g) appointments, and (h) face. Next, generate ideas for each of these elements.

- Watch hands—different shapes on ends, different colors, different designs
- Wrist strap—buckles, metal, different colors, transparent, different widths
- Date—flashing, multicolored, icons for months, written out
- Time—voice activated, voice response, flashing lights
- Second hand—digital, complementary color, gold plated, variable speed
- Battery—recharge in wall outlet, owner can replace
- Appointments—record appointments, beeper reminder, link appointments with other watches
- Face—celebrity faces, pictures of famous landmarks, spinning face

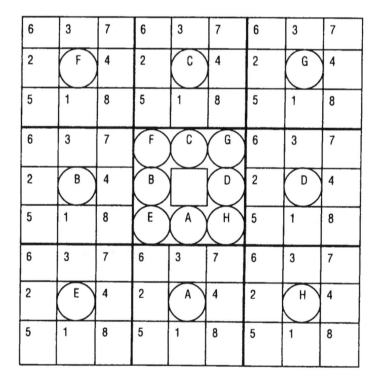

Figure 7.3. Lotus Diagram

44

Say Cheese

Background

When we first think of new ideas, they often flit about without defined shape. If we really concentrate, we can bring them into focus. These new ideas then become images we can capture in our mind's eye.

Frame. Focus. Click. There the images are. It's almost as if we photograph them with a camera. Van-Gundy (1983) used this comparison to suggest a procedure for stimulating ideas using an imaginary camera.

Objectives

- To help participants generate as many creative ideas as possible
- To help participants learn how to use the activities to generate ideas

Participants

Small groups of four to seven people each

Materials, Supplies, and Equipment

- For each group: markers, two flip charts, and masking tape for posting flip-chart sheets
- For each participant: one sheet each of three different colors of sticking dots (½″ diameter) and one pad of 4 x 6 Post-it® Notes
- Three sheets each of 8.5″ x 11″ paper and pens or pencils for each participant

Time

30 minutes

Related Activities

- Imaginary Mentor [42]

Procedure

1. Read the following to participants and ask them to respond individually:

   "Imagine you are looking at your problem through the viewfinder of a camera. Frame the picture and adjust the focus to view the entire problem in sharp detail. Move your mind forward or backward to adjust the focus. Add light to improve your view. Then make the image blurry to change perspective. Finally, add different lenses such as telephoto or wide angle to change perspectives again. Continue to make adjustments until your problem is centered clearly in your mind's eye. Push your mental shutter-release button and allow a picture of the problem to develop in your mind. Study the picture and try to absorb all relevant details. Write down on your paper any interesting features such as size, shape, texture, smells, movement. Finally, examine your descriptions and use them to prompt ideas."

2. Have each participant share his or her ideas, in turn, with the other group members, write them on Post-it® Notes (one idea per note), and place them on a flip chart to be evaluated later. Encourage them to consider any new ideas that might be prompted from others' ideas.

Debrief/Discussion

This technique is very similar to Imaginary Mentor [42] in that participants must rely on their visualization skills to help think of ideas. If any participants seem to struggle with creating ideas, tell them to try "playing off" of others' ideas. That is, let them know that they don't have to worry about their visualization abilities; instead, they can try to think of other ideas based on those produced by others (of course, they still can think of their own ideas!).

Also consider having participants debrief using the following questions:

- What was most helpful about this exercise?
- What was most challenging?
- What can we apply?
- How would you rate the value of this exercise to helping us with this issue?
- Will this exercise be helpful in the future for other sessions?
- What did you learn?
- What will we be able to use from this exercise?
- What ideas were generated, and which ones were most interesting?

45

Sense Making

Background

Our everyday language is colored by references to the five senses: "I hear you," "I see what you mean," "I feel for you," "That's a tasty idea," "I smell a rat!" Such phrases usually prompt a variety of sensory images, corresponding to whatever sense is involved. These images, in turn, help communicate meaning and increase understanding.

Just as our senses allow us to experience different stimuli, sensory images can help us experience the different perspectives needed to create ideas.

Objectives

- To help participants generate as many creative ideas as possible
- To help participants learn how to use the activities to generate ideas

Participants

Small groups of four to seven people each

Materials, Supplies, and Equipment

- For each group: markers, two flip charts, and masking tape for posting flip-chart sheets
- For each participant: one sheet each of three different colors of sticking dots (½" diameter) and one pad of 4 x 6 Post-it® Notes
- Three sheets each of 8.5" x 11" paper and pens or pencils for each participant

Handout

- Sense Making Ideas Handout

Time

30 minutes

Related Activities

- Say Cheese [44]
- We Have Met the Problem and It is We [48]

Procedure

1. Read the following to participants and ask them to respond individually:

   "Try to become as relaxed as possible. Breathe comfortably at an even rate. Listen to your breathing and let all stress flow out. Think about your problem in detail and try to experience it. Quickly smell it, see it, taste it, touch it, and hear it. Think of your sense of smell. Visualize different olfactory experiences you've had. For instance, you might think about some flowers you once smelled. Now, how might you use your sense of smell to generate ideas to solve your problem? Think of your sense of sight. Visualize different sight experiences you've had that have affected you emotionally. Now, how might you use your sense of sight to generate ideas to solve your problem? Continue this process with your senses of taste, touch, and hearing. Think of emotional experiences involving each of these senses."

2. Ask them to consider what ideas they might have thought of and to write them down on their individual sheets of paper. For sample ideas, refer them to the handout.

3. Have each participant share his or her ideas, in turn, with the other group members, write them on a Post-it® Note, and place them on a flip chart to be evaluated.

Debrief/Discussion

To help participants relate to this technique, you first might have them experience different items using their senses. For instance, you might place a number of objects varying in size and texture into a paper bag and have participants try to identify them using only their sense of touch. Or ask them to identify visually an object in a picture when only a small part of the object is visible. Although this technique may not be as "all-purpose" as others, it could be good enough to spark some useful ideas—and that's all it takes sometimes!

Also consider having participants debrief using the following questions:

- What was most helpful about this exercise?
- What was most challenging?
- What can we apply?
- How would you rate the value of this exercise to helping us with this issue?
- Will this exercise be helpful in the future for other sessions?
- What did you learn?
- What will we be able to use from this exercise?
- What ideas were generated, and which ones were most interesting?

Sense Making Ideas Handout

To illustrate this activity, consider a publisher's problem of how to increase book sales. Here are some ideas that this technique might spark:

- *Smell:* Produce books that contain fragrances that reflect literary themes.

- *Sight:* Include a page of slides to illustrate topics.

- *Taste:* Include free stamps to encourage book buyers to mail in coupons redeemable for discounts on future book purchases.

- *Touch:* Make book covers with different textures that invite people to touch them. Once people pick up a book, they will be more likely to buy it.

- *Hearing:* Put audio-digital computer chips (like those in greeting cards) in the inside covers of books. When someone opens the front cover, the book says, "Buy me, please!" or mentions some benefit of the book's contents.

46

Skybridging

Background

This technique involves working both forward and backward when generating ideas. Engineers call this method "reverse engineering." Doug Hall (1994) calls it Skybridging. It is based on a general definition of a problem as a gap between a current and a desired state of affairs. That is, we examine "what is" and "what should be" and then try to close the gap by working toward the goal and then back toward the current problem state. Thus, there may be many different roads to an objective.

Objectives

- To help participants generate as many creative ideas as possible
- To help participants learn how to use the activities to generate ideas

Participants

Small groups of four to seven people each

Materials, Supplies, and Equipment

- For each group: markers, two flip charts, and masking tape for posting flip-chart sheets
- For each participant: one sheet each of three different colors of sticking dots (½" diameter) and one pad of 4 x 6 Post-it® Notes

Handout

- Skybridging Handout

Time

20 minutes

Related Activities

- Brain Mapping [36]
- Idea Links [41]

Procedure

1. Tell each group to tape together two sheets of flip-chart paper, side-by-side, to a wall or other hard surface such as a table.

2. Distribute the Skybridging Handout, review the example with the participants, and answer any questions they may have.

3. Have them write down, on the left side, one to three words that define where they are today with respect to a current challenge (for example, if product improvement is the concern, they would list a current product's status).

4. Have them use one to three words and write them down, on the right side of the paper, where they would like to be with respect to the challenge (for example, what is the ideal result?).

5. Instruct them to draw a straight line between the current and desired states. Tell them to write on this line a sure thing and a boring thing, both of which represent ways to achieve the desired state.

6. Instruct them to draw another connecting line that bends in the middle, as shown in Figure 7.4. On the left side of the line, they should list an obvious idea; on the right side, a safe idea. Have them continue drawing lines and listing ideas as shown in the figure until they have generated all possible ideas. Note that, as they list ideas, they should try working from right to left on some of the lines.

7. After they have finished listing ideas, tell them to examine them and make any impractical ideas more practical, write all practical ideas on Post-it® Notes, and place them on a flip chart for evaluation.

Debrief/Discussion

You might want to note that words on the arches become more impractical the higher up they are. The diagram makes it relatively easy to see the range of ideas. Another thing to emphasize during this exercise is that the participants don't have to be too concerned with the "correctness" of their words or how concrete or abstract the ideas might be. The important thing is to generate a diversity of ideas.

Skybridging Handout

Figure 7.4 shows a sample skybridge based on generating ideas for improving a flashlight. The figure suggests several ideas, some directly and some indirectly:

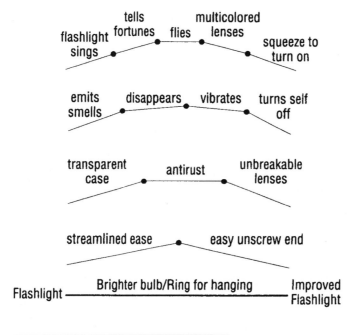

Figure 7.4. Skybridging Example

47

Tabloid Tales

Background

There you are, in line in the supermarket. The customer at the checkout counter just realized she has to pay for her groceries. She slowly gets out her checkbook and begins writing. After several minutes you notice she has finally written down the date. Unfortunately, it's July and she's had trouble remembering the date change from last year! She wrote down last year's date and has to start over.

You sigh and begin looking around for a distraction. You glance to your left at the magazine rack and you see it: "GIRL, 10, GIVES BIRTH TO CALF THAT LOOKS LIKE ELVIS." The headline sears into your brain and you shake your head as you struggle to reassert your rationality. You read on:

- WIFE MAKES SALAD DRESSING OF HUSBAND IN BLENDER
- BABY BORN WITH THREE HEADS, SIX TAILS, AND BLUE EYES
- WOMAN DIVORCES FROG—CLAIMS NO PRINCE
- BIGFOOT SPOTTED DANCING WITH ELVIS
- MAN GIVES BIRTH TO VW
- NEW DIET GROWS EXTRA TOES
- TRUCKER'S LUNG EXPLODES WHILE HE WAS SMOKING ON ROAD
- ALIENS RESPONSIBLE FOR LIGHT BULB BURNOUTS

You've just been victimized by tabloid headlines. But don't fret. You can salvage something positive from your experience by using tabloid headlines to prompt ideas. Doug Hall (1994) developed Tabloid Tales to help people distort facts and gain new perspectives on their problems.

Objectives

- To help participants generate as many creative ideas as possible
- To help participants learn how to use the activities to generate ideas

Participants

Small groups of four to seven people each

Materials, Supplies, and Equipment

- For each group: markers, two flip charts, and masking tape for posting flip-chart sheets
- For each participant: one sheet each of three different colors of sticking dots (½" diameter) and one pad of 4 x 6 Post-it® Notes
- An assortment of tabloid weekly newspapers such as *The Star*, *The National Enquirer*, and, especially, *Weekly News*

Handout

- Tabloid Tales Handout

Time

30 minutes

Related Activities

- A Likely Story [15]
- Fairy Tale Time [40]

Procedure

1. Distribute at least two tabloid publications to each group.
2. Distribute the Tabloid Tales Handout, review the example with the participants, and answer any questions they may have.
3. Instruct each group to list four key facts about their problem, product, service, or process.
4. Tell them to distort one aspect of each fact and make it sensational or more provocative by stating it as a tabloid headline.
5. For inspiration, suggest that participants thumb through the tabloids.
6. Have them use the distorted facts and review of the tabloids to generate practical ideas.
7. Direct them to write their ideas on Post-it® Notes and place them on the flip chart for evaluation later.

Debrief/Discussion

This can be a fun exercise for the participants. As some research has suggested, humor can enhance the creative output of groups. And many tabloid headlines and stories certainly can provoke mirth. However, the ideas in this exercise, while facilitated by humor, mostly will emerge from the headlines. This is because they typically are unrelated to the

101 Activities for Teaching Creativity and Problem Solving

problem and thus capable of triggering unique ideas. Because of these two elements, be sure to encourage the participants to have fun (although they may not need much encouragement).

Also consider having participants debrief using the following questions:

- What was most helpful about this exercise?
- What was most challenging?
- What can we apply?
- How would you rate the value of this exercise to helping us with this issue?
- Will this exercise be helpful in the future for other sessions?
- What did you learn?
- What will we be able to use from this exercise?
- What ideas were generated, and which ones were most interesting?

Tabloid Tales Handout

Assume you are an automobile insurance company and want to deal with the challenge of how to reduce auto theft. Four key facts are (1) auto thieves don't want to attract attention, (2) some cars are more likely to be stolen than others, (3) unlocked and unattended cars with running engines are likely theft candidates, and (4) alarms will deter some thieves. These facts suggest the following tabloid headlines:

- ELVIS SEEN HONKING HORNS OF PINK CADILLACS
- CAR THIEF HIDES CAR IN HIS PANTS
- PREVIOUSLY STOLEN CAR DRIVES SELF AWAY FROM THIEF
- STOLEN CAR BLOWS UP CLEVELAND

These headlines then prompt the following ideas:

- Car starts only when driver sings a specified Elvis song.
- Car starts only when driver's rear end fits specially molded car seat
- Hot-wired cars stop running after one minute
- Car started without special code sprays knockout gas in face of driver

48

We Have Met the Problem and It Is We

Background

A primary counseling skill is empathy—the ability to see and feel something from another's perspective. Some people say we can't really understand how others feel about something unless we can walk in their shoes and see the world with their eyes. "Change perspectives and you change understanding" is a principle that underlies many idea generation activities and applies especially well to this one.

Try to become our problems and we'll create new perspectives that may help spark new ideas. Of course, we can't literally become our problems. We can, however, bring life to our problems and alter how we see them. For this reason, We Have Met the Enemy and It Is We (with a nod to cartoonist Walt Kelly and his Pogo character) will probably work best with problems involving inanimate objects. This doesn't mean you shouldn't try it with people problems; it just may not be as effective.

Objectives

- To help participants generate as many creative ideas as possible
- To help participants learn how to use the activities to generate ideas

Participants

Small groups of four to seven people each

Materials, Supplies, and Equipment

- For each group: markers, two flip charts, and masking tape for posting flip-chart sheets
- For each participant: one sheet each of three different colors of sticking dots (½" diameter) and one pad of 4 x 6 Post-it® Notes

Handout

- We Have Met the Problem and It Is We Handout

Time

30 minutes

Related Activities

- Stereotype [10]
- Imaginary Mentor [42]
- What if. . . ? [49]

Procedure

1. Distribute the We Have Met the Enemy and It Is We Handout, review the example with the participants, and answer any questions they may have.

2. Recite the following instructions to the groups: "Think about what your problem would say, think, and feel about itself and its relation to its environment. What bugs it? What does it like? What are its major concerns, challenges, and opportunities? Write down your responses on a flip chart."

3. Tell them to use their descriptions as stimuli to brainstorm ideas, write them on Post-it® Notes, and place them on the flip chart for evaluation.

Variation

- Have individual group members take turns speaking the part of whatever object is chosen.

Debrief/Discussion

This is an especially useful exercise for people who are good at fantasizing and being playful. Because it requires users to suspend belief about inanimate objects talking, not everyone may excel at using it. However, most groups will have one or two people who can, and that's usually all it takes. Other group members then can use their thoughts to ignite ideas.

Consider having participants debrief using the following questions:

- What was most helpful about this exercise?
- What was most challenging?
- What can we apply?
- How would you rate the value of this exercise to helping us with this issue?
- Will this exercise be helpful in the future for other sessions?
- What did you learn?
- What will we be able to use from this exercise?
- What ideas were generated, and which ones were most interesting?

We Have Met the Problem and It Is We Handout

Assume your organization wants to generate ideas to improve a wastebasket. The wastebasket might "say" the following:

> "I'm sick and tired of being emptied so often. The food and cigarette ashes smell terrible. I also hate it when people bang me around and leave marks on my outside. It really irritates me when people knock me over and my insides spill out all over the carpet. I just hate all the messes. And they're not even my fault.

> "There is one nice thing about being a wastebasket. I just love it when some hotshot tries to impress his friends by throwing a paper wad in me from across the room. If the paper wad hits my rim, I sometimes can jiggle a little and knock it to the floor. This makes the hotshot look so foolish!"

This diatribe might spark the following ideas for improving a wastebasket:

- A built-in trash compactor
- A continuous roll of plastic lining that can be removed easily every time the wastebasket is emptied
- A built-in slot for a fragrance dispenser
- Suction cups, clamps, or Velcro® for attaching the wastebasket to the floor or a desk to prevent accidental spills
- A basketball-type net that can be raised above the rim for practicing paper wad shots

Free Association Activities: "Blue Skies"

49

What if...?

Background

    What if cows could fly?

    What if we grew telephones in our ears?

    What if we were all thumbs?

    What if diamonds were soft and cushions were rock hard?

    What if plants could talk?

    What if people who asked "What if. . . ?" all the time suddenly died?

Do you get the idea? As you read each of these questions, images formed in your mind. Most of these images probably were rather provocative. At least, they were a little out of the ordinary. Any time our minds encounter contradictions or paradoxical thinking, we experience a perspective shift. In this case, asking "What if. . . ?" frees our minds and opens them to possibilities we might never have thought of or explored. Asking "What if. . . ?" pushes out the boundaries of impossibilities and limits.

Objectives

- To help participants generate as many creative ideas as possible
- To help participants learn how to use the activities to generate ideas

Participants

Small groups of four to seven people each

Materials, Supplies, and Equipment

- For each group: markers, two flip charts, and masking tape for posting flip-chart sheets
- For each participant: one sheet each of three different colors of sticking dots (½" diameter) and one pad of 4 x 6 Post-it® Notes

Handout

- What if. . . ? Handout

Time

30 minutes

Related Activities

- Get Crazy [5]
- Imaginary Mentor [42]
- We Have Met the Problem and It Is We [48]

Procedure

1. Read the above Background information to the participants.
2. Distribute the What if. . . ? Handout, review the example with the participants, and answer any questions they may have.
3. Instruct the participants to brainstorm within their groups by saying the following:

   "Stretch your problem in as many ways as you can think of by asking 'What if. . . ?' Assume anything is possible. Don't worry about what won't work or why something can't be implemented. Just let your mind go. Have someone in your group write down all of the 'What if. . . ?' statements on a flip chart."

4. After they are finished writing, say the following:

   "Return to reality and examine each question while thinking, 'Well, we can't do that, but maybe we can. . . .' Brainstorm ideas by finishing this sentence and generate more practical ideas. Record all your ideas individually on Post-it® Notes and place them on flip-chart paper."

Debrief/Discussion

What if. . . ? is one of the simplest, yet most powerful, activities available. It is often overlooked, however, because it is so simple. If participants truly suspend belief during this exercise, the results can be outstanding. Ask participants how they think this approach compares with more traditional brainstorming activities and why.

Also consider having participants debrief using the following questions:

- What was most helpful about this exercise?
- What was most challenging?
- What can we apply?
- How would you rate the value of this exercise to helping us with this issue?
- Will this exercise be helpful in the future for other sessions?
- What did you learn?
- What will we be able to use from this exercise?
- What ideas were generated, and which ones were most interesting?

What if...? Handout

What if you were a car dealer who wanted to increase repeat business? To think of ideas, you might begin "Whatiffing" as follows:

- What if I gave repeat customers a free car?
- What if prospective repeat customers had to beg to let me sell them a new car?
- What if prospective repeat customers tried to pay double the price for a new car?
- What if a customer's current car hypnotized the customer into buying another car?
- What if new cars followed people around town until the people bought them?

    Next, use these questions as idea triggers. Here are some sample ideas:

- I can't give repeat customers a free car, but I could give them a substantial discount.
- I can't get repeat customers to beg me to sell them a new car, but I could contact customers on a regular basis to see if they have any problems. Such constant attention may encourage repeat sales.
- I can't double the price for a new car, but I could offer to pay customers double the difference of any better car deal they can get from another dealer.
- A customer's car won't hypnotize the customer into buying another car, but I could mount a relentless advertising campaign using all media.
- New cars won't follow customers around, but I could offer repeat customers free use of a cellular car phone for one year.

Chapter 8

Grab Bag: Miscellaneous Activities

Open the bag. Now reach right in and help yourself. Grab whatever you find. Don't be shy; take a risk and see what you get. You'll never know if you don't try.

A grab bag can't be beat when it comes to surprises. You never know what you're going to get. That also is true of this chapter. You don't know what you're going to get because this chapter contains miscellaneous activities.

Grab bag activities actually involve two different types of idea stimulators. The first type, "backward," includes activities that involve reversing or turning around a problem in some way. The second, "just alike only different," contains activities based on analogical thinking; that is, they generate ideas by focusing on similarities between a problem and something else.

Because these two types force us to look at our problems differently, these activities are especially useful for creating unique perspectives. Thus, the activities in this chapter possess considerable diversity in their approaches to generating ideas.

NOTE: FOR ALL ACTIVITIES, REMIND PARTICIPANTS
TO DEFER JUDGMENT WHILE GENERATING IDEAS.

"Backward" Activities: Reversals

Backward activities stimulate your brain by forcing you to reverse problem aspects and view things differently. This opposite tactic is not what most people expect to use when generating ideas. The typical reaction is to plunge right in and attack a problem by generating solutions—definitely a direct approach.

The point is, however, that reversals avoid the tendency to lock in on just one way of viewing a problem. Divergent, creative thinking requires many problem viewpoints.

50

Law Breaker

Background

Just as most societies have laws, so do most problems. Societal laws prescribe and govern social behavior. Similarly, problem laws govern the assumptions people use to perceive and define problems.

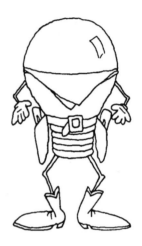

Our assumptions about the way we think things should be influence the way we generate ideas to solve problems. Unfortunately, most of these "shoulds" constrain our thinking and result in less creative ideas. Moreover, shoulds limit the number of solution categories we might consider. For instance, if we accept the notion that chocolate candy should be sold only in bars, all our ideas for chocolate candy will be based on bar products.

To overcome this creative thinking obstacle, Doug Hall (1994) designed Law Breaker as an activity to generate ideas by breaking assumptions about the way things should be.

Objectives

- To help participants generate as many creative ideas as possible
- To help participants learn how to use the activities to generate ideas

Participants

Small groups of four to seven people each

Materials, Supplies, and Equipment

- For each group: markers, two flip charts, and masking tape for posting flip-chart sheets
- For each participant: one sheet each of three different colors of sticking dots (½" diameter) and one pad of 4 x 6 Post-it® Notes

101 Activities for Teaching Creativity and Problem Solving

Handout

- Law Breaker Handout

Time

30 minutes

Related Activities

- Exaggerate That [39]
- Problem Reversals [51]
- Turn Around [52]

Procedure

1. Distribute the Law Breaker Handout, review it with the participants, and answer any questions they may have.
2. Instruct the groups to list all possible assumptions about their problems.
3. Tell them to break each assumption. Specifically, have them ask why the assumption is made about a particular aspect of a problem and write it down on flip-chart paper.
4. Direct them to use the broken assumptions to stimulate new ideas, write them on Post-it® Notes, and place them on a flip chart for evaluation.

Debrief/Discussion

Consider having participants debrief using the following questions:

- What was most helpful about this exercise?
- What was most challenging?
- What can we apply?
- How would you rate the value of this exercise to helping us with this issue?
- Will this exercise be helpful in the future for other sessions?
- What did you learn?
- What will we be able to use from this exercise?
- What ideas were generated, and which ones were most interesting?

Law Breaker Handout

Suppose you want to generate ideas for a new chocolate candy bar. First, list assumptions regarding candy bars:

- Rectangular bar form
- Solid brown in color
- Uniform sweetness
- Uniform taste
- May contain either peanuts or almonds in addition to chocolate, but nothing else
- Wrapped in aluminum foil
- Melts in the sun
- Weighs no more than three ounces

Next, generate ideas by breaking any of these "laws" governing chocolate candy bars. Here are some possible ideas:

- Triangular-shaped bar
- Different shades of brown in the same product
- Variable sweetness in different parts of the product
- Different fillings in the center
- Wrap in "theme" papers (for example, dinosaurs, space travel)
- High heat resistance for eating in the sun
- Variable weights ranging from one ounce to ten pounds—all with names reflecting the weights (for example, "air" bar, "monster" bar)

51

Problem Reversals

Background

Sometimes we have trouble solving problems because we attack them head-on and become immersed. The result is that we become too close to the problem and find ourselves unable to generate new perspectives.

This can't-see-the-forest-for-the-trees outcome can be avoided by entering the forest from a different direction. Change direction and we change perspectives. Instead of being blocked by our initial, unproductive perspectives, we will discover new ways of seeing our problems. New ideas then will flow.

Problem reversals have been widely used ever since brainstorming was popularized by Alex Osborn in the 1930s. Creativity consultant Edward de Bono (1972) also advocated reversals as one way to achieve his concept of "lateral thinking."

Stand-up comedians and cartoonists often use reversals to create the unexpected. Just look at Gary Larson's "The Far Side." One of his cartoons, for instance, depicts rifle-holding bears hunting people.

Everyday creative problem solving also benefits from reversing a problem statement. A popular approach to law enforcement is to reverse the problem of going out and getting the bad guys. Some police officers instead think of ways to get the bad guys to come to them.

Sounds far-fetched, doesn't it? Why would wanted criminals come to the police? One result of reversing thinking on this problem is for police to send out invitations to a special "party." The "guests" are arrested when they show up. Another is to notify wanted people they have won a prize and must show up in person to claim it. Thus, a simple change in problem definition provides a hot idea.

Objectives

- To help participants generate as many creative ideas as possible
- To help participants learn how to use the activities to generate ideas

Participants

Small groups of four to seven people each

Materials, Supplies, and Equipment

- For each group: markers, two flip charts, and masking tape for posting flip-chart sheets
- For each participant: one sheet each of three different colors of sticking dots (½" diameter) and one pad of 4 x 6 Post-it® Notes

Handout

- Problem Reversals Handout

Time

30 minutes

Related Activities

- Exaggerate That [39]
- Law Breaker [50]
- Turn Around [52]

Procedure

1. Distribute the handout, review it with the participants, and answer any questions they may have.
2. Instruct the groups to state their problems simply and clearly and write them on a flip chart for all to see.
3. Read the following aloud:

   "Reverse the direction of your problem statement. This reversal doesn't have to be a direct reversal of any particular problem aspect. You may change the verb, the goal, or any words in the definition. Thus, reversal is defined broadly as any change in a problem statement."

4. Tell them to write down on a flip chart each reversal as a new (possibly silly-sounding) problem statement, beginning with the phrase, "How might we. . .?
5. Direct them to use each reversal as a stimulus for new ideas, write the ideas on Post-it® Notes, and place them on a flip chart for evaluation.

Debrief/Discussion

Reversals have great potential for all-purpose idea generation. They provide an easy way to "force" people to view an initial problem differently. They figuratively force one out of a current "thinking box" and into another with the ability to trigger new ideas. You may want to emphasize that a reversal, as used in this exercise, does not have to be a direct or literal change. Changing any aspect of a problem often is all that is required.

Also consider having participants debrief using the following questions:

- What was most helpful about this exercise?
- What was most challenging?
- What can we apply?
- How would you rate the value of this exercise to helping us with this issue?
- Will this exercise be helpful in the future for other sessions?
- What did you learn?
- What will we be able to use from this exercise?
- What ideas were generated, and which ones were most interesting?

Problem Reversals Handout

Suppose you want to design a new soda can. Possible reversals include the following problem statements, each beginning with the same phrase. How might we design . . .

- an old soda can (classic picture or bottle shape)?
- a soda bottle?
- a soda can?
- a new beer can?
- a new trash can?

Next, use these reversals to help think of ideas:

- A can with a classic logo or picture
- A can in the shape of a bottle
- A can that decomposes after use
- A can with two compartments, with one side containing soda and one beer
- A can that beeps after being emptied until it is deposited in a recycling bin. The beeping stops after sensors are activated when the can is placed in the bin.

52

Turn Around

Background

Turn Around was originally developed by creativity consultant Steve Grossman (1984) as Assumption Reversals. It is a relative of the Law Breaker exercise [50] and generates ideas by reversing problem assumptions in any way possible. The difference between the two activities is that Law Breaker reverses what is commonly accepted as a "should" about a problem (for example, chocolate should be brown), whereas Turn Around reverses more general assumptions (for example, people eat chocolate).

Objectives

- To help participants generate as many creative ideas as possible
- To help participants learn how to use the activities to generate ideas

Participants

Small groups of four to seven people each

Materials, Supplies, and Equipment

- For each group: markers, two flip charts, and masking tape for posting flip-chart sheets
- For each participant: one sheet each of three different colors of sticking dots (½" diameter) and one pad of 4 x 6 Post-it® Notes

Handout

- Turn Around Handout

Time

30 minutes

Related Activities

- Exaggerate That [39]
- Law Breaker [50]

Procedure

1. Distribute the Turn Around Handout, review it with the participants, and answer any questions they may have.

2. Instruct the groups to state their problems simply and clearly and write them on a flip chart for all to see.

3. Tell them to list all assumptions about their problems on a flip chart. Remind them that even very obvious assumptions might be valuable.

4. Tell them to reverse each assumption in any way possible (as done in the handout) and write each one down on flip-chart paper.

5. Tell them to use each assumption as a trigger for new ideas, write each idea on a Post-it® Note, and place them on flip-chart paper for evaluation.

Debrief/Discussion

Some problem assumptions are extremely basic and fundamental; others may be more abstract and esoteric. For instance, a basic assumption of a problem involving attracting new bank customers would be that the customers have money to invest. A more abstract assumption might be that customers put their money in banks primarily to satisfy their needs for security. Either type of assumption is appropriate for this exercise. So encourage participants to consider whatever assumption they think of, even if it may not be correct technically.

Also consider having participants debrief using the following questions:

- What was most helpful about this exercise?
- What was most challenging?
- What can we apply?
- How would you rate the value of this exercise to helping us with this issue?
- Will this exercise be helpful in the future for other sessions?
- What did you learn?
- What will we be able to use from this exercise?
- What ideas were generated, and which ones were most interesting?

Turn Around Handout

Assume you are the president of a bank and want to attract new customers. You might list the following assumptions:

- Potential customers have money.
- Placing money in the bank satisfies security needs.
- Many potential customers are confused by banking procedures.
- Banks lend money to make money.
- People have to wait in line to get money.
- When you withdraw your money, it is not really the same money you deposited originally.
- Banks keep money in vaults.

Next, reverse these assumptions as shown in the following examples:

- Potential customers have no money.
- Putting money in the bank makes people insecure.
- Potential customers all are knowledgeable bankers.
- Banks lend money to lose money.
- People never have to wait to get money.
- Banks keep money in the open.

Finally, use these reversals to suggest ideas:

- Emphasize the lowest interest loans in town.
- Stress security measures taken to protect the customers' money.
- Develop commercials showing the professional expertise of the bank's officers and staff.
- Give customers who recruit other customers a higher interest rate.
- Offer home ATMs.
- Place a see-through bank vault door in the center of the bank.

"Just Alike Only Different" Activities: Analogies

People who like using analogies will take to them like a duck takes to water or a pig takes to mud. If people really like these activities, it will be like falling in love for the first time or the joy that comes from the birth of your first child. People may like these activities because they help them function as smoothly as a fine Swiss watch.

The previous paragraph represents analogical thinking—comparisons based on similarities. Whenever we say something is "like" something else, we make an analogy.

Such expressions enrich and enliven language and interpersonal communication in particular. Analogies also allow us to express ourselves creatively. Thus, all analogies are creative products.

Analogies can help explain difficult concepts and solve problems. For instance, educators use analogies extensively when trying to teach difficult concepts. Teachers pick one topic familiar to students and compare it with an unfamiliar topic. This enables students to understand the new topic more clearly based on their familiarity with the first topic. Outside of the classroom, we also may use analogies when trying to explain a difficult subject to someone.

Analogies have broad applicability in the business world. One of the most famous examples involves the use of analogies to develop Pringles® potato chips. A client of the Cambridge consulting firm Synectics, Inc., (Gordon, 1961) gave the firm a problem of how to put more potato chips on supermarket shelves. Regular bags of potato chips contain a lot of air and take up valuable space. If the product could be compressed, the company could increase its sales volume.

To solve this problem, firm members thought of other things in life that are compressed. One that stood out was leaves. When crushed and mixed with water, the leaves would still be there but would use less space. So the firm applied this concept to potato chips by mixing water with dehydrated potato flour, shaping the chips, stacking them, and putting them in small, cylindrical containers. Voila! An elegant solution using analogical thinking.

The activities that follow are based on this same process of applying analogies, but these activities add a few twists. The only exception is the I Like It Like That [55] exercise, which provides a more structured approach to analogical thinking.

53

Bionic Ideas

Background

Mother Nature is a pretty wise old gal. Among other things, she is a superior problem solver. Think about it. She has resolved countless problems for plants and animals (including humans). Many plants "know" how to turn toward a light source, for instance. And she helped bats to navigate without eyes, snakes to move without legs, and giraffes to eat leaves off tall trees.

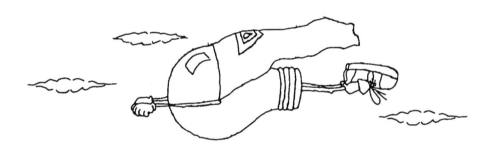

One specific type of analogy is known as "bionics." Whereas general analogies reflect similarities anywhere in life, the Bionic Ideas exercise looks to Mother Nature for similarities. Why invent the wheel if Mother Nature has already done it?

Research labs have resolved a variety of electronic, thermal, hydraulic, mechanical, and chemical problems using Bionic Ideas. For example, the eye of a beetle was used as an analogy to develop an aircraft ground-speed altitude indicator. Alexander Graham Bell used characteristics of the human ear to invent the telephone, and rattlesnake temperature-sensing organs helped suggest the guidance system for the Sidewinder heat-seeking missile.

One famous analogy involved a product that is analogous to the common cocklebur. A hunter walking through a field noticed how cockleburs caught on his trousers using a hook and loop mechanism. This closure system suggested the concept of Velcro®. An entire industry developed from this simple observation.

Objectives

- To help participants generate as many creative ideas as possible
- To help participants learn how to use the activities to generate ideas

Participants

Small groups of four to seven people each

Materials, Supplies, and Equipment

- For each group: markers, two flip charts, and masking tape for posting flip-chart sheets
- For each participant: one sheet each of three different colors of sticking dots (½" diameter) and one pad of 4 x 6 Post-it® Notes

Handout

- Bionic Ideas Handout

Time

45 minutes

Related Activities

- Chain Alike [54]
- I Like It Like That [55]

Procedure

1. Distribute the Bionic Ideas Handout, review it with the participants, and answer any questions they may have.
2. Have the groups state the problem as clearly as possible using an action verb and an object (for example, how to increase sales) and write it down on a flip chart.
3. Tell them to describe the major principle or process that underlies the problem. Cite, as an example, that increasing sales involves the principle of getting more of something.
4. Ask them to think of similar principles in nature (that is, biological or botanical analogies).
5. Instruct them to use these similar principles or processes to stimulate new ideas, writing them on Post-it® notes (one idea per note) to place on flip charts for evaluation.

Debrief/Discussion

Some people may have trouble generating analogies for this exercise. One way to help is to have the participants brainstorm more analogies than they might use. Another way to help would be to provide a list of processes and principles found in biology (for example, osmosis, cell structures). Such lists would be available in biology texts or on the Internet. Consider having participants debrief using the following questions:

- What was most helpful about this exercise?
- What was most challenging?
- What can we apply?
- How would you rate the value of this exercise to helping us with this issue?
- Will this exercise be helpful in the future for other sessions?
- What did you learn?
- What will we be able to use from this exercise?
- What ideas were generated, and which ones were most interesting?

Bionic Ideas Handout

Assume you are the manager of a department store. Your assistant has informed you that the store's losses due to shoplifting are greater than ever. To help resolve this problem, you decide to try Bionic Ideas.

You state the problem as "How could we prevent shoplifting in our store?" Next, you describe the major principle or process as prevention. You then make a list of things in nature that involve the concept of prevention:

- Most birds build their nests in trees to prevent predators from reaching the nests.
- Some animals change the color of their skin to blend in with their environment and prevent attacks from enemies.
- Squirrels put away nuts for the winter to prevent starvation during the cold months.
- Many animal couples take turns guarding their nests to prevent harm to their offspring.
- Camels store large quantities of water in their bodies to prevent thirst and dehydration.
- Turtles quickly pull into their shells to prevent predators from biting their heads or legs.
- Mother Nature installs a strong sex drive in most animals to prevent extinction of the species.
- Many plants turn toward a light source to prevent loss of growth (the so-called phototropic response).
- Leaves drop off many trees to prevent the trees from having to provide nourishment during the winter months.
- Many animals make loud noises to prevent enemies from attacking.

These comparisons might suggest the following ideas:

- Install cameras in ceilings to watch for shoplifters.
- Have security personnel pose as shoppers to blend in and nab any shoplifters.
- Save extra money to make up for stolen merchandise.
- Have employees rotate turns looking for shoplifters.
- Encourage customers to turn in shoplifters by having a lottery among customers who report shoplifting. The winner receives an ocean cruise.
- Install a sensor so that all the doors close automatically when the device detects that someone is trying to leave the store with stolen merchandise.
- Offer employees rewards to encourage them to help perpetuate profits for the store by catching shoplifters.

- Have all the store's lights begin flashing whenever someone attempts to leave with stolen items.
- "Drop" very expensive items into tall boxes to prevent people from reaching the items. Instead, expensive items must be retrieved electronically by a clerk.
- Install an alarm that sounds whenever someone tries to pick up an item before a clerk has turned off the alarm.

54

Chain Alike

Background

If you generate ideas using analogies, your source of stimulation is generally limited to comparisons with the basic problem principle. For instance, the problem of preventing shoplifting (the Bionic Ideas [53] illustration) is limited to analogies involving the principle of prevention. Although there is nothing wrong with this limitation, it does restrict the number of possible problem perspectives. And that's not good.

Fortunately, all is not lost. The Chain Alike activity attacks problems from multiple perspectives. And that's good.

Chain Alike is based on the Attribute Analogy Chains procedure developed by Koberg and Bagnall (1976). Ideas are generated by listing problem attributes, developing analogies for each attribute, and then using the analogies to prompt ideas.

Objectives

- To help participants generate as many creative ideas as possible
- To help participants learn how to use the activities to generate ideas

Participants

Small groups of four to seven people each

Materials, Supplies, and Equipment

- For each group: markers, two flip charts, and masking tape for posting flip-chart sheets
- For each participant: one sheet each of three different colors of sticking dots (½" diameter) and one pad of 4 x 6 Post-it® Notes
- (Optional) One paper or electronic thesaurus for each group

Handout

- Chain Alike Handout

Time

60 minutes

Related Activities

- Bionic Ideas [53]
- I Like It Like That [55]

Procedure

1. Distribute the handout, review it with the participants, and answer any questions they may have.
2. Tape a sheet of flip-chart paper lengthwise on a wall or table.
3. Read the following instructions aloud:

   "On the left side of the paper, list in a single column all major problem attributes (for example, name, form, parts, shape, structure, processes, materials, functions). For each attribute, list several subattributes that describe the attributes. Thus, 'round' and 'square' would be examples of two types of shapes. Write these in a line to the right of each attribute.

   "On a separate sheet of paper, write down several analogies or words similar in meaning for each subattribute. The word 'round,' for example, might spark 'circular,' 'a dog chasing its tail,' and 'a rolling ball. You may use paper or electronic thesauri to help select these words."

4. Tell them to examine each word analogy as a group, see what ideas are triggered, write them on Post-it® Notes (one per note), and place them on flip-chart paper for evaluation.

Debrief/Discussion

Chain Alike is slightly more complicated than other analogy-based activities. More work is required to set up the stimuli to use as idea triggers. Ask the participants if they felt the extra work was worth the effort and if the quality of ideas was any better than when compared with other activities.

Also consider having participants debrief using the following questions:

- What was most helpful about this exercise?
- What was most challenging?
- What can we apply?
- How would you rate the value of this exercise to helping us with this issue?
- Will this exercise be helpful in the future for other sessions?
- What did you learn?
- What will we be able to use from this exercise?
- What ideas were generated, and which ones were most interesting?

Chain Alike Handout

Assume you are the manager of a department store. Your assistant has informed you that the store's losses due to shoplifting are greater than ever. To help resolve this problem, you decide to try the Chain Alike activity.

- Customers
- Merchandise
- Money
- Security
- Observing customers

Next, list subattributes:

- *Name:* Shoplifting
- *Customers:* Children, elderly, middle-aged, rich, poor, educated, uneducated
- *Merchandise:* Electronics in display cases, clothing on shelves and racks
- *Money:* Dollar bills, coins, credit cards, debt, charging, exchange rates
- *Security:* Guards, cameras, alarms, lighting, electronic sensors
- *Observing Customers:* Watching, unobtrusive, disguises, equipment

Next, look at the subattributes and develop analogies for each one. For instance, some sample word analogies might include the following:

- *Name:* Disappearing merchandise
- *Customers:* Small people, money collectors, enhanced brains
- *Merchandise:* Electronic organizers, viewing boxes, stacking levels
- *Money:* Circular disks, plastic debits, substituting values
- *Security:* Caretakers, visual image capturing devices, illumination projection
- *Observing Customers:* Hidden recesses, cover-ups, electronic information processors

Finally, generate ideas using these word analogies:

- Lock all merchandise in display cases (from "disappearing merchandise").
- Install a system so that people must pay for merchandise on their way out to unlock an exit door. People who don't buy anything subject themselves to personal inspections (from "money collectors").
- Place video cameras on merchandise counters (from "viewing boxes").
- Provide educational seminars in schools on the pitfalls of shoplifting (from "substituting values").

- Place monitors throughout the store that show shoplifters being arrested (from "visual image capturing devices").
- Project onto the walls pictures of previous customers who were caught shoplifting (from "illumination projection").
- Put all merchandise in vending machines (from "hidden recesses").

55

I Like It Like That

Background

This activity is the grandparent of all the "just alike only different" activities. It is based on general analogical thinking that relies on the direct comparison of one thing or action to another. As with Bionic Ideas [53], comparisons are used to spark ideas. The difference is that the comparisons may be drawn from anywhere, not just from Mother Nature, as with Bionic Ideas. Once the similarities have been identified, they are elaborated and then used to stimulate ideas.

Objectives

- To help participants generate as many creative ideas as possible
- To help participants learn how to use the activities to generate ideas

Participants

Small groups of four to seven people each

Materials, Supplies, and Equipment

- For each group: markers, two flip charts, and masking tape for posting flip-chart sheets
- For each participant: one sheet each of three different colors of sticking dots (½" diameter)and one pad of 4 x 6 Post-it® Notes

Handout

- I like It Like That Handout

Time

45 minutes

Related Activities

- Bionic Ideas [53]
- Chain Alike [54]

Procedure

1. Distribute the I Like It Like That Handout, review it with the participants, and answer any questions they may have.

2. Tell group members to think of the major principle underlying their problem and use it to generate a list of things similar to the problem. To help generate this list, say, "This problem is like. . . ." (See the handout for an example.)

3. Instruct them to select one of the analogies and describe it in detail, elaborating as much as possible, listing parts, functions, or uses. Remind them to include many action-oriented phrases and, if possible, select an analogy that is controversial or out of the ordinary.

4. Have them review each description and use it to stimulate ideas that they should write on Post-it® Notes (one idea per note) and place on flip-chart paper for evaluation.

Debrief/Discussion

Some research suggests that analogies are more likely than other direct stimulation activities to yield unique ideas. Analogies also seem to work especially well for mechanical problems. For instance, analogies have been used to design a new type of thermos bottle closure and a way to attach spacesuit helmets. Although this activity may take a little more effort, it is quite useful for difficult problems.

Also consider having participants debrief using the following questions:

- What was most helpful about this exercise?
- What was most challenging?
- What can we apply?
- How would you rate the value of this exercise to helping us with this issue?
- Will this exercise be helpful in the future for other sessions?
- What did you learn?
- What will we be able to use from this exercise?
- What ideas were generated, and which ones were most interesting?

I Like It Like That Handout

Suppose you decide to use analogies to help recruit more engineers for your organization. The major principle in this case is, "getting more of something." Thus, you might think of analogies prompted by the phrase, "This problem is like . . ."

- asking your parents for an increase in your allowance.
- asking your boss for a raise.
- asking a cook for more food.
- asking your boss for more time to complete a project.
- an employee trying to get more power over another employee.
- a football team trying to win more games.
- a panhandler begging for more money.
- calling people to sell more magazines.

Select one of these analogies and elaborate.
A panhandler begging for more money involves the following things:

- Deciding which people to ask
- Not being too overbearing
- Watching out for the police
- Looking pathetic
- Using creative requests, such as asking for a quarter to call about graduate school admission
- Looking as presentable as possible
- Maintaining eye contact
- Finding the best location
- Using many different locations

Finally, use the elaborations to suggest ideas for recruiting engineers:

- Screen potential candidates using recommendations and background checks.
- Use a "soft sell" approach; don't seem overly interested.
- Conduct security checks.
- Tell top recruits how much you need them.
- Give prospects a toll-free number to call if they have questions.
- Scout out the best recruiting locations.
- Search for a variety of personality and ability types by recruiting from many different schools in various regions of the country.

56

What Is It?

Background

Advertising and marketing professionals frequently push products based on assumptions regarding core motivations and needs. Rather than appeal to people to buy a product based on its features, advertisers try to show potential customers how a product will satisfy some need.

For instance, one advertisement might push a brand of coffee because it tastes good. Another, in contrast, might emphasize how the product will satisfy the need to feel secure. Because security may be a stronger motivator than the taste of coffee, consumers may respond more positively to the need-satisfaction approach.

Here are some other possible examples:

- A convertible isn't a car, it's excitement.
- A watch isn't a timepiece, it's a piece of jewelry.
- A job position recruitment campaign isn't for a job, it's for prestige and recognition.
- A coat isn't for warmth, it's a fashion statement.

All of these relate to the question, What is it? Hall (1994) uses this question as the basis for an idea generation method by the same name. It generates ideas by thinking what else a problem is and then using these descriptions as idea stimuli.

Objectives

- To help participants generate as many creative ideas as possible
- To help participants learn how to use the activities to generate ideas

Participants

Small groups of four to seven people each

Materials, Supplies, and Equipment

- For each group: markers, two flip charts, and masking tape for posting flip-chart sheets
- For each participant: one sheet each of three different colors of sticking dots (½" diameter)and one pad of 4 x 6 Post-it® Notes

Handout

- What Is It? Handout

Time

45 minutes

Related Activities

- Essence of the Problem [38]
- Turn Around [52]

Procedure

1. Distribute the What Is It Handout, review it with the participants, and answer any questions they may have.
2. Tell the participants to describe their problems in at least six different ways that capture the "essence" of their problems (see the handout for examples).
3. Instruct them to use their descriptions to prompt ideas, write them on Post-it® Notes (one idea per note), and place them on a flip chart for evaluation.

Debrief/Discussion

This activity differs from most in its emphasis on human emotions and how they drive our creative abilities. It can be especially useful for new product development because of its ability to uncover consumer needs and supply ways to meet them. However, it also is extremely versatile in its ability to provide diverse problem perspectives by helping uncover hidden or unwarranted assumptions. You might ask participants to compare its ability to generate unique ideas with a an activity that relies on unrelated stimuli such as words, pictures, or objects.

Also consider having participants debrief using the following questions:

- What was most helpful about this exercise?
- What was most challenging?
- What can we apply?
- How would you rate the value of this exercise to helping us with this issue?
- Will this exercise be helpful in the future for other sessions?
- What did you learn?
- What will we be able to use from this exercise?
- What ideas were generated, and which ones were most interesting?

What Is It? Handout

Consider the problem of improving an office desk. First, describe what desks are. For instance, you might say that office desks are not just desks, they are

- Smooth writing areas
- Occupational centers
- Computer support stands
- Leg and lap covers
- Hollowed-out wooden boxes

Then use these descriptions to generate ideas:

- A variable-tilt writing surface built into the desk top
- Desks tailored to different occupations. For instance, a doctor's desk might have a place to hold a stethoscope, a blood pressure cuff, and other diagnostic tools, as well as a built-in computer screen with the *Physician's Desk Reference* on a CD
- A computer monitor that flips up when needed, a CPU under the desk, and a keyboard built into the desk top
- A desk with heating pads and foot warmers
- A desk that can be collapsed easily and stored in a compact area

Group Only
Activities

Chapter 9

Brainstorming with Related Stimuli

Brainstorming with related activities is classic brainstorming as developed and popularized by Alex Osborn. It's idea generation that focuses on the problem and uses the ideas of other group members as stimuli. The key to successful brainstorming is adherence to the following brainstorming principles.

1. Defer Judgment

Withhold all evaluation of ideas during idea generation. That is, separate generation from evaluation. Once you have listed all possible ideas, then go back and evaluate them. There's a lot of logic behind this principle. First, most groups don't follow it and, as a result, are less than productive. Second, deferring judgment increases the odds of finding at least one good idea. If you spend a lot of time evaluating each idea as you think of it, you may run out of time before you can list all possible ideas. It's a matter of probability.

Finally, separating evaluation from generation helps you avoid creating a negative group climate. Idea generation generally is a fun, positive experience. If you stop to criticize each idea as it is proposed, you're interjecting a negative process that disrupts the more positive aspects. Thus, you may never produce a climate healthy enough for effective idea generation. Separate the processes and you'll be amazed at how productive your group can be.

2. Quantity Breeds Quality

The more ideas you list, the more high-quality ideas you'll get. Again, it's all a matter of probability. Let's assume there is a potential pool of five hundred ideas. That's how many ideas you could generate hypothetically if you had all the brains and time in the world. Of these five hundred ideas, assume there are twenty-five you would consider as high quality. If you use the sequential generate-evaluate, generate-evaluate-generate-evaluate cycle, you may get "lucky" and produce a total of twenty-five ideas during a one-hour brainstorming session. Now, just what are the odds that a majority of these would be the same twenty-five high-quality ideas? The answer: not very high. The sequential approach relies on pure chance to produce a high-quality idea. It is more logical to increase the odds by first listing as many ideas as possible. You always can go back and evaluate them later. Moreover, each idea you list can help spark other ideas. So if you defer judgment and shoot for quantity, you may produce 125 ideas. Now what are the odds that one of those is a high-quality one? The answer: very high. You don't need to be a statistician to figure out this one.

3. The Wilder the Better

Although idea quantity is essential for idea quality, it may not always be sufficient. You can't always rely on the laws of probability. Thus, you need to free your mind and turn off censors and shake off constraints. Shoot for wild, crazy, silly, off-the-wall ideas. These ideas—and the ones they spark—are the ones you need for high-quality, winning ideas. Don't worry about practicality when generating ideas. Remember, you're supposed to separate generation and evaluation. Instead, focus on how many wild ideas you can think of. Some conventional ideas are O.K., too. But don't make a habit of it. Go for the unusual and see what results.

4. Combine and Improve Ideas

Another way to ensure high-quality ideas is to not let your ideas get lonely. Give them relatives and friends. That is, use your natural powers of free association and see how you can combine an existing idea with another one to form a completely new idea. Or encourage your ideas to be all they can be. Empower them to use their full potential. Take an existing idea and try to improve it. How else might it be implemented? What could you substitute, change, reverse, or make larger or smaller? What would make it better? Go for it and you'll increase your IQ (Idea Quotient) and generate better ideas as well.

NOTE: FOR ALL ACTIVITIES, REMIND PARTICIPANTS
TO DEFER JUDGMENT WHILE GENERATING IDEAS.

57

Be #1

Background

You want to be number one, don't you? Who doesn't? In the business world, it's important to carve out a niche and then work to dominate it.

Hall (1994) describes how you can use this emphasis on being number one to help generate ideas. All you do is list current benefits of some product or process and then transform them into winning, number one ideas.

Objectives

- To help participants generate as many creative ideas as possible
- To help participants learn how to use the activities to generate ideas

Participants

Small groups of four to seven people each

Materials, Supplies, and Equipment

- For each group: markers, two flip charts, and masking tape for posting flip-chart sheets
- For each participant: one sheet each of three different colors of sticking dots (½" diameter) and one pad of 4 x 6 Post-it® Notes

Handout

- Be #1 Handout

Time

30 minutes

Related Activities

- Idea Links [41]
- Skybridging [46]

Procedure

1. Have the groups tape a sheet of flip-chart paper lengthwise on a wall or table.

2. Distribute the Be #1 Handout, review it with the participants, and answer any questions they may have.

3. Tell the groups to list on the paper, in a single column, the current core benefits of their general business category. Prompt them to include both the trivial and the essential.

4. Have them create a second column in which they transform each benefit into its best state. Have them use the phrase "the best" or a word that ends in "est" (for example, "fastest").

5. Direct them, in column three, to list ways to achieve this elevated status. Note that these are their ideas.

6. Instruct them to repeat Steps 3 through 5, but to list in column one new benefits that currently do not exist.

7. Tell them to write down any ideas on Post-it® Notes (one idea per note) and place them on flip charts for evaluation.

Debrief/Discussion

An appealing feature of this exercise is that it may bring out a competitive spirit that can be translated into creative applications. More importantly, the matrix structure of this activity might provide the structure needed for some people to generate ideas instead of having to "pull them out of the air." It also provides a potentially useful visual focus for group members to direct their attention. If participants have trouble generating ideas with this exercise and time is available, consider having them start over but using new benefits.

Also consider having participants debrief using the following questions:

- What was most helpful about this exercise?
- What was most challenging?
- What can we apply?
- How would you rate the value of this exercise to helping us with this issue?
- Will this exercise be helpful in the future for other sessions?
- What did you learn?
- What will we be able to use from this exercise?
- What ideas were generated, and which ones were most interesting?

Be #1 Handout

Consider a problem involving a company that wishes to improve its line of floor cleaners. Examples of current benefits, being the best, and ideas are shown in Table 9.1.

Current Benefits	Being the Best	Ways to Realize (Ideas)
Shines floors	Best shine	Use luminescence
Cleans floors	The best cleaner	Antiseptic, good smell
Easy application	Easiest to apply	New, precise applicator

Table 9.1.   Example of Current Benefits

After generating ideas using current benefits, repeat the process using new benefits. Examples of new benefits, being the best, and ideas are shown in Table 9.2.

Current Benefits	Being the Best	Ways to Realize (Ideas)
Quick drying	Fastest drying	Dries instantly
Waxes floors	Best cleaner and waxer	Combination product
Easy-to-hold package	Best ergonomic design	Dispenser also cleans

Table 9.2.   Example of New Benefits

58

Blender

Background

A blender mixes two or more products together to produce something that may not even resemble the original products. Sometimes the final product is better than either of the originals. That's the philosophy behind the Blender activity.

According to Warfield, Geschka, and Hamilton (1975), Blender originally was developed by Helmut Schlicksupp at the Battelle Institute in Frankfurt, Germany. His name for the method was SIL, a German acronym meaning Successive Integration of Problem Elements. This activity combines elements of brainwriting and brainstorming, thus taking advantage of the strengths of each.

Objectives

- To help participants generate as many creative ideas as possible
- To help participants learn how to use the activities to generate ideas

Participants

Small groups of four to seven people each

Materials, Supplies, and Equipment

- For each group: markers, two flip charts, and masking tape for posting flip-chart sheets
- For each participant: one sheet each of three different colors of sticking dots (½″ diameter) and one pad of 4 x 6 Post-it® Notes

Handout

- Blender Handout

Time

30 minutes

Related Activities

- Force-Fit Game [74]

Procedure

1. Distribute the Blender Handout, review it with the participants, and answer any questions they may have.

2. Ask each person in the small groups to write, on Post-it® Notes (one idea per note), ideas for the problem, without speaking, for about 5 to 10 minutes.

3. Tell them to have two group members each read one of their ideas aloud.

4. Have the other group members attempt to integrate (blend) the two ideas into one idea and ask one group member to write it down on a Post-it® Note.

5. Instruct them to have a third group member read an idea aloud and have the groups integrate it with the result of Step 4 (that is, all three ideas now are integrated, because the third idea is integrated with the product of the first two ideas). Tell them that someone in their group should write down this new idea on a Post-it® Note.

6. Tell them to repeat this process until all ideas have been read and the group has attempted to integrate them (some ideas may defy integration).

7. Have the groups stop when the members find an integrated idea acceptable to all or time runs out.

8. Tell them to write down any other ideas on Post-it® Notes (one idea per note) and place all ideas generated on flip charts for evaluation.

Debrief/Discussion

This exercise has the potential to spark some unique ideas by blending together a number of concepts. One downside is that the potential limitations posed by integrating ideas, some of which might have been better as a stand-alone solution. To overcome this disadvantage, encourage the participants to write down any ideas on Post-its for evaluation, even if the idea is combined with another. This way, possibly valuable ideas won't be lost.

Also consider having participants debrief using the following questions:

- What was most helpful about this exercise?
- What was most challenging?
- What can we apply?
- How would you rate the value of this exercise to helping us with this issue?
- Will this exercise be helpful in the future for other sessions?
- What did you learn?
- What will we be able to use from this exercise?
- What ideas were generated, and which ones were most interesting?

Blender Handout

Assume you belong to a group of volunteer speakers. The group has met to brainstorm ways to improve their speeches. Group members silently generate ideas in writing for about 10 minutes. Then Mary reads her idea: "Ask the audience to submit questions on your topic before you speak."

Next, John reads his idea: "Tell an opening story to get the attention of the audience and to illustrate your major theme."

The group members think about these ideas and integrate them into one idea: "Ask the audience to submit brief stories illustrating a theme, take a break to analyze their responses, and then tell them the outcome."

After everyone agrees on this idea, Fred reads his idea: "Have audience members pair up with one other person to introduce themselves."

The group members attempt to integrate this idea and come up with this: "To illustrate how people miscommunicate, tell one audience member in a row a 'secret' and have that person tell it to the next person in the row who tells it to the next person and so forth. After the secret makes it to the end of the row, ask the last person to tell the entire audience the secret. The final version of the 'secret' usually is a gross distortion of the original."

Melvin then suggests his idea: "Project your image on screens around the room."

The group attempts to integrate this idea and comes up with the following: "Continually project audience members' facial reactions on a screen to demonstrate feedback through nonverbal communication."

59

Drawing Room

Background

You have probably browsed in a museum at one time or another. On a visit to a museum in Washington, D.C. (the Phillips Collection), I was struck with the variety of ideas expressed by the paintings from different periods: a Picasso from his blue period communicated some degree of depression, a Renoir showed a group of people enjoying themselves at a boating party luncheon, and a Degas showed ballet dancers preparing to perform. Of course, these are just my subjective impressions. You may not agree with what I see and experience. And that's just fine.

The paintings provide rich sources of stimulation to help us interpret and understand our world. Groups can use this principle of visual stimulation to generate ideas and have fun at the same time.

Objectives

- To help participants generate as many creative ideas as possible
- To help participants learn how to use the activities to generate ideas

Participants

Small groups of four to seven people each

Materials, Supplies, and Equipment

- For each group: markers, two flip charts, and masking tape for posting flip-chart sheets
- For each participant: one sheet each of three different colors of sticking dots (½" diameter), four sheets of 8.5" x 11" white paper, at least four crayons of different colors, and one pad of 4 x 6 Post-it® Notes

Time

30 minutes

Related Activities

- Picture Tickler [17]
- Rorschach Revisionist [18]
- Ideatoons [26]
- Doodles [37]
- Modular Brainstorming [62]

Procedure

1. Tell each group member to draw, individually, a picture representing a solution to the problem. Say that the picture may be either abstract or realistic and that artistic talent is not important.

2. When they have finished, tell them to tape their pictures to the walls or on a flip chart.

3. Instruct all participants from all groups to walk around the room and examine the drawings just as people would do in a museum. As group members examine the pictures, tell them to write down on Post-it® Notes any comments or new ideas triggered.

4. Instruct each group to reconvene and share their ideas, in turn, and try to think of any new ideas.

5. Tell them to write down any ideas on Post-it® Notes (one idea per note) and place them on flip charts for evaluation.

Debrief/Discussion

Participants don't need artistic talent for this exercise. In fact, this activity may work extremely well for visual thinkers who can play off of visual stimuli to help trigger ideas. Because some drawings may be more abstract than others, encourage participants to discuss whether they found more value in concrete or abstract drawings, or if it even made a difference.

Also consider having participants debrief using the following questions:

- What was most helpful about this exercise?
- What was most challenging?
- What can we apply?
- How would you rate the value of this exercise to helping us with this issue?
- Will this exercise be helpful in the future for other sessions?
- What did you learn?
- What will we be able to use from this exercise?
- What ideas were generated, and which ones were most interesting?

Variations

- Ask one-half of the group draw an abstract version and the other half a more realistic representation. Instruct the groups using Steps 2 through 4 above.

- Have participants pass their drawings around the table before finishing them. Encourage other participants to add to the drawings until each has gone around the table once. Instruct the groups using Steps 2 through 4 above.

60

Get Real!!

Background

We've all heard it before: "That's the stupidest idea I've ever heard!" "It'll never work!" "That's pretty dumb." "Get real!!" We seem to be conditioned to react negatively whenever we hear a new idea. Sometimes, the more innovative the idea, the more repulsed we are. It's as if our attitude is "If I haven't heard of it (or thought of it) before, then it can't be any good" (the "not-invented here syndrome").

Well, get real! Such a negative attitude isn't going to benefit us individually or in groups. In fact, this attitude can establish a negative climate that eliminates the possibility of developing any useful, innovative ideas. There is a bright side to such an attitude, however. It can be turned around and used to stimulate ideas.

Objectives

- To help participants generate as many creative ideas as possible
- To help participants learn how to use the activities to generate ideas

Participants

Small groups of four to seven people each

Materials, Supplies, and Equipment

- For each group: markers, two flip charts, and masking tape for posting flip-chart sheets
- For each participant: one sheet each of three different colors of sticking dots (½" diameter) and one pad of 4 x 6 Post-it® Notes

Handout

- Get Real!! Handout

Time

30 minutes

Related Activities

- Picture Tickler [17]
- Rorschach Revisionist [18]
- Ideatoons [26]
- Doodles [37]
- Drawing Room [59]

Procedure

1. Distribute the Get Real!! Handout, review it with the participants, and answer any questions they may have.
2. Instruct the participants in each group to brainstorm ideas for approximately 15 minutes.
3. Tell them to write down each idea, individually, on a Post-it® Note (one idea per note) and place it on a flip chart for all to see.
4. Have the group members select the two or three stupidest, most impractical, and most unworkable ideas from among those posted on the flip chart.
5. Direct the group members to examine each of these ideas and see what smart, practical, workable ideas the original ideas might stimulate.
6. Tell them to write down any ideas on Post-it® Notes (one idea per note) and place them on flip charts for evaluation.

Debrief/Discussion

This can be a fun and interesting exercise, especially for participants who tend to be highly judgmental. It can be surprising to see how supposedly "bad" ideas actually can be used to spark creative solutions. This information can be useful for training in creative thinking if participants will transfer it to other problem-solving situations. Ideas do not always have to be the perfect match for a problem; they also can be springboards to more practical ones.

Also consider having participants debrief using the following questions:

- What was most helpful about this exercise?
- What was most challenging?
- What can we apply?
- How would you rate the value of this exercise to helping us with this issue?
- Will this exercise be helpful in the future for other sessions?
- What did you learn?
- What will we be able to use from this exercise?
- What ideas were generated, and which ones were most interesting?

Get Real!! Handout

Suppose your organization wants to attract people to its arts foundation fund raisers. You and some others brainstorm some ideas and select two of the worst ones:

- Call all the people in town and ask them to attend.
- Offer to pick people up and drive them to the seminar.

  With these ideas as stimuli, the group generates some more practical ideas:

- Hire a marketing firm to call people most likely to benefit from such a seminar.
- Advertise on a radio show and offer a discount to the first twenty people who enroll by phone.
- Pay mileage to seminar participants.
- Lease buses to transport people from a common collection point.
- Raffle off a free rental car at the seminar.

61

Idea Showers

Background

Let the ideas rain on down. Flood your group with thoughts about how to solve your problem. Try for as much conceptual precipitation as you can generate. It's time for Idea Showers. Ideas Showers is another name for the classic brainstorming method developed years ago by advertising executive Alex Osborn.

Objectives

- To help participants generate as many creative ideas as possible
- To help participants learn how to use the activities to generate ideas

Participants

Small groups of four to seven people each

Materials, Supplies, and Equipment

- For each group: markers, two flip charts, and masking tape for posting flip-chart sheets
- For each participant: one sheet each of three different colors of sticking dots (½" diameter) and one pad of 4 x 6 Post-it® Notes.

Handout

- Idea Showers Handout

Time

30 minutes

Related Activities

- Get Crazy [5]

Brainstorming with Related Stimuli

- Idea Links [41]
- What if. . . ? [49]
- Phillips 66 [64]

Procedure

1. Distribute the Idea Showers Handout, review it with the participants, and answer any questions they may have.

2. After reviewing the handout, emphasize the importance of each of the four principles. Stress that the number one rule is to defer judgment.

3. Ask the groups to select a problem statement in the form of: "How might we. . . ?" For instance, "How might we better market our product or service?"

4. Instruct them to spend 15 minutes generating ideas to resolve this problem, with each person writing an idea on a Post-it® Note, after suggesting it verbally.

5. Call time and tell them place their ideas on flip charts for evaluation.

Debrief/Discussion

Ask the participants to discuss the following questions:

- Why is deferring judgment so important?
- Is it more important than the other three brainstorming principles? Why or why not?
- How feasible is it to defer judgment in practice?
- How might groups overcome obstacles to deferring judgment?
- Why are the other three principles important?

  Also consider having participants debrief using the following questions:

- What was most helpful about this exercise?
- What was most challenging?
- What can we apply?
- How would you rate the value of this exercise to helping us with this issue?
- Will this exercise be helpful in the future for other sessions?
- What did you learn?
- What will we be able to use from this exercise?
- What ideas were generated, and which ones were most interesting?

Idea Showers Handout

Advertising executive Alex Osborn's four principles for brainstorming are

- Defer judgment
- Quantity breeds quality
- The wilder the better
- Combination and improvement are sought

The trick is to translate these principles into workable brainstorming behaviors. The first principle suggests that your group should agree to think of all the ideas they can before evaluating any ideas. If you stick to this principle, you also should be successful with the second principle of quantity breeds quality. Separating generation from evaluation has been found to increase idea quantity, with a corresponding increase in quality. The third principle reinforces the second in that letting go and not being concerned with idea practicality is likely to increase idea quantity. Finally, the fourth principle—combination and improvement are sought—is likely to improve idea quality. Building on others' ideas helps improve existing ideas while triggering new ones.

62

Modular Brainstorming

Background

You've certainly heard the expression "A picture is worth a thousand words." Well, you might also say that a picture is worth a thousand ideas. Modular Brainstorming (also called "Component Detailing") was developed by Wakin (1985) to take advantage of the natural human tendency to use visualization during problem solving. This activity also helps provoke unique perspectives by positioning the pictures in a certain way.

Objectives

- To help participants generate as many creative ideas as possible
- To help participants learn how to use the activities to generate ideas

Participants

Small groups of four to seven people each

Materials, Supplies, and Equipment

- For each group: markers, two flip charts, and masking tape for posting flip-chart sheets
- For each participant: one sheet each of three different colors of sticking dots (½" diameter) and one pad of 4 x 6 Post-it® Notes

Handout

- Modular Brainstorming Handout

Time

45 minutes

Related Activities

- Picture Tickler [17]

101 Activities for Teaching Creativity and Problem Solving

- Rorschach Revisionist [18]
- Ideatoons [26]
- Doodles [37]
- Drawing Room [59]

Procedure

1. Distribute the Modular Brainstorming Handout, review it with the participants, and answer any questions they may have.
2. Tell the group members to generate a list of major problem components and sub-attributes for each component.
3. Instruct the group members to each select a different component, that is, one per person; if there are more attributes than components, have them each select an additional one. (If the problem involves a tangible product, you might give the groups an actual product.)
4. Tell the individual group members to study the component and its attributes, noting all details.
5. Have the individuals draw a picture of their components, being sure to include as much detail as possible.
6. Ask each group to collect their drawings and attach them to a wall or board or lay them out on a large table. Note that they should arrange the pictures so that their placement approximates the components of the actual problem/product.
7. Have the members of each group examine this collage to stimulate new ideas or improvements. Note that the individual drawings typically vary in size and proportion, thus instantly creating new perspectives.
8. Tell the participants to use the drawings to prompt ideas.
9. Tell them to write down any ideas on Post-it® Notes (one idea per note) and place them on flip charts for evaluation.

Debrief/Discussion

The visualizations and creative juxtapositions generated by this activity give it the potential to generate unique problem perspectives and innovative ideas. It is another visualization approach that can work well with people who can play off of concrete images. One unique aspect of this activity is that visual images of different sizes placed next to each other create unique perspectives not normally created with more traditional idea generation activities.

Also consider having participants debrief using the following questions:

- What was most helpful about this exercise?
- What was most challenging?
- What can we apply?

Brainstorming with Related Stimuli

265

- How would you rate the value of this exercise to helping us with this issue?
- Will this exercise be helpful in the future for other sessions?
- What did you learn?
- What will we be able to use from this exercise?
- What ideas were generated, and which ones were most interesting?

Modular Brainstorming Handout

To illustrate this activity, suppose you are a facilitator who agreed to help a company improve a common door lock. You ask group members first to list components such as knobs, latches, pins, tumblers, keys, bolts, springs, and a striking plate. Next, they list subattributes of each component. For instance, springs have such characteristics as being spiral in shape, under tension, capable of being stretched, and varied in size.

After group members draw pictures of the individual components, they arrange the pictures together and examine the collage for stimulation. Thus, the doorknob might suggest a new shape for a handle, and the bolt might be made larger and be designed to interlock with a different mechanism in the doorjamb.

63

Pass the Hat

Background

Doug Hall (1994) uses Pass the Hat as a combination brainstorming/brainwriting procedure for two or more groups. Unlike some brainwriting activities, this activity involves
generating problem attributes for stimuli instead of generating ideas. Other groups then
use the attributes to spark ideas.

Pass the Hat emphasizes blending together problem features to produce something
new. This "mix and match" process has been around for a while. Consider, for instance,
such products as wine coolers that blend wine and fruit juice.

Objectives

- To help participants generate as many creative ideas as possible
- To help participants learn how to use the activities to generate ideas

Participants

Small groups of four to seven people each

Materials, Supplies, and Equipment

- For each group: markers, two flip charts, and masking tape for posting flip-chart
  sheets
- For each participant: one sheet each of three different colors of sticking dots
  (½" diameter) and one pad of 4 x 6 Post-it® Notes
- One sheet of 5.5" x 8.5" paper for each group
- Pens or pencils for each group member

Handout

- Pass the Hat Handout

Time

30 minutes

Related Activities

- Brain Purge [82]
- Idea Pool [85]

Procedure

1. Distribute the Pass the Hat Handout, review it with the participants, and answer any questions they may have.

2. Give each small group a silly hat. (You can buy them from novelty stores or online.) If you don't have any hats, use small paper bags, wastebaskets, plastic sacks, or pillow cases. (Of course, you'll then need to change the name to "Pass the Plastic Sacks" or "Pass the Pillow Cases" or whatever.)

3. Have each group write down five problem attributes, characteristics, emotions, general perceptions, traits, features, or benefits of the challenge. (If there is more than one problem category—for example, different types of beverages such as punch, soda, and milk—instruct the groups to complete one list for each category, but no more than a total of three.)

4. Tell each group to place its list into a hat and pass the hat to another group.

5. Instruct each group to use the list it just received to think of ideas and write them on Post-it® Notes (one idea per note) to be placed on flip charts for evaluation.

6. Tell the groups that when they have finished with the list, to return it to the hat and pass it to another group, which then uses the list for stimulation.

7. After the groups have used all the available lists or time is called, stop the exercise (a time limit will generally be needed only when there are multiple lists).

Debrief/Discussion

Although Pass the Hat was originally developed for use with multiple groups, it will also work with just one group. Simply use the lists individuals generate instead of one passed to you by another group. One nice feature of this activity is that it provides problem-related stimuli that might help provoke new ideas. A more important feature, however, is its use of ideas from other groups to help spark new ideas. A more rich idea pool is likely to result. If time is available, you might ask the groups to discuss the advantages and disadvantages of sharing ideas with other groups.

Also consider having participants debrief using the following questions:

- What was most helpful about this exercise?
- What was most challenging?
- What can we apply?
- How would you rate the value of this exercise to helping us with this issue?
- Will this exercise be helpful in the future for other sessions?
- What did you learn?

- What will we be able to use from this exercise?
- What ideas were generated, and which ones were most interesting?

Pass the Hat Handout

Suppose you are concerned with packaging and marketing water in plastic bottles. Your group lists five attributes of this product:

- The bottle has a screw-on cap.
- The water is perceived as being pure and free from contamination.
- The bottle can easily be recycled.
- Different flavors will enhance the taste of the water.
- The bottle is unbreakable and lighter than a glass bottle.

You place this list in a hat and pass it to the next group. This group examines the list and generates the following ideas:

- Design a novelty bottle shaped like a water faucet.
- Stress product purity in advertisements and label designs.
- Demonstrate environmental awareness by providing recycling instructions on the label.
- Use different colors of plastic that match different flavors.
- Package water in bottles shaped like the fruit used to flavor the water.
- Advertise by dropping plastic and glass bottles on a hard surface.

64

Phillips 66

Background

Does the name of this activity make you want to gas up your car? Do you have a sudden urge to buy stock in an oil company? If you answered "yes" to either of these questions, you may be a little strange.

The Phillips 66 activity has nothing to do with gasoline, the Phillips Petroleum Company, or your personality. It has a lot to do, however, with the name of the person who devised this activity: Donald Phillips.

Phillips (1948), a former president of Hillsdale College, created Phillips 66 (also known as the Phillips 66 Buzz Session) to help increase audience participation in large groups.

Objectives

- To help participants generate as many creative ideas as possible
- To help participants learn how to use the activities to generate ideas
- To involve a large audience in small group brainstorming

Participants

Small groups of six people each

Materials, Supplies, and Equipment

- For each group: markers, two flip charts, and masking tape for posting flip-chart sheets
- For each participant: one sheet each of three different colors of sticking dots (½" diameter) and one pad of 4 x 6 Post-it® Notes
- One overhead projector, transparency markers, and at least one transparency sheet for each small group

Time

45 minutes

Related Activities

- Idea Showers [61]

Procedure

1. Tell the groups to select a discussion leader and a secretary/recorder who will record and report the group's ideas.

2. Have the groups generate ideas for 6 minutes and record them on a flip chart. (If more time is available, allow the groups 15 to 20 minutes.)

3. Tell each group to evaluate its ideas and select the best ones.

4. Instruct the spokesperson for each group to read aloud the group's best ideas to the large group.

5. The facilitator (you or someone you appoint) should record each group's best ideas on a flip chart or overhead transparency visible to all.

6. Give the final list of ideas to an individual or committee for additional evaluation, or ask the larger group to discuss the ideas if time permits. Record any new ideas that result.

Debrief/Discussion

This is a rather simplistic version of traditional brainstorming with the twist of sharing ideas from the other groups. When it first was created years ago, it was novel in providing a structured way to solicit ideas from a large group of participants—even several hundred. By breaking down the audience into small groups, everyone is ensured of a chance to participate and the structure can produce more ideas than otherwise might result. You probably should consider using the brainwriting variation separately or in conjunction with brainstorming. This should ensure more ideas and higher quality ones.

Consider having participants debrief using the following questions:

- What was most helpful about this exercise?
- What was most challenging?
- What can we apply?
- How would you rate the value of this exercise to helping us with this issue?
- Will this exercise be helpful in the future for other sessions?
- What did you learn?
- What will we be able to use from this exercise?
- What ideas were generated, and which ones were most interesting?

Variation

- Use brainwriting within the groups. Have each person write at least one idea on a Post-it® Note and pass it around the group for others to use for stimulating ideas. The group then would select the best ones to present to the large group.

65

Play by Play

Background

Play by Play is another Doug Hall (1994) brainchild that he describes as a step-by-step adventure. This activity is much like doing a mini-commercial for television. It is especially appropriate for process or new product improvements. However, it also could apply to other types of problems such as those involving marketing or human resources.

Objectives

- To help participants generate as many creative ideas as possible
- To help participants learn how to use the activities to generate ideas

Participants

Small groups of four to seven people each

Materials, Supplies, and Equipment

- For each group: markers, two flip charts, and masking tape for posting flip-chart sheets
- For each participant: one sheet each of three different colors of sticking dots (½″ diameter) and one pad of 4 x 6 Post-it® Notes.
- One camera for each group capable of taking instant pictures or a digital camera and small printer capable of printing photos on demand (either directly from the camera or via a computer)
- For each group, examples of products or processes that might need improvement and any associated accessories. For instance, if you want to improve fruit drinks, you would bring existing fruit drinks, fruit, drink containers, drinking cups, straws, ice, et cetera.

Time

75 minutes (requires preparation one week prior to the activity)

Related Activities

- Picture Tickler [17]
- SAMM I Am [33]
- Say Cheese [44]

Handout

- Play by Play Handout

Procedure

1. Distribute the Play by Play Handout, review it with the participants, and answer any questions they may have.

2. Distribute one camera to each group or ask them, in advance, to bring a camera.

3. Discuss using the cameras to be sure everyone understands how to use them.

4. Instruct them to photograph each step involved in using a product or process, starting from as far back as possible, and to try to go far into the future. In the fruit drink example, a group might start with a picture of different types of fruit and end with some exotic looking concoction.

5. After they have taken all the pictures, have the groups arrange their pictures in order and examine them.

6. Instruct them to look for moments that might be improved, moments that seem to have best captured the essence of the product or process, and the most intriguing moments.

7. Tell them to redo any pictures that need improvement.

8. Direct the groups to examine all the pictures again and use them to help generate new ideas.

9. Have them write their ideas on Post-it® Notes (one idea per note) and place them on a flip chart for evaluation.

Debrief/Discussion

This exercise typically is very popular because of its fun, hands-on approach and its use of individual creative talents and visual images. To ensure successful implementation, plan ahead for technical problems that might arise, such as cameras not working properly to take or print pictures. A couple of extra cameras probably would be a good idea. This also is an excellent exercise to use for a group discussion of what else could be added to make it more interesting or useful.

Also consider having participants debrief using the following questions:

- What was most helpful about this exercise?
- What was most challenging?

Brainstorming with Related Stimuli **275**

- What can we apply?
- How would you rate the value of this exercise to helping us with this issue?
- Will this exercise be helpful in the future for other sessions?
- What did you learn?
- What will we be able to use from this exercise?
- What ideas were generated, and which ones were most interesting?

Play by Play Handout

Assume you manufacture soup and want to improve sales. You might create scenes in which a small child is shown:

- Walking into a kitchen
- Pushing a chair toward a cabinet
- Smiling as she reaches for a can of soup in the cabinet
- Retrieving a can opener from a drawer
- Opening the can of soup with her tongue projecting from one corner of her mouth
- Retrieving a pan from underneath a counter
- Pouring soup into the pan
- Stirring the soup
- Ladling the soup into a bowl
- Eating the soup with it dripping from her mouth
- Drinking the soup from the bowl
- Sitting and smiling

With these pictures as stimuli, a soup company brainstorming group might think of the following types of ideas:

- Easy-open cans for children
- "Cartoon" soups with appropriate themes and pictures
- A soup can with a built-in heating pan
- A can with a pour spout
- A can with a built-in or attached "classic" soup spoon
- Ready-to-eat cold soups with straws
- Soup cans with small mirrors on the label in which a child's face can be seen as the head of some cartoon character

66

Rice Storm

Background

Not all brain activities help all people. If one activity doesn't seem helpful, try another. But if you find yourself totally stumped during idea generation, it may be time to back up instead of plunging blindly ahead with more ideas. The solution may not be trying more activities or finding more creative people. Instead, you may need to devote some time to ensuring that the problem is understood.

This need for clarifying a problem is especially critical in groups. The more people involved in problem solving, the greater the number of perceptions that must be dealt with. Each individual may see a problem from a different perspective. In such situations, the group won't be able to generate ideas until all group members are aligned in their perceptions.

Rice Storm (also called the TKJ Method) is a Japanese activity developed by Kobayashi and Kawakita as described in Michalko (1991). It has two stages: (1) understanding the problem and (2) solving the problem. Understanding involves ensuring that each group member grasps the essence of the problem; solving involves encouraging individuals to participate in idea generation.

Objectives

- To help participants generate as many creative ideas as possible
- To help participants learn how to use the activities to generate ideas

Participants

Small groups of four to seven people each

Materials, Supplies, and Equipment

- For each group: markers, one flip chart, masking tape for posting flip-chart sheets, and one deck of 4 x 6 index cards.
- For each participant: one sheet each of three different colors of sticking dots (½" diameter) and one pad of 4 x 6 Post-it® Notes

Handout

- Rice Storm Handout

Time

60 minutes

Related Activities

- Picture Tickler [17]
- Rorschach Revisionist [18]
- Ideatoons [26]
- Doodles [37]
- Drawing Room [59]

Procedure

1. Distribute the Rice Storm Handout, review it with the participants, and answer any questions they may have.

Problem Definition

1. Tell group members to write pertinent facts about the problem on index cards (one fact per card).

2. Have someone in each group collect and redistribute the cards among the group members so that no one receives his or her original card.

3. Instruct the groups to have one person read one card aloud.

4. Tell the group members to select facts on their cards that are related to the one read. They are then to read these facts aloud to the other members, thus building a set of facts.

5. Have someone record these facts on a flip chart.

6. Instruct the groups to label the set of facts using a name that reflects the set's essence. Tell them to derive this name by considering all the facts and then boiling them down to extract essential features. This name must be (a) verifiable using the facts from which it was generated; (b) specific (not too general); and (c) a simple combination of the subset of facts.

7. Have them repeat this process (Steps 4 through 7) until all the facts have been distilled into name sets.

8. Instruct the groups to combine all the sets until there is one all-inclusive group of sets that they must name. This name must (a) reflect the essence of the all-inclusive problem definition set and (b) include all of the previously discussed facts and essences.

9. Tell the group members they should affirm individually this final definition and feel that a consensus has been reached.

Problem Solution

1. Tell group members to write potential solutions to the problem on index cards (one idea per card).

2. Have someone in each group collect and redistribute the cards among the group members so that no one receives his or her original card.

3. Instruct the groups to have one person read one card aloud.

4. Tell the group members to look over the solutions on their cards and select the ones related to the solution just read. Have the members share these related solutions and use them to build solution-set card piles.

5. Have the groups name each set and place a name card on it.

6. Instruct them to continue this process (Steps 3 through 5) until an all-inclusive solution set is achieved.

7. Emphasize that the essence of this final solution should incorporate all the previous solutions and capture the essence of all the solutions.

8. Ask, "What is the essence of the properties and characteristics that are indispensable to these ideas? Use your answers to this question to trigger new ideas."

9. Encourage the groups to select and combine the best suggestions into a final solution set, writing the ideas on Post-it® Notes (one idea per note) and placing them on flip-chart paper for evaluation.

Debrief/Discussion

This can be a powerful exercise because it exploits the close interplay between problem elements and eventual solutions. That is, the more a problem is understood by gathering and analyzing facts, the more likely a solution is to emerge. *A well-defined problem is a solved problem.* For instance, if a group discusses what they know about a problem, they are exploring its different facets that lead to different perspectives, which, in turn, can result in solutions popping up. Thus, Rice Storm provides a structured way to explore a problem prior to focusing on idea generation. This relationship between problems and solutions could provide an interesting discussion topic for the groups.

Also consider having participants debrief using the following questions:

- What was most helpful about this exercise?
- What was most challenging?
- What can we apply?
- How would you rate the value of this exercise to helping us with this issue?
- Will this exercise be helpful in the future for other sessions?
- What did you learn?
- What will we be able to use from this exercise?
- What ideas were generated, and which ones were most interesting?

101 Activities for Teaching Creativity and Problem Solving

Rice Storm Handout

To illustrate Rice Storm, Michalko (1991) describes a group of computer specialists using Rice Storm to consider ways to improve the home computer. The group first lists verifiable, relevant problem facts:

- We can produce computers that operate twenty to fifty times faster than standard computers.
- Computer screens can be mounted on walls.
- Fiberoptics make higher resolution possible.
- Full-motion video can be mixed with computer graphics.
- Laptops are becoming more portable.

After considering these and other facts, you describe the essence of its challenge as follows: "In what ways might we develop a home computer that is faster, multiuse, multimedia, and high resolution with multiscreens for a variety of purposes?"

Next, group members individually generate ideas. The following ideas are suggested:

- A portable computer so small that you could carry it while holding two bags of groceries
- A merger of video and computer capabilities with a very high bandwidth link for video access to every movie ever made
- Electronic publishing involving home computer access to data banks about education, travel, medicine, sports, and so on
- Cellular transponders in wall outlets to permit placement of computer screens anywhere, allowing movies to be embedded in such novel objects as desks or work areas

These and other solutions are grouped into sets, named, renamed, and grouped again into an all-solution set that best describes the essence of all the previous solutions: "A home multimedia *Roger Rabbit*." This solution involves a home computer networking system with such features as entertainment (access to every movie ever made); handwriting machines that transfer thoughts automatically to the computer; a scanner; smart software agents to scan databases for useful information and store it in the computer; and custom-designed screens that can be embedded in desks, hung on walls, or carried around.

67

Spin the Bottle

Background

Around and around it goes. Where it stops, only the bottle knows. Do you remember playing "Spin the Bottle" as a child (or even as an adult)? The Spin the Bottle idea generation exercise, developed by Hall (1994), is very similar, except you don't have to kiss anyone. Instead, groups use a bottle to point to someone who must suggest an idea.

Objectives

- To help participants generate as many creative ideas as possible
- To help participants learn how to use the activities to generate ideas

Participants

Small groups of four to seven people each

Materials, Supplies, and Equipment

- For each group: markers, two flip charts, and masking tape for posting flip-chart sheets
- For each participant: one sheet each of three different colors of sticking dots (½" diameter) and one pad of 4 x 6 Post-it® Notes
- One empty, glass, long-necked bottle per group (or, as Hall suggests, light beer bottles for "less substantial ideas")

Time

60 minutes

Related Activities

- Picture Tickler [17]
- Rorschach Revisionist [18]
- Ideatoons [26]

- Doodles [37]
- Drawing Room [59]

Procedure

1. Give each group one bottle.
2. Tell each small group to sit on the floor in a circle with a bottle in the center, lying on its side.
3. Tell the groups to have one of the group members spin the bottle.
4. Say that the person to whom the bottle points must suggest an idea.
5. Have the groups discuss the idea for 107 seconds and try to use it as a springboard for additional ideas (Hall prefers using a more unconventional way of approaching time to further emphasize creative perspectives).
6. Tell them that the person who suggested the previous idea must spin the bottle again and the group repeats Steps 5 and 6 until everyone has suggested several ideas.
7. Tell them to write down any ideas on Post-it® Notes (one idea per note) and place them on flip charts for evaluation.

Debrief/Discussion

Spin the Bottle is a relatively simple exercise that most participants should experience as a fun activity, although the quality of ideas will depend on the creativity of the participants. This is an exercise you should monitor to ensure that each group's energy level is maintained and that they don't run out of ideas. If they do, you should move to another activity or have participants change groups.

Consider having participants debrief using the following questions:

- What was most helpful about this exercise?
- What was most challenging?
- What can we apply?
- How would you rate the value of this exercise to helping us with this issue?
- Will this exercise be helpful in the future for other sessions?
- What did you learn?
- What will we be able to use from this exercise?
- What ideas were generated, and which ones were most interesting?

68

Story Boards

Background

Story Boards originated with Walt Disney, who created series of pictures to illustrate major scenes during animated films. Each scene then was used as a point around which a complete story could be built. A variety of related procedures for generating ideas has evolved since then. Although there are significant differences among these procedures, these activities all share the common feature begun by Walt Disney: laying out key concepts that are linked together to form a complete whole.

Objectives

- To help participants generate as many creative ideas as possible
- To help participants learn how to use the activities to generate ideas

Participants

Small groups of four to seven people each

Materials, Supplies, and Equipment

- For each group: markers, two flip charts, and masking tape for posting flip-chart sheets
- For each participant: one sheet each of three different colors of sticking dots (½" diameter) and one pad of 5 x 7 (or larger) Post-it® Notes

Handout

- Story Boards Handout

Time

45 minutes

Related Activities

- Ideas in a Box [25]
- Parts Is Parts [30]
- SAMM I Am [33]

Procedure

1. Distribute the Story Boards Handout, review it with the participants, and answer any questions they may have.

2. Tell group members to brainstorm solution categories (attributes) and write each one on a large Post-it® Note and place them in a row approximately five feet above the floor along a wall.

3. Instruct group members to use each category as a stimulus for problem solutions and write these solutions on new notes.

4. Have them place the solution notes below the appropriate category card.

5. Have the group members examine the solutions and try to generate additional ideas from them or combine solutions across categories and use them as stimuli for new ideas.

6. Tell the participants to continue this process (Steps 4 and 5) until the group generates a sufficient number of ideas or time runs out.

7. Direct them to write down any ideas on Post-it® Notes (one idea per note) and place them on flip charts for evaluation.

Debrief/Discussion

This is an "oldie but goodie" approach that provides some structure to the idea generation process while providing a fun, energizing activity. Unlike most other activities, Story Boards allows people to walk around and be active during idea generation—a feature found in some research to be conducive to creative thinking. Because of the flexibility the large Post-it® Notes provide, you might ask participants to devise their own variations of this procedure. For instance, you might suggest that they experiment with "affinity groups" and use the notes to cluster together related ideas.

Also consider having participants debrief using the following questions:

- What was most helpful about this exercise?
- What was most challenging?
- What can we apply?
- How would you rate the value of this exercise to helping us with this issue?
- Will this exercise be helpful in the future for other sessions?
- What did you learn?
- What will we be able to use from this exercise?
- What ideas were generated, and which ones were most interesting?

Story Boards Handout

Suppose you are an automobile manufacturer and your problem is developing ways to reduce auto theft. You get together a group of your best engineers and decide to use Story Boards. You generate problem attributes and write them on cards, as shown in Figure 9.1. Next, you use each category to help stimulate ideas. Finally, you examine all the solutions and see what new solutions might be suggested.

The nine ideas listed in Figure 9.1 suggest additional solutions when combined. For instance, someone who tries to break a window might receive a shock (from "break-proof glass" and "car shocks when touched"). Or the car might automatically photograph anyone who walks within five feet of it (from "flashing lights" and "automated voices").

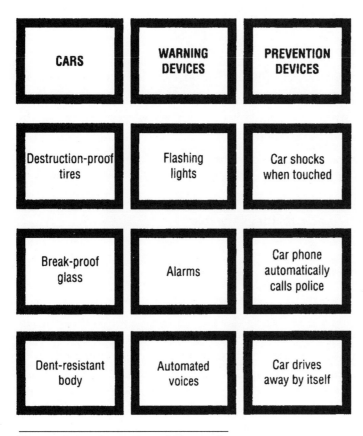

Figure 9.1.   Story Board Example

69

That's the Ticket!

Background

This activity is "the ticket" to enhancing your group's creativity. And it's well worth the price of admission. All you have to do is turn in your tickets and watch the ideas flow. It's as simple as that. That's the Ticket! is a relatively uncomplicated brainstorming variation I developed as another form of brainwriting (that is, ideas are generated silently and in writing), which has been shown to result in more ideas than traditional brainstorming activities.

Objectives

- To help participants generate as many creative ideas as possible
- To help participants learn how to use the activities to generate ideas

Participants

Small groups of four to seven people each

Materials, Supplies, and Equipment

- For each group: markers, two flip charts, and masking tape for posting flip-chart sheets
- For each participant: one sheet each of three different colors of sticking dots (½" diameter) and one pad of 4 x 6 Post-it® Notes
- As many blank paper tickets as there are participants (the same size as movie theater tickets, approximately one inch by three inches) available at novelty stores and party shops (Tickets can also be cut from blank pieces of paper or index cards)

Handout

- That's the Ticket! Handout

Time

20 minutes

Related Activities

- Pass the Hat [63]
- Idea Pool [85]

Procedure

1. Distribute the That's the Ticket! Handout, review it with the participants, and answer any questions they may have.
2. Give each group member ten blank tickets.
3. Tell them to write one idea on each ticket and place them in the center of a table.
4. Have one group member withdraw two tickets and read them aloud to the group.
5. Instruct the groups to use the combination of the two ideas as possible stimulation for new ideas.
6. Tell them to return the two tickets to the middle of the table and have another group member select two more tickets.
7. Ask them to repeat the process of choosing tickets and generating ideas until all group members have selected two tickets at least once or time has expired.
8. Tell them to write down any ideas on Post-it® Notes (one idea per note) and place them on flip charts for evaluation.

Debrief/Discussion

This activity has three primary strengths. The first is that it is a brainwriting variation in that ideas are generated in writing. Research (Diehl & Stroebe, 1991; VanGundy, 1993) indicates that brainwriting will result in substantially more ideas than conventional brainstorming, since multiple ideas are generated more or less at the same time—unlike brainstorming, in which one idea at a time is contributed. However, it also provides verbal brainstorming when combining two tickets, thus offsetting the brainwriting weakness of lacking verbal interaction. The second is that you are guaranteed at least ten ideas per group member (assuming each member follows the instructions). Thus, if you have five group members, you'll get at least fifty ideas before beginning brainstorming. The third and less important strength is that the activity provides a more interesting way to generate ideas.

Also consider having participants debrief using the following questions:

- What was most helpful about this exercise?
- What was most challenging?
- What can we apply?
- How would you rate the value of this exercise to helping us with this issue?
- Will this exercise be helpful in the future for other sessions?
- What did you learn?
- What will we be able to use from this exercise?
- What ideas were generated, and which ones were most interesting?

That's the Ticket! Handout

Suppose your problem involves improving a telephone. Two ideas might be (1) a padded ear piece and (2) a built-in radio that either listener can hear if put on hold. These two ideas together suggest the idea of a built-in radio with volume control (from "padded ear piece," which suggests the concept of making something soft).

70

What's the Problem?

Background

"So, exactly what is the problem?" That's a frequently heard query in brainstorming groups as they struggle to analyze and define a problem. Groups should devote considerable time to understanding a problem before generating ideas. But by then, it may be too late. They've already corrupted any potential ideas.

Creative problem solving is a "darned if you do, darned if you don't" situation. Defining problems and generating ideas often lead to a paradox. Effective creative problem solving demands that you analyze and define a problem to ensure that you start from the most productive perspective. There is nothing inherently wrong with this. Things get challenging, however, when we start generating ideas following extensive analysis and redefinition.

The more we analyze a problem, the more we understand it. The more we understand it, the closer and more involved we become. Although these outcomes may produce fresh perspectives, they also limit our ability to generate unique ideas. Too much problem knowledge tends to lead to conventional, mundane solution proposals. Thus, this is another case of a little knowledge being a dangerous thing.

To overcome this problem, William Gordon (1961), a cofounder of the Synectics consulting firm, developed this activity. What's the Problem? attempts to counter our natural tendency to exhaust all conventional solutions and then declare we have run out of ideas. Because Gordon developed his procedure while working at the Arthur D. Little consulting firm, VanGundy (1988) referred to Gordon's procedure as the Gordon/Little method.

Objectives

- To help participants generate as many creative ideas as possible
- To help participants learn how to use the activities to generate ideas

Participants

Small groups of four to seven people each

Materials, Supplies, and Equipment

- For each group: markers, two flip charts, and masking tape for posting flip-chart sheets

- For each participant: one sheet each of three different colors of sticking dots
(½″ diameter) and one pad of 4 x 6 Post-it® Notes

Handout

- What's the Problem? Handout

Time

45 minutes

Related Activities

- Essence of the Problem [38]

Procedure

Note: There are two ways to facilitate this exercise. One is to guide all of the groups through the steps. The other is to train individual facilitators for each group. The procedure below assumes that you are facilitating all of the groups at once. It also assumes that the group members are not aware of what the challenge is—although that is not essential.

1. Distribute the What's the Problem? Handout, review it with the participants, and answer any questions they may have.

2. Describe a general, abstract problem without revealing the "real" problem. This abstract problem should describe the general principle underlying the real problem (see the handout).

3. Ask the participants to generate ideas for the abstract problem.

4. Describe a slightly less abstract, more specific version of the real problem and ask the groups to generate ideas for it.

5. Describe an even more specific version of the real problem and ask the groups to generate ideas for it.

6. Reveal the real problem and instruct the group members to examine the ideas for the two abstract problems and use them as stimuli for new ideas.

7. Tell them to write down any ideas on Post-it® Notes (one idea per note) and place them on flip charts for evaluation.

Debrief/Discussion

This activity stands alone among idea generation activities. Its premise is different from all other activities in that it assumes that the participants are not aware of the problem. As a result, this approach helps participants get outside of themselves (or "outside the box") in a way not possible with other activities. If the participants are not aware of the problem, then they are prevented from making unwarranted assumptions that typically block most people when trying to resolve a problem.

Consider having participants debrief using the following questions:

- What was most helpful about this exercise?
- What was most challenging?
- What can we apply?
- How would you rate the value of this exercise to helping us with this issue?
- Will this exercise be helpful in the future for other sessions?
- What did you learn?
- What will we be able to use from this exercise?
- What ideas were generated, and which ones were most interesting?

What's the Problem? Handout

Suppose the problem involves ways to develop a snack that would surprise children. The group leader first might ask the group to think of ways to catch people's attention. The group might make the following suggestions:

- Tap them on the shoulder.
- Yell at them.
- Expose yourself to them.

Next, the leader asks the group to think of ways to shock people. They suggest these ideas:

- Electrocute them.
- Urinate in public.
- Swear at them.
- Do something sexually provocative.

Then the leader asks the group to think of ways to surprise children—a problem even more closely related to the real problem. For this problem, the group generates such ideas as:

- Play peek-a-boo.
- Short-sheet their beds.
- Burst a balloon.

Finally, the leader reveals the problem and asks the group to use all the ideas as stimuli to generate new ideas:

- When a child unwraps candy, a scary face appears (from "peek-a-boo").
- A telescopic candy bar (from "short-sheet their beds").
- Insert a small voice box in candy that yells "ouch!" when bitten (from "yell at them").
- Candy-coated small balloons that burst harmlessly when eaten (from "burst a balloon").
- Candy shaped like a toilet bowl (from "urinate in public").

Chapter 10

Brainstorming with Unrelated Stimuli

The activities in this chapter use unrelated problem stimuli to help generate ideas. For some problems and some groups, brainstorming with unrelated stimuli may result in better ideas. Unrelated stimuli can help create different perspectives, because they are not similar to the problem. Therefore, there is more likelihood that unique ideas will result. (All the "tickler" activities in Chapter 5 also rely on unrelated stimuli, so they also may produce more novel solutions.)

Remember the old saying "You can't see the forest for the trees"? The "trees" are problem elements that encourage you to focus all your attention on the problem. In other words, there may be parts of a problem that distract you from a more central focus. Such use of related stimuli provides a narrow focus, limits your perspectives, and actually may make it more difficult to generate creative ideas.

Although unrelated stimuli may help you generate better ideas, there is no guarantee. Many other factors also are involved. Problem solving success is determined by the type of problem, the degree to which it is understood and structured, and the personalities and creative abilities of the group members. Nevertheless, the unrelated activities in this chapter will increase your odds of getting unique ideas.

NOTE: FOR ALL ACTIVITIES, REMIND PARTICIPANTS
TO DEFER JUDGMENT WHILE GENERATING IDEAS.

71

Battle of the Sexes

Background

Gender wars rage all around us—at least in the minds of people who pay attention to such things. Regardless of your interest in the battle of the sexes, gender differences play a significant role in many areas of life as women strive to gain equality. Gender differences are, of course, not necessarily bad. Remember, "Vive la difference!"

Males and females can make unique contributions in many situations, including creative problem solving. And that's exactly what Doug Hall (1994) had in mind when he developed this activity.

Objectives

- To help participants generate as many creative ideas as possible
- To help participants learn how to use the activities to generate ideas

Participants

Small groups of four to seven people each

Materials, Supplies, and Equipment

- For each group: markers, two flip charts, and masking tape for posting flip-chart sheets
- For each participant: one sheet each of three different colors of sticking dots (½" diameter) and one pad of 4 x 6 Post-it® Notes
- For each group of males: an assortment of male-oriented magazines such as *Esquire*, *Field & Stream*, and *Men's Health*.
- For each group of females: an assortment of female-oriented magazines such as *Redbook*, *Cosmopolitan*, and *Mademoiselle*.

Handout

- Battle of the Sexes Handout

Time

45 minutes

Related Activities

- Picture Tickler [17]
- Text Tickler [20]

Procedure

1. Distribute the Battle of the Sexes handout, review it with the participants, and answer any questions they may have..
2. Divide a large group into smaller groups of all women and all men, four to seven people per group.
3. Instruct the group members to generate two ideas using these criteria:
    - The perfect solution from the perspective of their gender
    - The perfect solution from the perspective of the opposite gender
4. Distribute to the male groups a variety of male-oriented magazines such as *Esquire, Field & Stream,* and *Men's Health.*
5. Give the female groups several women's magazines such as *Redbook, Cosmopolitan,* and *Mademoiselle.*
6. Tell the groups to look through the magazines and examine words and pictures for potential idea stimulation that would be either stereotypically feminine or masculine.
7. Have the groups write down on Post-it® Notes, individually, any ideas suggested, and place them on a flip chart.
8. Tell the male and female groups to share their best ideas and for the large group to try to think of any additional ideas.
9. Tell them to write down any ideas on Post-it® Notes (one idea per note), and place them on flip charts for evaluation.

Debrief/Discussion

A unique aspect of this activity is that it can create some friendly competition between groups. You may want to make some mild comments to encourage such competition, such as asking the participants to predict which sex can produce the greater number of ideas. After all the ideas have been generated, ask the members to discuss if the gender of the groups played a significant role in each group's ability to generate ideas.

Variation

- Use mixed-sex groups.
- Give the male groups female-oriented magazines and the female groups male-oriented magazines. Have the members try to adopt the attitudes of the other sex and use them to generate ideas.

Battle of the Sexes Handout

Consider a problem of how to decrease employee absenteeism. The female groups might suggest "feminine" ideas such as holding teas to develop support systems and "masculine" ideas such as organized sports teams. The male groups might suggest "masculine" ideas such as having managers and workers socialize in bars after work and "feminine" ideas such as sewing circles during lunch periods. Although some or all of the ideas might not be practical, all group participants would then develop more workable solutions.

72

Best of ...

Background

Remember how some children grow up taunting their friends that their father is smarter, stronger, richer, or nicer than someone else's father? Or have you noticed how athletes on television point their index fingers upward while chanting, "We're number one"?

Our society seems to have an insatiable appetite for the best of everything. Hall (1994), creator of this activity, once conducted a computer search of newspaper abstracts from 1991 and 1992 and found more than 11,000 instances of headlines containing the word "best." Every day some television show or magazine bombards us with a "Top Ten" list or other ratings of movies, books, plays, and music. We're a people obsessed with who or what is best.

One benefit of these "best of" lists is that they have value as idea stimulators. According to Hall, brainstorming groups can use such lists to generate ideas.

Objectives

- To help participants generate as many creative ideas as possible
- To help participants learn how to use the activities to generate ideas

Participants

Small groups of four to seven people each

Materials, Supplies, and Equipment

- For each group: markers, two flip charts, and masking tape for posting flip-chart sheets
- For each participant: one sheet each of three different colors of sticking dots (½" diameter) and one pad of 4 x 6 Post-it® Notes

Handout

- Best of . . . Handout

Time

45 minutes (requires preparation prior to the activity)

Brainstorming with Unrelated Stimuli

Related Activities

- Text Tickler [20]

Procedure

1. Prior to the exercise, tell the participants to collect, as individuals, a variety of "best of" lists. The lists may or may not be related to any specific problem, and they don't need to be "official." If group members don't have access to official lists, they may generate their own lists by reading movie reviews, brainstorming the best books of the year, the best cars, et cetera, or search the Internet.

2. Divide the participants into groups of four to seven people.

3. Distribute the Best of . . . Handout, review it with the participants, and answer any questions they may have.

4. Have the groups select one of the member's lists and generate traits that make each item a certifiable "best."

5. Tell the group to use the traits for each item to spark ideas, write them on Post-its and place them on a flip chart for evaluation.

6. Instruct the groups to repeat Steps 4 and 5 until they have generated a sufficient number of ideas.

Debrief/Discussion

The lists used for this exercise are not as important as their diversity and number. In other words, the more stimuli the groups have, the greater the number of ideas they are likely to produce. The lists themselves also can introduce a humorous element that, of course, is conducive to creative thinking.

Also consider having participants debrief using the following questions:

- What was most helpful about this exercise?
- What was most challenging?
- What can we apply?
- How would you rate the value of this exercise to helping us with this issue?
- Will this exercise be helpful in the future for other sessions?
- What did you learn?
- What will we be able to use from this exercise?
- What ideas were generated, and which ones were most interesting?

Variation

- Instead of having the participants bring lists to the sessions, ask each group to generate its own lists at the start of the exercise. This may help engage all of the participants immediately and serve as a warmup for generating ideas.

Best of . . . Handout

Imagine you are part of a group charged with inventing a new coat hanger (Hall, 1994). One of the lists involves Top Ten television shows, and the group develops traits and ideas for the top three from the list.

Top TV Show: "Roseanne"

Traits: Irreverent, loud, earthy, big, salty, disrespectful, working-class family

Ideas: Extra-strength coat hangers for large or bulky clothes

Top TV Show: "Cheers"

Traits: Friends, leisure time, flippant, beer, sports

Ideas: Hangers with built-in deodorant properties for hanging sweat clothes in lockers

Top TV Show: "60 Minutes"

Traits: Exposes, shocks, champion of the little person, ambushes, confronting

Ideas: A hanger with a heating tube that dries clothes still wet from the wash, thereby eliminating scandalous shrinkage and the blight of dryer wrinkles

73

Brain Splitter

Background

One management approach that has received considerable attention over the years is the concept of left- and right-brain thinking. Although much of the literature exaggerated or misunderstood how the brain hemispheres actually function during thinking, the basic processes are relatively straightforward.

The right brain is considered the seat of creative, holistic, artistic, nonlinear thinking; the left is the center of logical, analytical, non-artistic, linear thinking. The right brain is emotional, disorderly, experiential, subjective, nonjudgmental, fantasy-like, and concerned with spatial relations and metaphorical meanings. The left brain, in contrast, is more rational, orderly, intellectual, objective, judgmental, realistic, and concerned with verbal relations and literal meanings.

We all have right- and left-brain hemispheres. Although there is evidence that many people have developed certain hemispheric functions more highly than others, no normal, healthy human is truly a left- or right-brain person. The human mind relies on both hemispheres to think and solve problems. The structure that transfers information between the hemispheres is a bundle of nerve fibers known as the "corpus collosum."

You may wonder what all this has to do with brainstorming ideas in groups. Well, you can use the stereotypical aspects of brain functions to prompt ideas (VanGundy, 1983). And it can be a fun experience as well!

Objectives

- To help participants generate as many creative ideas as possible
- To help participants learn how to use the activities to generate ideas

Participants

Small groups of four to seven people each

Materials, Supplies, and Equipment

- For each group: markers, two flip charts, and masking tape for posting flip-chart sheets

- For each participant: one sheet each of three different colors of sticking dots (½″ diameter) and one pad of 4 x 6 Post-it® Notes.

Handout

- Brain Splitter Handout

Time

45 minutes

Related Activities

- Get Crazy [5]
- Blender [58]
- Force-Fit Game [74]

Procedure

1. Tell the participants that this will be an exercise based on the metaphor of brain hemispheric dominance. Briefly explain the differences between right- and left-brained thinking as described in the Background section.

2. Divide the participants into smaller groups of four to seven people based on their professed right- or left-brain dominance. That is, ask them to decide which type of thinking best would characterize them in general. (If necessary, you may have to assign people arbitrarily to one of the two categories to equalize the size of the groups.) Try to create an equal number of left- and right-brained groups. (If you want to be more precise in dividing the participants, you could have them complete the Hermann Brain Dominance Questionnaire, available at: www.hbdi.com.)

3. Distribute the Brain Splitter Handout, review it with the participants, and answer any questions they may have.

4. Instruct the left-brain group members to generate as many practical, conventional, and logical ideas as they can in 20 minutes.

5. Tell the right-brainers to generate as many far-out, unconventional, and illogical ideas as they can in 20 minutes.

6. After they have verbalized their ideas, have all participants write them down on sheets of flip-chart paper.

7. Ask the members of each group to count off by twos. Have all of the left-brain "ones" move to a group with right-brained "ones" and the left-brained "twos" with the right-brained "twos." There now should be at least two groups composed of one-half left-brain thinkers and one-half right-brained thinkers. These groups represent symbolically the "corpus collosum" function of the human brain.

8. Tell the group members originally in a right-brain-only group to share with their new left-brain group members a copy of their idea lists, so that each combination group now has one list of left-brain ideas and one list of right-brain ideas.

9. Have the groups randomly select one idea from each list and use the combination to help think of new ideas, write new ideas down on Post-it® Notes, and place them on flip charts for evaluation.

Debrief/Discussion

This activity exploits the natural tendency of people to generate logical, practical ideas that, of course, rarely lead to breakout ideas. By insisting that people intentionally think of illogical ideas instead, participants are forced to create new perspectives and consider more innovative approaches. You might suggest that the participants discuss how well they were able to demonstrate right- and left-brained thinking and whether combining the two types of thinking made a difference in the quality of ideas produced.

Also consider having participants debrief using the following questions:

- What was most helpful about this exercise?
- What was most challenging?
- What can we apply?
- How would you rate the value of this exercise to helping us with this issue?
- Will this exercise be helpful in the future for other sessions?
- What did you learn?
- What will we be able to use from this exercise?
- What ideas were generated, and which ones were most interesting?

Brain Splitter Handout

Assume you manufacture umbrellas and want to develop improved designs and features. First, the groups generate two lists:

Left-Brain Ideas

1. Use a more durable fabric.

2. Strengthen metal supports.

3. Design the handle like a pistol grip.

4. Improve the ability of fabric to shed water.

5. Use less expensive materials.

Right-Brain Ideas

6. Create an umbrella that automatically opens when wet and closes when dry.

7. Add air jets that blow down from the top edges of the umbrella to keep rain off the lower body.

8. Create an umbrella that repels rain before it hits the fabric.

9. Make an umbrella that is small enough to carry in a wallet.

The groups combine ideas from each list to produce the following ideas:

Combination Ideas

- 1 & 6: Develop a faster-drying fabric.
- 1 & 8: Make an umbrella that vibrates off water.
- 1 & 9: Make a wallet that doubles as an umbrella.
- 2 & 7: Put air jets in the ends of the metal spikes to rotate the umbrella automatically, throwing off water.
- 2 & 8: Eliminate the need for metal supports.
- 2 & 9: Develop a carrying device designed like a hip or shoulder holster.
- 3 & 6: Use compressed-air capsules to open the umbrella.
- 3 & 9: Have the umbrella double as a pistol.
- 4 & 5: Develop an inexpensive fabric that can be replaced easily when damaged.
- 4 & 7: Build in air pockets so the umbrella can double as a flotation device.
- 4 & 8: Eliminate fabric and use only air jets to repel water.
- 5 & 9: Design a plastic, foldable parka with an umbrella hat.

74

Force-Fit Game

Background

Even the best groups sometimes have trouble generating ideas. Idea generation activities usually help when this occurs. There are times, however, when even basic idea generation activities fail, such as when a group simply lacks the necessary motivation. Thus, it's not so much the fault of the activity as it is the people.

One way to motivate groups under these circumstances is to introduce a little friendly competition. Brain Splitter [73] does this a little, but competition is not included as a basic mechanism. (Force-Fit Game is similar to Brain Splitter, however, in that each technique generates ideas from stimulation provided by both practical and impractical ideas.) To ensure competition, you have to use a procedure based on competitive elements. And that's exactly what the Force-Fit Game does as developed by Helmut Schlicksupp (in Warfield, Geschka, and Hamilton, 1975).

Objectives

- To help participants generate as many creative ideas as possible
- To help participants learn how to use the activities to generate ideas

Participants

Small groups of four to seven people each

Materials, Supplies, and Equipment

- For each group: markers, two flip charts, and masking tape for posting flip-chart sheets
- For each participant: one sheet each of three different colors of sticking dots (½″ diameter) and one pad of 4 x 6 Post-it® Notes

Time

45 minutes

Related Activities

- Blender [58]
- Brain Splitter [73]

Procedure

1. Arrange small tables capable of seating four to seven people so that pairs of tables are placed close enough for members from both tables to hear each other.

2. Divide the large group into sets of two small groups each of four to seven people. For example, if there are twenty people, you would divide them into four groups of five people each. Groups 1 and 2 are one set and Groups 3 and 4 are another. (You do not have to have an equal number of people in each group, however.)

3. Ask for one volunteer from each set (not each group) to assume the role of referee/recorder. In the example in Step 2, there now would be two sets of groups with two, five-person groups in each set. Label the first set, Set A and the second, Set B.

4. Direct one group of each set to start by suggesting an idea that is silly or remote from the problem.

5. Give the second group of each set 2 minutes to develop a practical solution from this idea.

6. Tell the referee/recorder for each set to write down the idea on a flip chart and award the second group 1 point if he or she judges the idea to be practical; if the referee/recorder determines the group was unsuccessful, he or she gives the first group the point.

7. After 30 minutes, ask the referee/recorder to declare the group in each set with the most points the winner.

8. Tell them to write down all ideas generated on Post-it® Notes (one idea per note) and place them on flip charts for evaluation.

Debrief/Discussion

There are at least four unique aspects of this activity: (1) having one group suggest impractical ideas; (2) using these ideas as stimuli for more practical ideas; (3) having two groups interact with each other; and (4) awarding points based on an idea's practicality. All of these can make for an engaging and productive group experience. If time is available after generating ideas, you might ask the participants to discuss what worked well and what did not and to suggest ways to improve on the exercise. One approach, for instance, would be to ask participants to share written ideas on paper airplanes thrown at the other group.

Also consider having participants debrief using the following questions:

- What was most helpful about this exercise?
- What was most challenging?
- What can we apply?

- How would you rate the value of this exercise to helping us with this issue?
- Will this exercise be helpful in the future for other sessions?
- What did you learn?
- What will we be able to use from this exercise?
- What ideas were generated, and which ones were most interesting?

75

Grab Bag Forced Association

Background

This activity is similar to Tickler Things [21], except Hall (1994) modified it for groups instead of individuals. It is especially effective for people who respond well to tangible stimuli and are good at visual thinking.

Objectives

- To help participants generate as many creative ideas as possible
- To help participants learn how to use the activities to generate ideas

Participants

Small groups of four to seven people each

Materials, Supplies, and Equipment

- For each group: markers, two flip charts, and masking tape for posting flip-chart sheets
- For each participant: one sheet each of three different colors of sticking dots (½″ diameter) and one pad of 4 x 6 Post-it® Notes
- For each group: one grocery sack containing various small items and toys such as little cars, funny glasses, balloons, corks, spinning tops, buttons, squirt guns, novelty items, and so forth (Novelty and toy stores are excellent sources for these items)

Time

30 minutes

Related Activities

- Idea Shopping [14]
- Tickler Things [21]

Procedure

1. Distribute to each group one grocery bag containing the items listed above.

2. Tell the participants that one group member should reach into the bag without looking and retrieve one item.

3. Instruct all of the group members to describe the characteristics and traits of the item and then use them to trigger ideas.

4. Have them write down all ideas on Post-it® Notes (one idea per note) and place them on a flip chart for evaluation.

5. Tell them to have another group member select a second item and use it to suggest ideas and record the ideas as described in Steps 3 and 4.

6. Have the groups continue this process until they have used all of the items in their bags or all members have selected at least one item to use for stimulation.

Debrief/Discussion

As mentioned, Grab Bag Forced Association is similar to "Tickler Things" [21] in that it uses unrelated stimulus objects to help groups generate ideas. However, instead of the groups thinking of objects to use, the Grab Bag approach provides the objects and allows them to be selected randomly. In this respect, it is more of a "hands on" activity because the group members actually touch the objects. It also introduces an element of surprise that can be conducive to a creative climate within the groups.

Consider having participants debrief using the following questions:

- What was most helpful about this exercise?
- What was most challenging?
- What can we apply?
- How would you rate the value of this exercise to helping us with this issue?
- Will this exercise be helpful in the future for other sessions?
- What did you learn?
- What will we be able to use from this exercise?
- What ideas were generated, and which ones were most interesting?

76

It's Not My Job

Background

Have you ever been curious about other people's jobs? What exactly do they do? How do they do it? How do they feel about it? Henry Andersen (1991), a former marketing manager for Mitsubishi Heavy Industries Europe, Ltd., had a similar curiosity. One difference was that his curiosity was directed more at how ideas could be generated by borrowing from different work disciplines.

Andersen developed "The Diamond Idea Group" to promote use of multidisciplinary perspectives during idea generation. He envisioned the Diamond Idea Group as a worldwide resource organizations could use to generate ideas for any number of problems. His primary activity for generating ideas is what he calls "Trans-Disciplinary Analogy" (TDA).

Objectives

- To help participants generate as many creative ideas as possible
- To help participants learn how to use the activities to generate ideas

Participants

Small groups of four to seven people each

Materials, Supplies, and Equipment

- For each group: markers, two flip charts, and masking tape for posting flip-chart sheets
- For each participant: one sheet each of three different colors of sticking dots (½" diameter) and one pad of 4 x 6 Post-it® Notes

Handout

- It's Not My Job Handout

Time

30 minutes

Related Activities

- I Like It Like That [55]
- Rolestorming [77]

Procedure

1. Divide participants into small groups of four to seven people each.

2. Assign a facilitator to each group (or solicit volunteers).

3. Distribute the It's Not My Job Handout, review it with the participants, and answer any questions they may have.

4. Ask each group to select a discipline (professional or nonprofessional activity) of interest to the group members. This discipline does not have to be a group member's primary occupation or a traditional academic discipline. It even may be some activity such as gardening or building model airplanes. However, the group should be relatively knowledgeable about the choice.

5. Tell the groups to identify central concepts or themes from the discipline selected.

6. Instruct the facilitator in each group to record these concepts on a flip chart.

7. Have the groups select one of the concepts or themes and ask the contributor to describe it in some detail.

8. Tell the groups to use the descriptions to generate ideas, record them on Post-its, and place them on flip-chart paper for evaluation.

9. Have the groups repeat Steps 4 to 8 until enough ideas are generated or time is called.

Debrief/Discussion

This activity helps personalize the idea stimuli by using group members' knowledge of different disciplines. Although it is similar to analogies, the familiarity involved with the disciplines could be either a positive or negative factor. One positive feature is the familiarity that results in increased problem understanding; a negative is that too much familiarity might make it more difficult to think of unique ideas. Because of the relatively unusual nature of this approach, you might ask the group members to discuss its pros and cons and any ways it might be improved.

Also consider having participants debrief using the following questions:

- What was most helpful about this exercise?
- What was most challenging?
- What can we apply?
- How would you rate the value of this exercise to helping us with this issue?
- Will this exercise be helpful in the future for other sessions?
- What did you learn?
- What will we be able to use from this exercise?
- What ideas were generated, and which ones were most interesting?

101 Activities for Teaching Creativity and Problem Solving

It's Not My Job Handout

Suppose you want to improve a bathtub. One group member's interest area is gardening and he decides that its central concept is nurturing. The group selects this concept and the group member describes it as follows:

- Watering as needed
- Tilling to eliminate weeds
- Spraying insecticide to eliminate bugs
- Covering small plants during cold weather
- Adding fertilizer to promote growth

Next, the group uses these descriptions to suggest the following ideas:

- Button on top of tub (closer to hands) that adds more water when pushed
- Tub with built-in planter
- Tub that automatically sprays disinfectant inside tub after use
- Designer cover or cabinet to hide tub
- Tub that can be raised or lowered hydraulically to create a sunken tub look or to make it easier for older or disabled people to enter

77

Rolestorming

Background

We all play various roles in our lives: butcher, baker, candlestick maker, mother, father, brother, teacher, friend, and so on. In one sense, we all are actors strutting on the stage of life (with apologies to The Bard). Life requires that we wear many different hats to interact with various people. We act our way through most interpersonal situations.

Most of our "acting" is genuine in that we aren't intentionally trying to become someone else. Rather, we may act out little scenarios to add spice to our interactions. Thus, we might sometimes put a little twist in our behavior and temporarily pretend we're someone else or act slightly out of character. Such role-playing behavior helps emphasize a point and simply makes life more interesting.

Role playing also provides new perspectives. Marriage counselors often ask spouses to role play a dialog from the other spouse's point of view. This allows both spouses to see things differently and increases their understanding of the other. As a result, they may think of new ways to interact.

Griggs (1985) devised the Rolestorming activity to capitalize on the advantages of role playing. Griggs believes that many brainstorming sessions are unproductive because people feel inhibited. We take a risk every time we suggest something new. If our ideas are not received well, we stand to lose face.

To help prevent inhibition, Griggs suggested that group members generate ideas from someone else's perspective, which is the premise of this exercise.

Objectives

- To help participants generate as many creative ideas as possible
- To help participants learn how to use the activities to generate ideas

Participants

Small groups of four to seven people each

Materials, Supplies, and Equipment

- For each group: markers, two flip charts, and masking tape for posting flip-chart sheets

- For each participant: one sheet each of three different colors of sticking dots (½" diameter) and one pad of 4 x 6 Post-it® Notes

Time

60 minutes (requires prior participant activity)

Related Activities

- It's Not My Job [76]

Procedure

1. Tell group members to defer judgment and brainstorm twenty to thirty ideas for their problem (before the role-playing process), record them individually on Post-it® Notes, and place them on a flip chart (this serves as an "idea purge").

2. Instruct each participant to think of an historical figure they have admired. Tell them to take about 5 minutes and write down what they know about this person. Have them think about the attitudes, preferences, opinions, and beliefs of the person, and pretend that the person has a stake in the group's problem.

3. Direct them to have one member in each group share whom they chose.

4. Tell the group members to generate ideas based on what they think this person might say about the problem. Encourage the person who suggested the person to say such things as: "My person would try to. . . ." or "My person would want to. . . ."

5. Repeat Steps 3 to 4.

6. Tell them to write down any ideas on Post-it® Notes (one idea per note) and place them on flip charts for evaluation.

Debrief/Discussion

This exercise builds on empathetic design (that is, using another's perspective) and any dramatic flair participants may have. If the group members have trouble describing the person they selected, tell them that it is not important to be accurate. Instead, they should focus on being as descriptive, detailed, and dramatic as possible. The goal is to create stimuli to help trigger ideas.

Also consider having participants debrief using the following questions:

- What was most helpful about this exercise?
- What was most challenging?
- What can we apply?
- How would you rate the value of this exercise to helping us with this issue?
- Will this exercise be helpful in the future for other sessions?

- What did you learn?
- What will we be able to use from this exercise?
- What ideas were generated, and which ones were most interesting?

Variation

- Have the participants use people personally known to everyone. This person could be a co-worker, manager, secretary, staff person, or anyone else known to them. Caution them to be careful about any inappropriate characterizations that might be harmful or disrespectful to others.

78

Roll Call

Background

Are you an extrovert? Did you always try to answer teachers' questions in school? Do you like to shout out ideas when brainstorming? Do you shoot from the hip? If you answered yes to any of these questions, then you and others like you probably will enjoy this activity.

Although we have been taught to think before we speak, this advice may sometimes be counterproductive. If we think too much before we talk during idea generation, we may judge our ideas prematurely and restrict our creativity. Self-censors are the enemies of all creative thought and that is the basis for this activity, developed by Hall (1994).

Objectives

- To help participants generate as many creative ideas as possible
- To help participants learn how to use the activities to generate ideas

Participants

Small groups of four to seven people each

Materials, Supplies, and Equipment

- For each group: markers, two flip charts, and masking tape for posting flip-chart sheets
- For each participant: one sheet each of three different colors of sticking dots (½" diameter) and one pad of 4 x 6 Post-it® Notes

Handout

- Roll Call Handout

Time

45 minutes

Related Activities

- Text Tickler [20]
- Blender [58]
- Force-Fit Game [74]

Procedure

1. Divide the participants into groups of six people.
2. Distribute the Roll Call Handout, review it with the participants, and answer any questions they may have.
3. Ask half the members of each group to call out one word each. Explain that the words should be whatever pops into their heads. Note also that they shouldn't think very long about what word to say and that the words should be unrelated to the problem.
4. Give the group members 104 seconds to create a practical idea based on combining the three words or using the individual words for stimulation. (Hall doesn't say why he chose 104 seconds, but probably just to be different.)
5. Instruct them to write down their ideas on Post-it® Notes (one idea per note) and place them on a flip chart for evaluation.
6. Ask the participants to repeat Steps 3 to 5, but have the remaining group members call out the words.
7. Repeat this process again using the original three members to call out new words and continue until time is called.

Debrief/Discussion

Unlike many situations in life, this activity works best when you talk before you think. Its major strength is that it encourages spontaneity and helps eliminate judgmental thinking. Group members are forced to leap to conclusions instead of leaping to ideas. Thus, they have little choice but to defer judgment and the result should be more novel ideas than had they constrained themselves.

Also consider having participants debrief using the following questions:

- What was most helpful about this exercise?
- What was most challenging?
- What can we apply?
- How would you rate the value of this exercise to helping us with this issue?
- Will this exercise be helpful in the future for other sessions?

- What did you learn?
- What will we be able to use from this exercise?
- What ideas were generated, and which ones were most interesting?

Roll Call Handout

Assume your group is dealing with the problem of how to improve a kitchen table. Group members call out such words as "radio," "penguin," and "icicle." The group then uses these words to prompt ideas:

- Radio built into the table
- Musical lazy Susan with a cooling mechanism that keeps food cold
- Table designed with a tuxedo motif
- Table with holders to keep drinks cold
- Table with an "arctic" motif
- A "penguin table" with leaves that resemble penguin wings

79

Sculptures

Background

For many people, a sculpture is a place for pigeons to light; for others, a sculpture may represent a sublime representation of the agonies of displaced human frailties (or some other equally esoteric line of art babble). However you perceive sculptures, they all represent different interpretations of reality. As such, they also are stimuli capable of prompting different perspectives.

Most of the activities in this book help prompt different perspectives. An "aha!" should be going off in your head right now. Why not use sculptures to generate ideas?

Unfortunately, most people don't have ready access to sculptures. Although I might like to have a sculpture garden in my backyard, it will probably be a few years before that becomes a reality—if ever. Although most of us don't have the resources for our own sculpture collection, we could visit a local museum. But that's not always convenient or possible.

Another option is to create our own sculptures. Such a method has been used for years as a management training activity. I learned of this version while visiting a management consultant in Oslo, Norway. The consultant, Ole Faafeng (1986), devised this activity to help groups get more involved in brainstorming and to provide a source of unrelated stimuli.

Objectives

- To help participants generate as many creative ideas as possible
- To help participants learn how to use the activities to generate ideas

Participants

Small groups of four to seven people each

Materials, Supplies, and Equipment

- For each group: markers, two flip charts, and masking tape for posting flip-chart sheets
- For each participant: one sheet each of three different colors of sticking dots (½" diameter) and one pad of 4 x 6 Post-it® Notes

- For each group: a variety of materials unrelated to the problem to be solved, for instance: string, rope, blocks of wood, wire, books, colored paper, tape, scissors, paper clips, clay, cardboard, glue sticks, dowel rods, crayons, small chairs, and rubber balls (Toy, craft, and novelty stores are good sources for these items)

Handout

- Sculptures Handout

Time

45 minutes

Related Activities

- Tickler Things [21]
- Museum Madness [86]

Procedure

1. Distribute the Sculptures Handout, review it with the participants, and answer any questions they may have.

2. Tell each group to look over the materials and construct a sculpture that represents an abstract version of their problem.

3. Give them at least 20 minutes for this activity.

4. When all groups have finished, ask the group members to discuss their sculptures among themselves and to note structures, parts, relationships, and any other observations they might care to make.

5. Tell them to use these observations as stimuli, write down any ideas on Post-it® Notes (one idea per note), and place them on flip charts for evaluation.

Debrief/Discussion

This is another activity that can help generate ideas while also creating a climate conducive to creative thinking. It makes it easier for participants to express themselves creatively, and that could lead to more unique ideas. The activity level also is a plus since it encourages equal participation and may stimulate ideas just from physically moving around.

Consider having participants debrief using the following questions:

- What was most helpful about this exercise?
- What was most challenging?
- What can we apply?

- How would you rate the value of this exercise to helping us with this issue?
- Will this exercise be helpful in the future for other sessions?
- What did you learn?
- What will we be able to use from this exercise?
- What ideas were generated, and which ones were most interesting?

Variation

- Have the groups construct a sculpture completely unrelated to the problem and then use it as a stimulus for ideas.

Sculptures Handout

Imagine you are in a group using Sculptures to improve communication within an organization (Faafeng, 1986). Part of the sculpture you create involves a string stretched between two objects. The string reminds one group member of a communication network within the organization. He then thinks of a way to alter a communication line in a novel way. Other group members join in and refine and elaborate on his idea, including such ideas as giving everyone "walkie-talkie" type cell phones for more instantaneous communication and reducing the number of intermediate people as communication networks because they might slow down message transmittal.

80

Super Heroes

Background

"Look! Up in the sky! It's a bird! It's a plane!" These words, which describe the super hero Superman, may evoke childhood memories of super deeds and exploits—days when a fantasy character could come to our rescue. Then we grew up and learned that our super heroes are imaginary and may not always be there for us. Well, fret not. The Super Heroes have returned! And now they can help us solve some real-world problems.

Consultants Steve Grossman and Katherine Catlin (1985) developed Super Heroes as a way to introduce a playful spirit during brainstorming sessions. (See VanGundy, 1988, for a more detailed description.) Group members assume the identity of various super heroes and use the characters' perspectives to prompt ideas. It is similar to Rolestorming [77], but differs in the added stimuli provided by the various powers of the super heroes.

Objectives

- To help participants generate as many creative ideas as possible
- To help participants learn how to use the activities to generate ideas

Participants

Small groups of four to seven people each

Materials, Supplies, and Equipment

- For each group: one roll of cellophane tape for attaching yarn to signs, markers, two flip charts, and masking tape for posting flip-chart sheets
- For each participant: one 8.5" x 11" sheet of paper, yarn to attach to the paper, one sheet each of three different colors of sticking dots (½" diameter), and one pad of 4 x 6 Post-it® Notes

Handout

- Super Heroes Handout

Time

75 minutes

Related Activities

- Fairy Tale Time [40]
- Imaginary Mentor [42]
- Rolestorming [77]

Procedure

1. Distribute the Super Heroes Handout, review the different super heroes with the participants, and answer any questions they may have.
2. Tell each group member to select a character and assume that character's identity. If group members really want to get into the spirit, they may don their characters' costumes; if not, each group member wears a sign around his or her neck with the name of the character on it.
3. Have individual group members read their character descriptions silently. Tell them to summarize these descriptions aloud, describing special powers, strengths, weaknesses, habits, and other special characteristics.
4. After hearing each character description, direct all the group members to use the descriptions as stimuli for ideas. For instance, Superman's x-ray vision might suggest using hidden cameras to detect employee and customer theft in a store.
5. Tell them to write down any ideas on Post-it® Notes (one idea per note) and place them on flip-chart paper for evaluation.

Debrief/Discussion

This is another role-playing exercise in which trying to view the world from another's perspective can create unique insights. Well-suited for drama kings and queens, Super Heroes is sure to invigorate a lethargic group. To ensure that the role playing is sufficient to help produce ideas, be sure to allow at least 10 minutes for the participants to learn about their characters and think of ways to play them to help trigger ideas in themselves and others. When you are reviewing the descriptions of Super Heroes, you might encourage participants to suggest other Super Heroes to use to generate ideas.

Also consider having participants debrief using the following questions:

- What was most helpful about this exercise?
- What was most challenging?
- What can we apply?
- How would you rate the value of this exercise to helping us with this issue?
- Will this exercise be helpful in the future for other sessions?

- What did you learn?
- What will we be able to use from this exercise?
- What ideas were generated, and which ones were most interesting?

Super Heroes Handout

Here are some sample Super Heroes and their major characteristics:

- *Batman*—first-rate detective; can outwit the worst criminals; uses bat paraphernalia such as a Batmobile, a Batplane, a Batcycle, Batrollerskates, and a Batrope. Batman's alter ego is millionaire Bruce Wayne.

- *Captain America*—represents the ultimate in American ideals (truth, justice, mom, apple pie), has a winning personality with great powers of persuasion, maintains a positive outlook on life, is very athletic, and uses his Captain America Shield to protect himself from harm.

- *Dr. Strange*—a skilled magician and sorcerer who can create numerous illusions. He can also cure sicknesses, control people and situations, and transform objects into other objects. He often has temporary losses of concentration.

- *Mr. Fantastic*—the smartest man in the world; can stretch his body into any length and has tremendous flexibility.

- *The Human Torch*—a short-tempered hothead who has the power to emit and control fire without burning himself. He also can fly.

- *The Invisible Girl*—can make herself or other people and things invisible and make them reappear. When in danger, she creates an invisible shield that protects her from harm.

- *Spiderman*—can shoot webs out from his wrists and quickly swing from different buildings. Has the ability to attach himself to ceilings or hang upside down. Dedicated to helping people in trouble.

- *Superman*—has x-ray vision and super hearing, can fly faster than a speeding bullet, and is the strongest man on earth. Clark Kent, mild-mannered newspaper reporter, is his alter ego. Can be weakened only by Kryptonite. Is able to leap tall buildings in a single bound. Often mistaken for birds or airplanes.

- *Wonder Woman*—a true Super-woman with super strength, agility, and athletic ability who can overpower anyone. Has magical bracelets that deflect bullets, and she can capture almost anything or anyone with her magical lasso. Once lassoed by Wonder Woman, a person must tell the truth. Flies an invisible airplane.

- *Storm*—a character in the X-Men movie series, she has the power to control the weather, to call up fierce winds, blinding snow or rain, or intense heat, among other weather-related outcomes. She originally was from Africa, where she was orphaned when her parents were killed and their house destroyed, trapping Storm inside. For the rest of her life she was afraid of being in closed-in places. Local tribes worshipped her as a god until she moved to the United States.

Chapter 11

Brainwriting with Related Stimuli

The group activities in this chapter produce ideas using silent, written idea generation with stimuli related to the problem. Ideas typically are written on Post-it® Notes and then retained for evaluation or shared with other group members to help prompt new ideas. These activities may not produce ideas as unique as ideas generated using unrelated stimuli. However, the right combination of group members can spark ideas regardless of the stimuli used.

As with other brainwriting activities, some activities in this chapter require group members to share their ideas, whereas others involve no sharing. (Activities in this chapter that do not involve sharing during idea generation include Group Not [83], Organizational Brainstorms [87], and Your Slip Is Showing [90].) Research suggests that sharing should produce more ideas and higher-quality ideas (VanGundy, 1993).

Brainwriting, with or without sharing, may be one of the best ways to guarantee large numbers of ideas in a group. When compared to conventional brainstorming activities, the Brain Purge activity [82] described in this chapter has been found to be especially useful for increasing idea quantity in groups. Research by VanGundy (1993) has shown that Brain Purge groups generate four times as many ideas as conventional brainstorming groups. And, as you may know, idea quantity is often linked directly to idea quality.

So what makes brainwriting so special? Brainwriting activities compensate for a serious deficiency of most brainstorming groups. Specifically, only one person can generate ideas at a time during brainstorming. This is known as "production blocking." Brainwriting overcomes production blocking by enabling all group members to generate ideas at the same time since they all are writing down ideas—more or less—at the same time.

Most brainwriting activities also are simple and easy to use. What more could you want in a group activity? After all, the objective of most idea generation sessions is to think of lots of ideas.

Unfortunately, the downside of brainwriting is that most people enjoy the social satisfaction that accompanies brainstorming. In brainstorming groups, productivity often takes a back seat to satisfaction of social needs. So what to do? Use both brainstorming and brainwriting. They complement each other nicely.

NOTE: FOR ALL ACTIVITIES, REMIND PARTICIPANTS
TO DEFER JUDGMENT WHILE GENERATING IDEAS.

81

As Easy As 6–3–5

Background

As Easy As 6–3–5, originally known as Method 6–3–5 (VanGundy, 1988), is a very basic brainwriting procedure that structures how people interact and generate ideas. There are at least three versions of this activity, so you get three activities in one! You may want to read through all of the versions to choose the one that would work best with your situation.

John Warfield and his colleagues (1975) developed the first version of this activity; German creativity consultant Horst Geschka and his associates (1981) developed the second (Some claim it is the first brainwriting method); the third version was originated by creativity consultants in Germany and Holland and then developed further by University of Manchester (U.K.) business professor Tudor Rickards (1974). It is similar to the other versions except that it is slightly more structured and no time limit is imposed.

Objectives

- To help participants generate as many creative ideas as possible
- To help participants learn how to use the activities to generate ideas

Participants

Small groups of six people each

Materials, Supplies, and Equipment

- For each group: markers, two flip charts, and masking tape for posting flip-chart sheets
- For each participant: one sheet each of three different colors of sticking dots (½" diameter) and one pad of 4 x 6 Post-it® Notes

Time

20 minutes

Related Activities

- Brain Purge [82]
- Group Not [83]
- Organizational Brainstorms [87]
- Your Slip Is Showing [90]

Procedure: Version 1

1. Have six people sit around a table and discuss the problem.
2. Tell the group members to write down, individually, on a sheet of paper, three ideas in a 5-minute period.
3. At the end of the 5 minutes, tell the group members to pass their papers to the person on their right.
4. Inform them that the person receiving a paper should examine the ideas and try to generate new ideas or elaborations.
5. Continue this process until each group member receives his or her original paper.
6. Have the group members transfer all of their ideas to Post-it® Notes and place them on a flip chart for evaluation. Or write the ideas on a flip chart for evaluation.

Procedure: Version 2

1. Have six people sit around a table and discuss the problem.
2. Instruct the participants to draw three equal sized, vertical columns (lengthwise) on a sheet of paper and write down one idea at the top of each column.
3. After 5 minutes, tell them to pass their papers to the person on their right and write down at least one idea that improves on the one listed at the top of each column. (If they can't think of a way to improve an idea, instruct them to write down new ideas.)
4. Continue this process of writing down improvements or new ideas until each person receives his or her original paper or time is called.
5. Have the group members transfer all of their ideas to Post-it® Notes and place them on a flip chart for evaluation. Or write the ideas on a flip chart for evaluation.

Procedure: Version 3

1. Have six people sit around a table and discuss the problem.
2. Assign a member number to each group participant so that each group contains members one through six.
3. Give each group member a pad of 4 x 6 Post-it® Notes and instruct them to write

down one idea each on three of the notes. (In each group, there now should be a total of eighteen ideas on the notes.)

4. Direct them to pass their notes to another, pre-selected member. For instance, group member 1 may be instructed to pass his or her notes to member 2; member 2 to member 3, and so forth.

5. Tell the members receiving the notes to read them and write any new ideas or improvements on a separate note.

6. Continue this process until group members have responded to each idea five times.

7. Have the group members place all of their Post-it® Notes on a flip chart for evaluation.

Debrief/Discussion

If you will be facilitating a number of idea generation sessions, it might be interesting to experiment and see which of the three versions seem to work best (if any) and which ones are preferred by the participants. To do this, you might consider evaluating them with respect to idea quantity and quality as well as ease of use.

Also consider having participants debrief using the following questions:

- What was most helpful about this exercise?
- What was most challenging?
- What can we apply?
- How would you rate the value of this exercise to helping us with this issue?
- Will this exercise be helpful in the future for other sessions?
- What did you learn?
- What will we be able to use from this exercise?
- What ideas were generated, and which ones were most interesting?

82

Brain Purge

Background

Before we can think of creative solutions, we often must purge ourselves of more traditional or obvious ideas. Brain Purge, originally developed by Geschka (1979) as Pin Cards, allows you to flush out ideas you can think of immediately or ideas you have been waiting to express. However, don't use this activity just to get rid of conventional ideas. It also is a handy way to generate many ideas—in a relatively short time—for almost any problem situation. You'll find that Brain Purge is similar to As Easy As 6–3–5 [81], but not as structured.

Objectives

- To help participants generate as many creative ideas as possible
- To help participants learn how to use the activities to generate ideas

Participants

Small groups of four to seven people each

Materials, Supplies, and Equipment

- For each group: markers, two flip charts, and masking tape for posting flip-chart sheets
- For each participant: one sheet each of three different colors of sticking dots (½″ diameter) and one pad of 4 x 6 Post-it® Notes

Time

20 minutes

Related Activities

- Idea Pool [85]
- Organizational Brainstorms [87]

- Your Slip Is Showing [90]
- The Shirt Off Your Back [101]

Procedure

1. Give each member of a group a pad of Post-it® Notes and pens or pencils.

2. Tell each participant to write one idea on a Post-it® and pass it to the person on his or her right.

3. Instruct the group members to read the ideas on the Post-its they just received and use these ideas to stimulate improvements or entirely new ideas.

4. Tell them to write any improvements or new ideas on new Post-its and pass them to the persons on their right.

5. Allow this process to continue for about 10 to 15 minutes.

6. Call time and ask group members to sort the Post-its into categories of similar ideas for evaluation. Tell them to do this on a table, a flip chart, or a wall.

Debrief/Discussion

This is one of the original brainwriting activities developed in Germany and one of the most popular activities in use today throughout the world. It is a natural complement to brainstorming and should be used whenever at least 15 minutes of time is available. Many trainers and facilitators use this approach as a way to kick off a brainstorming session in that it can serve as a purging activity to allow participants to share their pre-session ideas without having to wait.

Perhaps the most useful discussion question to use with this exercise is to ask participants to discuss why this method would generate more ideas than traditional brainstorming or brainwriting activities in which the ideas are not shared.

Also consider having participants debrief using the following questions:

- What was most helpful about this exercise?
- What was most challenging?
- What can we apply?
- How would you rate the value of this exercise to helping us with this issue?
- Will this exercise be helpful in the future for other sessions?
- What did you learn?
- What will we be able to use from this exercise?
- What ideas were generated, and which ones were most interesting?

83

Group Not

Background

The title of this activity refers to an interesting question in small-group problem solving: When is a group not a group? The answer is that a group isn't a group when members don't interact during a group activity. Such "nongroups" are known as "nominal" groups.

Group Not is based on one of the most heavily researched small-group idea generation activity: the Nominal Group Technique (NGT), developed by Delbecq and Van de Ven (1971). Although this activity allows group members to discuss their ideas, the members do so only after all the ideas have been generated.

Objectives

- To help participants generate as many creative ideas as possible
- To help participants learn how to use the activities to generate ideas

Participants

Small groups of four to seven people each

Materials, Supplies, and Equipment

- For each group: markers, two flip charts, and masking tape for posting flip-chart sheets
- For each participant: one sheet each of three different colors of sticking dots (½" diameter) and one pad of 4 x 6 Post-it® Notes

Time

45 minutes

Related Activities

- As Easy As 6–3–5 [81]

Brainwriting with Related Stimuli

Procedure

1. Divide participants into small groups and give each member a pad of Post-it® Notes and pens or pencils.

2. Ask group members to write down ideas individually on their Post-its without sharing them with others. Stress that they should write down only one idea per Post-it®.

3. Tell the group members to take turns reading aloud one of their ideas and have a leader/recorder write down these ideas and number them on a flip chart. Emphasize that, during this activity, they are not supposed to discuss ideas.

4. Ask the leader in each group to point to each idea listed and ask for discussion. Note that the purpose of this activity is to clarify the meaning, purpose, or logic behind each idea.

5. Instruct the group members to select, individually, between five and nine favorite ideas and write each on a separate Post-it® Note.

6. Have them write the number of the idea (from the master list) in the upper left corner of each note and record their rating of the idea (1 = not important; 5 = important) in the lower left corner.

7. Tell the group leaders to collect all the notes and record the votes on a flip chart. (You may want to allow all the groups to take a break while the group leaders tally the votes.) Have the group leaders note the idea receiving the greatest number of votes. If a clear winner emerges, tell them that the process is finished.

8. If no clear winner emerges or there is some doubt about the vote tallies, tell the group members to examine the vote tally sheets for peculiar patterns (for example, if an idea receives many high and low votes). If they notice an odd pattern, tell group members to discuss the item to clarify why that pattern resulted.

9. If necessary, have the groups conduct a final vote using the procedure outlined in Steps 6 and 7.

Debrief/Discussion

As with similar activities, a major disadvantage of NGT is that group members don't see each other's ideas during idea generation. On the other hand, this activity provides a highly structured process for both idea generation and evaluation. Unlike the other activities, Group Not builds in a specific process to achieve decision-making closure on the ideas. This structure can be especially valuable when there is little time for decision making. On the other hand, the structure itself may limit decision quality if closure is forced before adequate discussion of an idea's strengths and weaknesses. You might want to ask the participants to discuss how they experienced the structure.

Also consider having participants debrief using the following questions:

- What was most helpful about this exercise?
- What was most challenging?
- What can we apply?

- How would you rate the value of this exercise to helping us with this issue?
- Will this exercise be helpful in the future for other sessions?
- What did you learn?
- What will we be able to use from this exercise?
- What ideas were generated, and which ones were most interesting?

84

Idea Mixer

Background

I don't know much Japanese, so I have to assume that Hiroshi Takahashi is correct when he says that NHK is a Japanese acronym for the Japan Broadcasting Corporation. Takahashi developed what I call Idea Mixer while he worked for NHK (he calls the method NHK Brainstorming). Although he refers to it as a brainstorming activity and it involves some oral idea generation, Idea Mixer actually is a combination brainwriting/brainstorming activity.

Objectives

- To help participants generate as many creative ideas as possible
- To help participants learn how to use the activities to generate ideas

Participants

Small groups of four to seven people each

Materials, Supplies, and Equipment

- For each group: markers, two flip charts, and masking tape for posting flip-chart sheets
- For each participant: one sheet each of three different colors of sticking dots (½" diameter) and one pad of 4 x 6 Post-it® Notes
- (Optional) One overhead projector, at least ten blank transparencies, and markers

Procedure

1. Divide participants into small groups and give each member of a group a pad of Post-it® Notes and pens or pencils.

2. Ask group members to write down ideas individually on their Post-its without sharing them with others. Stress that they should write down only one idea per Post-it. Allow no more than 10 minutes for this step.

3. Have each individual read aloud, in turn, one of his or her ideas.

4. Tell the other group members to write down, on a Post-it, any new ideas that might come to mind (one idea per note).

5. Repeat Steps 3 and 4 until each group member has read aloud at least one of his or her ideas. If you want more ideas, have them repeat the round.

6. Instruct the groups to collect and group the ideas into categories of related themes, using a flip chart or a wall.

7. Ask the participants to form new groups of two or three people, brainstorm ideas for the themes at their new tables, and write the ideas on Post-it® Notes, one idea per note.

8. After one hour or less, ask each group to sort its ideas by themes and present them to the larger group. Write down these ideas on a flip chart or overhead transparencies visible to all.

9. Have the participants form new groups of ten people, brainstorm ways to improve the ideas listed, write them down on Post-its (one idea per note), and place them on flip charts for evaluation.

Debrief/Discussion

This exercise introduces several "wrinkles" into a brainwriting/brainstorming process that should yield a fairly large number of ideas. It takes advantage of the strengths of both brainwriting and brainstorming while mixing up group composition.

This latter feature can be effective to keep groups from becoming stale and to continually bring in new perspectives. A downside to changing group composition is that groups that are "clicking" together and cranking out ideas fluently could be broken up and lose their productivity when combined with others.

Also consider having participants debrief using the following questions:

- What was most helpful about this exercise?
- What was most challenging?
- What can we apply?
- How would you rate the value of this exercise to helping us with this issue?
- Will this exercise be helpful in the future for other sessions?
- What did you learn?
- What will we be able to use from this exercise?
- What ideas were generated, and which ones were most interesting?

85

Idea Pool

Background

Idea Pool (also known as Brainwriting Pool) is a close relative of the Brain Purge activity [82]. It was developed at the Battelle Institute in Frankfurt, Germany (Geschka, Schaude, and Schlicksupp, 1973). One difference between the two activities is in how the ideas are shared among the group members. In Brain Purge, members pass ideas around the group, whereas in Idea Pool members put ideas in the center of a table to form a "pool."

Objectives

- To help participants generate as many creative ideas as possible
- To help participants learn how to use the activities to generate ideas

Participants

Small groups of four to seven people each

Materials, Supplies, and Equipment

- For each group: markers, two flip charts, and masking tape for posting flip-chart sheets
- For each person: one sheet of 8.5 x 11 paper (lined or unlined) and pens or pencils.

Procedure

1. Give each group member one sheet of 8.5 x 11 paper.
2. Tell them to silently write down, individually, four ideas on the sheet of paper.
3. Instruct each group member to place the sheet of paper in the center of the table and exchange it for another sheet.
4. Instruct participants to examine the ideas on the new sheet and write down improvements or new ideas.
5. Have them place this sheet in the center of the table and exchange it for a new one.

6. After 10 to 15 minutes of this activity, tell them to collect the idea sheets and tape them to flip charts for evaluation.

Debrief/Discussion

Idea Pool is another quick way to generate a relatively large number of ideas in a short time. As with Brain Purge, Idea Pool relies on the ideas of others to help trigger new ones. It differs, however, in that each person has at least four ideas to respond to as stimuli.

Also consider having participants debrief using the following questions:

- What was most helpful about this exercise?
- What was most challenging?
- What can we apply?
- How would you rate the value of this exercise to helping us with this issue?
- Will this exercise be helpful in the future for other sessions?
- What did you learn?
- What will we be able to use from this exercise?
- What ideas were generated, and which ones were most interesting?

86

Museum Madness

Background

Museum Madness (also known as the Gallery Method) is another of the many group activities originally developed at the Battelle Institute in Frankfurt, Germany, by Horst Geschka and his associates (1981). It is similar to other group activities that use unrelated stimuli. However, it is different in one significant way: instead of passing ideas around the group, members walk around to the ideas. Thus, Museum Madness reverses the process that most group brainwriting activities use. The title of the activity derives from the way people browse around a museum looking at works of art.

Objectives

- To help participants generate as many creative ideas as possible
- To help participants learn how to use the activities to generate ideas

Participants

Small groups of four to seven people each

Materials, Supplies, and Equipment

- At least one sheet of flip-chart paper for each participant (if there are fewer than thirty people; if more than thirty, use one sheet for every two people)
- Masking tape for posting flip-chart sheets
- One dark-colored marker for each participant

Procedure

1. Attach sheets of flip-chart paper to the walls of a room (flip charts on stands also can be used).
2. Tell the participants to silently write several ideas on a sheet of flip-chart paper.
3. After about 10 to 15 minutes of writing, ask the participants to spend 15 to 20 minutes walking around the room, read each other's ideas, and take notes on thoughts that might pop up.

101 Activities for Teaching Creativity and Problem Solving

4. Ask the group members to generate ideas again, silently, on one sheet of flip-chart paper. This time, however, tell them to try to use the other ideas to stimulate improvements or new ideas and write them down on a flip chart.

5. At the end of the second round of idea generation, have the participants evaluate all the ideas.

Debrief/Discussion

This is a great activity to use after lunch or at the end of the day during a brainstorming session. Research indicates that people often are more creative if they can move around. Although it may be frustrating to some to remain silent during idea generation, the result typically will be a relatively large quantity of ideas. Remind the participants that they will have an opportunity to talk during idea evaluation.

Also consider having participants debrief using the following questions:

- What was most helpful about this exercise?
- What was most challenging?
- What can we apply?
- How would you rate the value of this exercise to helping us with this issue?
- Will this exercise be helpful in the future for other sessions?
- What did you learn?
- What will we be able to use from this exercise?
- What ideas were generated, and which ones were most interesting?

87

Organizational Brainstorms

Background

John Haefele (1961), an employee of Procter & Gamble, developed this activity and called it the Collective Notebook Method. It is unique among the group activities in this book in that it is the only activity in which ideas are not generated in a small-group setting. Instead, ideas come from a select group of employees throughout an organization.

The original version of Organizational Brainstorms is somewhat similar to Group Not [83] and Your Slip Is Showing [90]. All these activities involve generating ideas without sharing them with other participants. A variation, however, does permit limited idea sharing.

Objectives

- To help participants generate as many creative ideas as possible
- To help participants learn how to use the activities to generate ideas

Participants

Selected participants from throughout an organization

Materials, Supplies, and Equipment

- One notebook and pens or pencils for each participant

Procedure

1. Pre-select participants from throughout an organization (representing different areas of knowledge related to the problem) and give each a notebook containing problem information and instructions on the process.
2. Instruct the participants to write one idea per day in their notebooks.
3. At the end of one month, instruct the participants to summarize their best ideas.
4. Collect all the notebooks, record and categorize the ideas, and prepare a summary.
5. Provide the participants a copy of the summary and invite them to discuss the ideas generated during a face-to-face meeting.

Debrief/Discussion

This activity obviously was developed years before email became a common way of communicating. Computer technology now makes it possible for organizations to collect ideas via intranets. According to *Business Week*, IBM demonstrated the power of global brainstorming over the Internet when it received ideas from thousands of international employees (November 24, 2003). Organizational Brainstorms differs in that it requires at least one idea per day for a month. Nevertheless, new technology makes this exercise almost obsolete. The new emphasis in many organizations is on "idea management," where companies use enterprise idea management software to solicit and process ideas. (One of the leading companies in this area is Imaginatik.com.)

Also consider having participants debrief using the following questions:

- What was most helpful about this exercise?
- What was most challenging?
- What can we apply?
- How would you rate the value of this exercise to helping us with this issue?
- Will this exercise be helpful in the future for other sessions?
- What did you learn?
- What will we be able to use from this exercise?
- What ideas were generated, and which ones were most interesting?

Variations

- Alan Pearson (1978) has used this activity with one significant variation: participants proceed as just described, except they exchange their notebooks with another person after two weeks. Tell the participants to use the ideas in the new notebooks to trigger additional ideas over the remaining two weeks.
- Another variation is to collect the ideas daily via email. It then would be relatively easy to share all of the ideas with the participants on a daily basis. The result might be a greater idea quantity.

88

Out-of-the-Blue Lightning Bolt Cloudbuster

Background

Hall (1994) developed this activity to spark ideas during extended group idea generation sessions. As with some other activities in this chapter, written ideas are shared among group members. However, the procedure used to share ideas is much more unstructured (to say the least). Group members write their ideas on paper airplanes and throw them about. The result can be a lot of fun. And where there's fun, there are often many creative ideas.

Objectives

- To help participants generate as many creative ideas as possible
- To help participants learn how to use the activities to generate ideas

Participants

Small groups of four to seven people each

Materials, Supplies, and Equipment

- At least five sheets of multi-colored, bright (for example, AstroBrites®), 8.5" x 11" paper for each participant, plus pens or pencils
- For each group: markers, two flip charts, and masking tape for posting flip-chart sheets
- For each participant: one sheet each of three different colors of sticking dots (½" diameter) and one pad of 4 x 6 Post-it® Notes

Procedure

1. Distribute the paper to each participant, making sure that they receive a variety of different colors.

2. If necessary, demonstrate how to fold a paper airplane. If some aren't able to make a paper airplane, instruct them to write an idea on a piece of paper and crumple it into a ball that they then would throw instead.

3. During an extended idea generation session, tell the participants that whenever they think of an idea, they should write it on a wing of an airplane and throw the plane into a designated location (for example, a non-burning fireplace, a box, wastebasket, or a corner of the room).

4. At the end of the idea session, distribute the airplanes to the group members and ask the participants to fly the planes to someone else, all at the same time.

5. Tell the participants to examine the idea written on an airplane, write down any improvements or new ideas, and then launch the airplane again. Encourage participants to write whatever comes to mind and repeat this process until each participant has thrown a plane four or five times.

6. Tell the groups to collect airplanes, write down the ideas on Post-it® Notes (one idea per note), and place them on flip charts for evaluation.

Debrief/Discussion

This exercise has proven to be an excellent approach for jump-starting a group and creating a fun environment conducive to creative thinking. I have used it numerous times in practice and it always has been well-received because it introduces the "Fun Factor." Use it to kick off an idea generation session or when an energy burst is needed. It also works extremely well when very little time is available since it is a brainwriting variation and doesn't require verbal interaction.

Also consider having participants debrief using the following questions:

- What was most helpful about this exercise?
- What was most challenging?
- What can we apply?
- How would you rate the value of this exercise to helping us with this issue?
- Will this exercise be helpful in the future for other sessions?
- What did you learn?
- What will we be able to use from this exercise?
- What ideas were generated, and which ones were most interesting?

Variation

- Instead of having participants arbitrarily write down ideas during a session and fly them to a designated location, instruct them to fly their planes (with ideas) as the core part of this exercise. In other words, tell them to write one idea on an airplane and then fly it to others upon command and then follow Steps 4 to 6.

89

You're a Card, Andy!

Background

Many people play cards to relax and enjoy the company of others. Others play cards to escape their troubles. For instance, I remember fellow students in college who loved to play cards. Unfortunately, many of them loved playing cards more than they loved studying. After less than a year, most of these folks found that they had all the time in the world to play cards—no college education, but plenty of time for cards.

One conclusion from this story may be that playing cards can be unproductive. This is true if card playing is taken to extremes. It is possible, however, to play cards while generating ideas. Thus, you can have fun while also being productive. You're a Card, Andy! is a brainwriting activity developed by Goodman and Shields (1993). It is similar to Brain Purge [82] but has the potential to generate a more fun atmosphere. Just be careful that the group doesn't pay more attention to playing cards than to generating ideas!

Objectives

- To help participants generate as many creative ideas as possible
- To help participants learn how to use the activities to generate ideas

Participants

Small groups of four to seven people each

Materials, Supplies, and Equipment

- For each group: one deck of 100, 4 x 6 or 3 x 5 index cards, markers, two flip charts, and masking tape for posting flip-chart sheets
- For each participant: pens or pencils and one sheet each of three different colors of sticking dots

Time

30 minutes

Related Activities

- As Easy As 6–3–5 [81]
- Brain Purge [82]
- Idea Mixer [84]
- Idea Pool [85]
- Out of the Blue Lightning Bolt Cloudbuster [88]

Procedure

1. Tell the groups to select one member to be the "dealer."
2. Ask the dealer in each group to deal the others (and the dealer) seven index cards each as their "starting hands."
3. Tell them to write one idea on a card and pass it to anyone they choose in the group. Have them continue this process for 10 minutes or until there is a lull in activity.
4. The only restriction is that each member must receive at least two cards each.
5. Have each member show his or her "hand" (that is, read aloud the ideas) and then place the cards in the center of the table.
6. Instruct the groups to create a "pot" of additional ideas. To do this, note that each person should ante up his or her cards (put them in the center of the table) in turn, after writing an idea on each card.
7. Tell all participants that the last person in each group with an additional idea when time is called (15 minutes) will win some prize such as a dream date, vacation, or whatever prize the group decides is appropriate. You also might offer a prize for the group with the most ideas.
8. Direct the group members to pin the cards to a bulletin board, foam boards, or just lay them out on a table in logical clusters involving commonalities (aka "affinity groups").
9. Ask the group members to review the ideas and see if any new ideas are prompted. If so, have them add new idea cards to the clusters and evaluate the ideas using Post-it® Notes on flip charts.

Debrief/Discussion

This activity capitalizes on the fun people can have playing cards in addition to individual competitiveness. Most idea generation activities exhort participants to generate a given number of ideas. Although this can be motivating, the desire to "win" a game can be even stronger. If your participants include some who are familiar with card games, you might ask for suggestions on variations of this exercise.

Also consider having participants debrief using the following questions:

- What was most helpful about this exercise?

- What was most challenging?
- What can we apply?
- How would you rate the value of this exercise to helping us with this issue?
- Will this exercise be helpful in the future for other sessions?
- What did you learn?
- What will we be able to use from this exercise?
- What ideas were generated, and which ones were most interesting?

90

Your Slip Is Showing

Background

This activity (also known as Crawford Slipwriting) may be the "mother of all formal small group idea generation activities"—at least in terms of being a progenitor of brainwriting activities. Dr. C.C. Crawford developed this activity in the United States in the 1920s (see Crawford & Demidovitch, 1983; Whiting, 1958), and Charles Clark (1978) has popularized the method over the years. It is especially useful when you want to gather ideas from a large number of people, such as participants at a conference.

Although it can accommodate a large number of people, Your Slip Is Showing differs from Organizational Brainstorms [87] in two ways. First, the participants in Organizational Brainstorms are members of the same organization, submit ideas individually, and typically are by themselves when submitting their ideas. The second difference is that participants in Your Slip Is Showing generate their ideas while in small groups in the presence of other people, although they do not have to share their ideas with others.

Objectives

- To help participants generate as many creative ideas as possible
- To help participants learn how to use the activities to generate ideas

Participants

Thousands or as many as there are resources to process all the ideas. They may be in small groups, but do not have to be since all ideas are generated by individuals and not shared.

Materials, Supplies, and Equipment

- For each participant, one pad of 3 x 5 or 4 x 6 Post-it® Notes and pens or pencils (If Post-its are not available, substitute slips of paper, giving each person at least ten slips)

Time

30 minutes

Related Activities

- As Easy As 6–3–5 [81]
- Group Not [83]
- Idea Pool [85]
- Museum Madness [86]
- Organizational Brainstorms [87]

Procedure

1. Distribute the Post-its or paper slips to all participants.
2. Tell them to begin writing one idea on each slip.
3. After 5 to 10 minutes, tell them to stop writing and collect the notes or slips.
4. Appoint a task force to evaluate the ideas. This task force first should sort the ideas into categories according to frequency of occurrence or degree of usability. Have the task force select the best ideas and develop them into workable ideas.

Debrief/Discussion

This represents the most basic form of brainwriting. Its primary advantage is audience participation and the ability to collect a large number of ideas from a large number of people in a short period of time. If you accept the premise that quantity breeds quality, then it theoretically should be possible to produce some high-quality ideas (that is, ideas capable of resolving a problem).

Also consider having participants debrief using the following questions:

- What was most helpful about this exercise?
- What was most challenging?
- What can we apply?
- How would you rate the value of this exercise to helping us with this issue?
- Will this exercise be helpful in the future for other sessions?
- What did you learn?
- What will we be able to use from this exercise?
- What ideas were generated, and which ones were most interesting?

Variations

- Clark also suggests some variations, such as using abstract graphics to prompt ideas. Or participants could divide into pairs and one person in the pair could record ideas for both people—a sort of mini-brainstorming group.

- As with Organizational Brainstorms [87], ideas also could be submitted electronically. For instance, at a conference where the participants are in attendance, they might submit ideas via their personal laptops or computers set up just for the conference.

Chapter 12

Brainwriting with Unrelated Stimuli

The activities in Chapter 11 are all based on stimuli related to the problem. Theoretically this means that the resulting ideas may not be as unique as those generated with unrelated stimuli. Of course, that's not always the case, because other factors (such as a highly creative personality) may determine the quality of a group's ideas. All things being equal, however, unrelated stimuli are more likely to lead to winning ideas.

The activities in this chapter are based on sources of stimulation not related directly to the problem. In that respect, they resemble the unrelated brainstorming activities in Chapter 10. The difference, of course, is that the activities in this chapter are based on basic brainwriting methods (the silent, written generation of ideas in a group).

As noted in Chapter 3, some research suggests that brainwriting may outperform brainstorming, regardless of the stimulus source. Thus, unrelated brainwriting activities have the highest hypothetical potential to produce the "best" ideas. This is only a conclusion based on some research. The best activities may represent all categories, depending on the user and the problem.

NOTE: FOR ALL ACTIVITIES, REMIND PARTICIPANTS
TO DEFER JUDGMENT WHILE GENERATING IDEAS.

91

Altered States

Background

Many of the activities in this book are based on changing perspectives. Creating a new way of seeing things disrupts locked-in viewpoints. Although many people fear change, changing perspectives should be welcomed in creative thinking. Altering a dysfunctional or narrow perspective can provide the insights needed to generate breakthrough ideas. Change your perspective and you'll open up new worlds of thought.

Hall (1994) developed Altered States to help people change their frames of reference and see their problems differently. Once a person's perspective has changed, new ideas should flow more freely.

Objectives

- To help participants generate as many creative ideas as possible
- To help participants learn how to use the activities to generate ideas

Participants

Small groups of four to seven people each

Materials, Supplies, and Equipment

- For each group: markers, two flip charts, and masking tape for posting flip-chart sheets
- For each participant: one sheet each of three different colors of sticking dots (½" diameter) and one pad of 4 x 6 Post-it® Notes

Handouts

- Altered States Handout
- Altered States Questions Handout

Time

45 minutes

Related Activities

- As Easy As 6–3–5 [81]
- Brain Purge [82]
- Idea Mixer [84]
- Idea Pool [85]
- Museum Madness [86]

Procedure

1. Distribute the Altered States Handout, review it with the participants, and answer any questions they may have.
2. Distribute to each group members one copy of the Altered States Questions Handout.
3. Instruct the participants to answer the four questions, individually and in writing, and list three bizarre, wild, altered states for each question. Encourage them to avoid over-analyzing or being too concerned with practicality, and try to be spontaneous.
4. After they have finished answering the questions, instruct the group members to pass their lists to another group member.
5. Instruct the group members to examine the lists they receive, use the responses to trigger ideas, write them down on Post-it® Notes (one idea per note), and place the notes on a flip chart for evaluation.

Debrief/Discussion

One positive feature of this exercise is that the questions force participants to move out of their narrow perceptions about a problem and create novel ones. Of course, the altered states themselves may seem bizarre at first to people not accustomed to using unrelated stimuli. However, most people catch on relatively quickly, especially after reviewing the Altered States Handout. Another positive is that group members use the altered states of others, rather than the ones they generated. This is another wasy to force people to think differently about a problem to which they may have become too close.

Also consider having participants debrief using the following questions:

- What was most helpful about this exercise?
- What was most challenging?
- What can we apply?
- How would you rate the value of this exercise to helping us with this issue?
- Will this exercise be helpful in the future for other sessions?
- What did you learn?
- What will we be able to use from this exercise?
- What ideas were generated, and which ones were most interesting?

Altered States Handout

Suppose you want to generate cereal product ideas. First, list bizarre, wild, altered states:

- When is the product or service consumed or purchased?

  Response 1: In the bathtub

  Response 2: When the user craves vampire blood

  Response 3: When the user is rolling on the floor

- Why is the product or service consumed or purchased?

  Response 1: To alleviate boredom

  Response 2: To cure cancer

  Response 3: To impress the neighbors

- Where is the product or service consumed or purchased?

  Response 1: In Martian vending machines

  Response 2: In public restrooms

  Response 3: In butcher shops

- What components, ingredients, or elements make up the product or service?

  Response 1: Silly Putty

  Response 2: Light bulbs

  Response 3: Bricks

If you received this list of responses, it might help you think of such ideas as:

- Cereal boxes shaped like bathtubs
- Cereal shaped like blood clots to "gross out" children
- Designer cereal boxes with snob appeal
- Cereal sold in vending machines
- Meat-flavored cereal that doubles as pet food
- Transparent cereal boxes
- Cereal boxes that, when empty, can be used as molds for bricks to build homes for the homeless

Altered States Questions Handout

1. When is the product or service consumed or purchased?

   Response 1: _____

   Response 2: _____

   Response 3: _____

2. Why is the product or service consumed or purchased?

   Response 1: _____

   Response 2: _____

   Response 3: _____

3. Where is the product or service consumed or purchased?

   Response 1: _____

   Response 2: _____

   Response 3: _____

4. What components, ingredients, or elements make up the product or service?

   Response 1: _____

   Response 2: _____

   Response 3: _____

92

Balloon, Balloon, Balloon

Background

The fun factor is an important ingredient during any idea generation session. Several activities in this book incorporate fun elements to heighten creative perceptions and increase the potential for large numbers of ideas. Developed by Hall (1994), Balloon, Balloon, Balloon is one of these fun factor activities. Although it is similar to others, it can provide the lift a group needs to generate hot ideas. Try it right after lunch or at the end of a day and I guarantee no one will fall asleep.

Objectives

- To help participants generate as many creative ideas as possible
- To help participants learn how to use the activities to generate ideas

Participants

Small groups of four to seven people each

Materials, Supplies, and Equipment

- For each group: markers, two flip charts, and masking tape for posting flip-chart sheets
- For each participant: one sheet each of three different colors of sticking dots (½" diameter) and one pad of 4 x 6 Post-it® Notes
- For each participant: two balloons of different colors, approximately 9" to 12" in diameter

Handout

- Balloon, Balloon, Balloon Handout

Time

45 minutes (requires prior preparation)

101 Activities for Teaching Creativity and Problem Solving

Related Activities

- As Easy As 6–3–5 [81]
- Group Not [83]
- Idea Pool [85]
- Out of the Blue Lightning Bolt Cloudbuster [88]

Procedure

1. Before the session, prepare two sets of paper slips, small enough to be inserted into the balloons. For the first set (for example, for blue balloons), write one silly, abstract, nonsensical phrase unrelated to the problem on each slip (for example, "rhubarb ink javelins," "worm lips on parade," "rotating cat lemons", "vibrating elephants in your ear"). On each slip in the second set (for example, red balloons), write one word or phrase related to the problem—any of its features, benefits, or attributes. (If time is available, you might have the participants come up with these words and insert them into the balloons).

2. Insert the slips into their respective color of balloon, then blow up and tie all of the balloons. (Or wait until the session and ask the participants to help you.)

3. Begin the session by distributing the Balloon, Balloon, Balloon Handout, reviewing it with the participants, and answering any questions they may have.

4. Turn on some high energy, rock music, and tell the members of all groups to tap the balloons back and forth (if there is only one group, the individual members tap the balloons around within that group).

5. Stop the music after about 2 minutes and ask the participants to gather at least one balloon of each color. Have them sit on their balloons or pop them with a pen, pencil, or other sharp object. (Warn them not to do this too close to their eyes—which shouldn't be a problem for those who sit on the balloons!)

6. Instruct the participants to find one slip from each color balloon and return to their respective tables.

7. Have one of the group members read aloud what is on the two slips, and use the combination as a stimulus for new ideas. (You might suggest that one member of each group could write these words on a flip chart for all group members to view.)

8. Have the person who suggests an idea write it down on a Post-it® Note and pass it to the person on the right. Tell the people receiving the notes to think of possible new ideas and write them on

Post-it® Notes. (This procedure of writing new ideas on the notes helps ensure that no ideas are left out of consideration.)

9. Tell them to repeat this process (Steps 7 and 8) until they have considered all possible pairs of stimuli (that is, related and unrelated from the different balloon colors) and generated as many ideas as possible, writing them on Post-it® Notes (one idea per note) and placing them on flip charts for evaluation.

Debrief/Discussion

This approach is similar to using paper airplanes (Out of the Blue Lightning Cloudbuster [88]) in terms of the amount of fun involved. As a facilitator you will want to manage how much fun the groups have, so that they keep focused on the task of generating ideas. In addition to creating a climate conducive for idea generation during this exercise, the fun factor also can help spark a productive climate in subsequent idea generation sessions.

Also consider having participants debrief using the following questions:

- What was most helpful about this exercise?
- What was most challenging?
- What can we apply?
- How would you rate the value of this exercise to helping us with this issue?
- Will this exercise be helpful in the future for other sessions?
- What did you learn?
- What will we be able to use from this exercise?
- What ideas were generated, and which ones were most interesting?

Variation

1. Use any combination of balloon colors and give each participant two balloons.
2. Have them write, on a small slip of paper, an idea for resolving the problem, insert their papers into the balloons, and blow them up.
3. Tell them to tap the balloons around the large group as described above, pop two balloons each, and return to their tables with the two slips of paper.
4. Ask each person in a group to read one of the ideas aloud and have the other group members try to improve it or think of another idea.
5. Ask another person to read one of the ideas on their paper slips and again have the other group members think of improvements or new ideas.
6. Once everyone has shared one of his or her two original ideas, repeat the process (Steps 4 and 5) using the second slips of paper.

Balloon, Balloon, Balloon Handout

Assume you want ideas about how to sell more office chairs. Your group examines several slips from the balloons and comes up with the following ideas:

- Pen holders built into a chair's arms (from "arms" and "rhubarb ink javelins")
- A self-propelled office chair (from "wheels" and "rhubarb ink javelins")
- A chair with a drink holder for different cup sizes (from "arms" and "rotating cat lemons")
- A built-in vibrating seat and back (from "back" and "vibrating elephants in your ear")
- A built-in stereo radio in the top of the seat back (from "back" and "vibrating elephants in your ear")

93

BOUNCING BALL

Background

You've probably heard the expression "Let's bounce that idea around." Well, this activity allows a group to do almost exactly that. Bouncing Ball is a fun activity, and it's probably one of the easiest activities to implement as well.

Objectives

- To help participants generate as many creative ideas as possible
- To help participants learn how to use the activities to generate ideas

Participants

Small groups of four to seven people each

Materials, Supplies, and Equipment

- For each group: markers, two flip charts, and masking tape for posting flip-chart sheets
- For each participant: one sheet each of three different colors of sticking dots (½" diameter) and one pad of 4 x 6 Post-it® Notes
- For each group, at least three foam balls approximately four inches in diameter (they should be heavy enough to throw and be caught easily)

Time

45 minutes

Related Activities

- Spin the Bottle [67]
- Roll Call [78]
- Out of the Blue Lightning Bolt Cloudbuster [88]
- Balloon, Balloon, Balloon [92]

Procedure

1. Have each group select a recorder to write down ideas on a flip chart.
2. Tell the members of each group to stand in a small circle and throw the balls to each other for a few minutes.
3. From each group, collect all the balls except one.
4. Say that whoever is holding this ball must throw it to another group member.
5. Say that whoever catches the ball must shout out a random word or phrase.
6. Tell this person to throw the ball to another person, who then shouts out a word related to the problem.
7. Instruct the recorders in each group to write down on a flip chart these two words as a combination.
8. Have the entire group use this combination to stimulate new ideas and ask individual members to write down their ideas on Post-it® Notes (one idea per note) to be placed on flip-chart paper for evaluation.
9. After all ideas are exhausted for that combination, tell the last person to catch the ball to throw it to someone else and repeat Steps 5 through 8.

Debrief/Discussion

The basic elements of Bouncing Ball are virtually identical to those of Balloon, Balloon, Balloon [92]. A major difference is in how the random and nonrandom words are selected. Bouncing Ball is easier to implement, but Balloon, Balloon, Balloon will probably provide more sustained fun.

Also consider having participants debrief using the following questions:

- What was most helpful about this exercise?
- What was most challenging?
- What can we apply?
- How would you rate the value of this exercise to helping us with this issue?
- Will this exercise be helpful in the future for other sessions?
- What did you learn?
- What will we be able to use from this exercise?
- What ideas were generated, and which ones were most interesting?

Variation

- Simplify and use this exercise as a warm-up exercise. Instead of requiring related and unrelated words, just have whoever catches the ball shout out an idea that then is written on a flip chart or Post-it® Note by a recorder.

94

BRAINSKETCHING

Background

If you're like many people, you may enjoy drawing doodles and sketches of various objects. You may do this absentmindedly while talking on the phone, for instance, or intentionally while trying to visualize some problem aspect.

Brainsketching draws on this natural activity and applies it in a group setting.

Brainsketching was developed by Pickens (1980) as a modification of the Brain Purge activity [82]. The primary difference is that Brainsketching involves passing pictures around a group instead of ideas. Another distinction is that the sketches may be more abstract and symbolic than the ideas used by the Brain Purge activity.

Objectives

- To help participants generate as many creative ideas as possible
- To help participants learn how to use the activities to generate ideas

Participants

Small groups of four to seven people each

Materials, Supplies, and Equipment

- For each group: markers, two flip charts, and masking tape for posting flip-chart sheets
- For each participant: one sheet each of three different colors of sticking dots (½" diameter) and one pad of 4 x 6 Post-it® Notes
- For each participant: one 8.5" x 11" sheet of paper, a small box of crayons, and a pen or pencil

Time

45 minutes

Related Activities

- Rorschach Revisionist [18]
- Drawing Room [59]
- Modular Brainstorming [62]
- Brain Purge [82]
- Idea Pool [85]
- Museum Madness [86]
- Doodlin' Around the Block [95]

Procedure

1. Tell each group member to draw a sketch of a problem solution. Say, "This sketch doesn't need to represent a direct, clear-cut solution; it may be relatively abstract and symbolic. Don't be concerned if you are not artistic; what you draw is more important than how you draw it. No talking is permitted while sketching, and please do not share your sketches while drawing them."

2. After 5 minutes, tell group members to pass their sketches to the person on their right.

3. Instruct the group members receiving a sketch to review it and try to improve it by adding to the sketch, making brief comments, or drawing an entirely new sketch.

4. When they have completed Step 3, tell them to pass this drawing to the person on their right.

5. Tell the participants to repeat Steps 3 and 4 until time is called.

6. Have them collect all the sketches and review them, in turn, with other group members. (You might suggest that they tape each sketch on a flip chart.)

7. Direct them to examine each sketch and use it to brainstorm ideas.

8. Have them record any new ideas stimulated by the sketches on Post-it® Notes (one idea per note) and place them on a flip chart for evaluation.

Debrief/Discussion

Artistic types or "doodlers" should especially enjoy this exercise. Drawing is a physical activity that also can help our thinking. Both the act of drawing and the images created can help prompt new perspectives. Sharing the sketches with others can spark new ideas, just as revealing intangible thoughts can. This exercise also can serve as an excellent warm-up to get everyone involved before a brainstorming session that requires full participation to be effective.

Also consider having participants debrief using the following questions:

- What was most helpful about this exercise?
- What was most challenging?
- What can we apply?
- How would you rate the value of this exercise to helping us with this issue?
- Will this exercise be helpful in the future for other sessions?
- What did you learn?
- What will we be able to use from this exercise?
- What ideas were generated, and which ones were most interesting?

95

DOODLIN' AROUND THE BLOCK

Background

This activity is a little like Brainsketching [94] in that it involves some doodling. Brainsketching uses doodles of pictures and abstract symbols; Doodlin' Around the Block, in contrast, uses a very specific type of doodle: a square or rectangle. It also differs in that it introduces some game-like competition, much like The Name Game [97].

Objectives

- To help participants generate as many creative ideas as possible
- To help participants learn how to use the activities to generate ideas

Participants

Small groups of four to seven people each

Materials, Supplies, and Equipment

- For each group: markers, two flip charts, and masking tape for posting flip-chart sheets
- For each participant: one sheet each of three different colors of sticking dots (½" diameter) and one pad of 4 x 6 Post-it® Notes
- For each participant: markers or crayons, at least one per person
- Small prizes for the winning group

Handout

- Doodlin' Around the Block Handout

Time

30 minutes

Brainwriting with Unrelated Stimuli

Related Activities

- Rorschach Revisionist [18]
- Doodles [37]
- Drawing Room [59]
- Brainsketching [94]

Procedure

1. Ask participants to place a sheet of flip-chart paper on a table or on a floor hard enough to be written upon.

2. Direct one group member to draw a large rectangle on the paper, approximately one by two feet in size.

3. Have each group member write inside the rectangle one word unrelated to the problem. Tell them to write the words approximately the same distance from each other and spread them out within the rectangles.

4. Note that if there are six group members, for example, there should be six words spread around within different rectangles. Refer them to the Doodlin' Around the Block Handout.

5. Direct the participants by saying:

   "When I tell you to start, each one of you simultaneously will begin drawing squares—about two inches by two inches—from the edges of the paper. Use the unrelated words as stimuli and write down ideas inside the boxes, one idea per box. Your will receive one point for each box with an idea. You may draw squares in any direction as long as they are connected. However, you must draw each square without lifting up your pen or pencil, so that each square will be connected. You may retrace lines if you wish. Group members who no longer can connect squares must stop writing."

6. Refer them to the Doodlin' Around the Block Handout for an example and instruct the participants to begin drawing.

7. After all squares have been completed, ask each group to total their ideas and report to the large group.

8. Award the winning group small prizes and ask all the groups to record their ideas on Post-it® Notes (one idea per note) and place them on a flip chart for evaluation.

Debrief/Discussion

Although it may seem counterintuitive, some of the best ideas from this exercise might result when participants quickly draw the squares and generate ideas. Hesitation can result in more conventional, analytical thinking. If participants are involved and motivated to complete this exercise, more unique ideas may pop out, so it is important that participants do not spend too much time contemplating where to draw their boxes. The fact that they may retrace lines should help facilitate this aspect.

Doodlin' Around the Block Handout

Assume that you manufacture food products and decide to generate some snack food ideas. As shown in Figure 12.1, a group member draws a large rectangle and the others write in one word each.

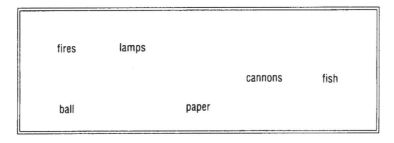

Figure 12.1.   Sample Doodlin' Word Rectangle

The members then begin taking turns and draw boxes around three of the unrelated stimulus words and generate seven snack food product ideas for a total of seven boxes with ideas (Figure 12.2). Another session might result in a different number of boxes and ideas, depending on the number of participants and time available.

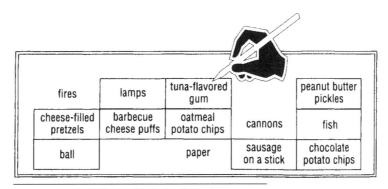

Figure 12.2.   Sample Doodling' Exercise

96

GREETING CARDS

Background

There is little doubt that a playful group atmosphere is more likely to result in quality ideas than a more staid, serious environment. Several research studies have found that humor and creativity go hand in hand (Dovidio, Gartner, Isen, & Lowrence, 1995; Russ, 1993). When laughter is present, good ideas seem to appear.

Many of the activities in this book help create a fun environment. Prominent among these are Spin the Bottle [67], Battle of the Sexes [71], Sculptures [79], Super Heroes [80], and Balloon, Balloon, Balloon [92]. In addition, the Greeting Cards activity seems to work especially well for making creative thinking fun.

Greeting Cards (Pickens, 1985) is a hands-on activity that allows group members to express themselves in an environment conducive to creative thinking. Unlike most activities, the group leader should avoid telling the group the problem if possible (the problem will be revealed later as part of the process).

Objectives

- To help participants generate as many creative ideas as possible
- To help participants learn how to use the activities to generate ideas

Participants

Small groups of four to seven people each

Materials, Supplies, and Equipment

- For each group: markers, two flip charts, masking tape for posting flip-chart sheets, four or five magazines and catalogs (for pictures), ten sheets of colored construction paper, and two to three each: glue sticks, boxes of crayons, and rolls of adhesive tape
- For each participant: pens or pencils, markers, and one pad of 4 x 6 Post-it® Notes

Handout

- Greeting Cards Handout

Time

45 minutes (requires prior preparation)

Related Activities

- Brain Purge [82]
- Museum Madness [86]
- Altered States [91]
- Brainsketching [94]

Procedure

1. Give out copies of the Greeting Cards Handout and answer any questions the members may have.
2. Provide each group with the materials needed to create greeting cards.
3. Instruct group members to look through the catalogs and magazines and cut out about ten pictures that look interesting.
4. Tell the group members to paste the pictures onto sheets of paper folded in half and write catchy text. Indicate that the most effective cards use humor for traditional themes such as belated birthday, divorce, friendship, or get well.
5. After all the cards are constructed, reveal the problem to the participants.
6. Direct the group members use the text, pictures, and themes of the cards as stimuli for ideas.
7. Have them write down their ideas on Post-it® Notes (one idea per note), and place them on flip charts for evaluation.

Debrief/Discussion

This is an excellent exercise to allow participants to express their creativity, to create a climate conducive to creative ideas, and to generate ideas. It obviously is a "hands on" exercise that can keep participants engaged in a fun activity and generate some ideas as well. As with many group idea generation activities, this activity also can provide a team-building function due to the type of interactions required.

Also consider having participants debrief using the following questions:

- What was most helpful about this exercise?
- What was most challenging?
- What can we apply?

- How would you rate the value of this exercise to helping us with this issue?
- Will this exercise be helpful in the future for other sessions?
- What did you learn?
- What will we be able to use from this exercise?
- What ideas were generated, and which ones were most interesting?

Variation

- If there is more than one group, ask the groups to exchange cards and use them to trigger additional ideas.

Greeting Cards Handout

Imagine your group is trying to help an airline generate ideas to attract international passengers (VanGundy, 1988). One of the participants created a card for a recently divorced male friend. The front of the card read, "True, the judge may have awarded her the alimony . . ." When the card is opened, a picture of a male torso in underwear is revealed. The caption under this picture reads ". . . So we're awarding you support." The group members then used this card to think of designing seats with adjustable support (such as an inflatable lumbar device).

97

THE NAME GAME

Background

In developing The Name Game (also known as the Brainwriting Game), Woods (1979) sought to create an activity that was fun but did not require a high degree of leader or participant skills. Although this exercise is slightly more complex than other brainwriting activities, it still is relatively easy to implement.

Objectives

- To help participants generate as many creative ideas as possible
- To help participants learn how to use the activities to generate ideas

Participants

Small groups of four to seven people each

Materials, Supplies, and Equipment

- For each group: markers, two flip charts, and masking tape for posting flip-chart sheets
- For each participant: one sheet each of three different colors of sticking dots (½″ diameter) and one pad of 4 x 6 Post-it® Notes
- For each participant: five to ten pennies (or poker chips)

Time

60 minutes

Related Activities

- Get Real!! [60]
- Brain Purge [82]
- Altered States [91]

Procedure

1. Tell participants that the objective of this exercise is to develop the most improbable idea and that whoever suggests the least probable idea wins the game.

2. Have each group select a leader and give each leader a pad of Post-it® Notes.

3. Ask the leaders in each group to assign to each group member—including themselves—a consecutive number beginning with "1." Thus, if there were five members, they would use the numbers 1 to 5.

4. Tell each group member to buy one of the numbered (but otherwise blank) notes from the leader at one cent each and write their assigned numbers in the upper right-hand corner of the note (for identification later).

5. Instruct all participants to write, on the notes they just purchased, the most improbable idea they can imagine.

6. Repeat Steps 4 and 5 until at least five notes have been purchased by each person and one idea has been written on each one.

7. Once all ideas are written, tell them to place their notes on the flip chart for the entire group to read.

8. Tell the groups to study all ideas as individuals, and think of ways to make them more practical to reduce the idea owner's chances of winning. Note that they may not talk during this activity.

9. Instruct them to write down any new or more practical ideas on Post-it® Notes and place them at the bottom of the flip-chart paper or on another sheet.

10. After 15 to 20 minutes, ask the group members to vote for the two most improbable ideas. The person whose idea receives the most votes is awarded the money that was exchanged for the cards.

11. Divide each group into two subgroups, and give each subgroup one-half of the Post-its (with the ideas written on them).

12. Have the groups use these ideas to stimulate a minimum of six practical problem solutions.

13. After 20 minutes, have each group try to "sell" its ideas to another group and for both groups to try to agree on a final list of the best ideas. (This step is optional, of course, if there is only one group.)

14. Have them write down their ideas on Post-it® Notes (one idea per note) and place them on flip charts for evaluation.

Debrief/Discussion

The Name Game provides competition to motivate group members and is unique in that it uses impractical ideas as a source for practical solutions. Improbable ideas (which are also used as the basis for the Get Real!! activity [60]) have great potential to trigger workable ideas. If time is available, you might ask the participants to discuss the somewhat paradoxical value of impractical ideas and why it exists. That is, impractical ideas shouldn't be very practical, by definition. However, their very impracticality may serve as stimuli for practical ideas.

Also consider having participants debrief using the following questions:

- What was most helpful about this exercise?
- What was most challenging?
- What can we apply?
- How would you rate the value of this exercise to helping us with this issue?
- Will this exercise be helpful in the future for other sessions?
- What did you learn?
- What will we be able to use from this exercise?
- What ideas were generated, and which ones were most interesting?

98

PASS THE BUCK

Background

"Passing the buck" is an old expression meaning avoiding responsibility by blaming or otherwise involving someone else. Various take-charge presidents and business executives helped popularize the expression by asserting that "the buck stops here." Hall (1994) created a new use for the phrase "pass the buck" by developing an activity using the expression.

Pass the Buck was designed for use by four different small groups. It can be modified easily, however, for just one group.

Objectives

- To help participants generate as many creative ideas as possible
- To help participants learn how to use the activities to generate ideas

Participants

Small groups of four to seven people each

Materials, Supplies, and Equipment

- For each group: markers, one sheet of 8.5" x 11" paper, two flip charts, and masking tape for posting flip-chart sheets
- For each participant: one sheet each of three different colors of sticking dots (½" diameter) and one pad of 4 x 6 Post-it® Notes
- A musical CD or cassette player with relatively loud, high-energy music

Time

20 minutes

Brainwriting with Unrelated Stimuli   **379**

Related Activities

- As Easy as 6–3–5 [81]
- Idea Mixer [84]
- Museum Madness [86]

Procedure

(*Note:* The following procedure is designed for four groups.)

1. Ask the group members to take one sheet of 8.5" x 11" paper and draw a rectangle on it lengthwise so that there is about a one-half inch border. Then tell them to divide the rectangle into four cells by drawing straight lines. Have them number the cells as: "1" in the upper left, "2" in the upper right, "3" in the lower left, and "4" in the lower right.

2. Play loud music while each group generates an "Absurd, Bizarre, Exotic Idea" and writes it in cell 1 on the worksheet.

3. Have each group pass its worksheet to another group.

4. Tell the groups receiving the worksheets to examine the first idea, write a "Somewhat Realistic" version of this idea in cell 2, and pass this worksheet to another group.

5. Instruct the groups to examine the worksheets passed to them, write an idea that is "A Little More Realistic" in cell 3, and pass this worksheet to another group.

6. Have the groups then write down the final, most realistic idea in cell 4 and title it "The Buck Stops Here."

7. Ask the groups to share all their ideas with the other groups, record any new ideas on Post-its (one idea per note), and place them on flip charts for evaluation.

Debrief/Discussion

A distinguishing feature of this activity is that it provides an opportunity for multiple groups to interact with each other. In addition to the competitive spirit and social satisfaction this interaction can provide, involving other groups also increases the number of perspectives available for resolving a problem. It also is a relatively structured activity, which sometimes can be an advantage for groups lacking energy or wanting more boundaries instead of a free flow of ideas. On the other hand, this structure might limit the number of ideas, so consider the tradeoffs involved. Ask the participants to discuss how the structure might have affected them in comparison to more traditional brainstorming.

Also consider having participants debrief using the following questions:

- What was most helpful about this exercise?
- What was most challenging?
- What can we apply?
- How would you rate the value of this exercise to helping us with this issue?

- Will this exercise be helpful in the future for other sessions?
- What did you learn?
- What will we be able to use from this exercise?
- What ideas were generated, and which ones were most interesting?

Variation

- If you have just one group, you can modify this activity easily, especially if you have only four group members. Just have one group member write an idea in each of the cells. If you have more than four members, have them double up to fill in the cells.

99

POST IT, PARDNER!

Background

Those semi-sticky Post-it® Notes are good for something besides general office work such as memos. They also can help generate ideas in a group and provide a fun experience as well.

Post It, Pardner! is a relative of Museum Madness [86], in which group members write ideas on flip-chart sheets attached to a wall and then browse around the room using others' ideas as stimuli for new ideas. Post It, Pardner! uses a similar process, except it relies on unrelated stimuli to help trigger ideas. Specifically, instead of using ideas to prompt new ideas, group members use free associations generated by other group members.

Objectives

- To help participants generate as many creative ideas as possible
- To help participants learn how to use the activities to generate ideas

Participants

Small groups of four to seven people each

Materials, Supplies, and Equipment

- For each group: markers, two flip charts, and masking tape for posting flip-chart sheets
- For each participant: one sheet each of three different colors of sticking dots (½″ diameter) and one pad of 4 x 6 Post-it® Notes
- A room with a variety of objects, including fixtures and furniture such as lamps, windows, doors, tables, chairs, coffeepot, cups, glasses, table cloths, light switches, and plants

Handout

- Post It, Pardner! Handout

Time

30 minutes

Related Activities

- Brain Purge [82]
- Group Not [83]
- Idea Pool [85]
- Museum Madness [86]

Procedure

1. Distribute the Post It, Pardner! Handout, review it with the participants, and answer any questions they may have.
2. Tell each group member to peel off three Post-it® Notes.
3. Have all participants select an object in the room and use it as the stimulus for free associations (thoughts that can represent anything, not necessarily the original object).
4. Instruct them to write one free association on each note and stick the note on or near the object.
5. Have all participants from all groups examine the free associations written by other group members and use them to spark new ideas that they should write down on new notes, one idea per note.
6. Ask them to place their Post-its® on a flip chart and evaluate them later.

Debrief/Discussion

This activity combines a number of features, including brainwriting, physical movement, free associations, and unrelated stimuli. Alone, these features could help trigger unique ideas; when used in combination, they can increase the number of ideas possible.

This would be an ideal exercise to engage the participants in some discussion regarding its positive and negative aspects and any difficulties they had in using unrelated stimuli and free associations to generate ideas. If a large number of participants have trouble using this activity, you might skip the free associations and use just the selected objects.

Also consider having participants debrief using the following questions:

- What was most helpful about this exercise?
- What was most challenging?
- What can we apply?
- How would you rate the value of this exercise to helping us with this issue?
- Will this exercise be helpful in the future for other sessions?
- What did you learn?
- What will we be able to use from this exercise?
- What ideas were generated, and which ones were most interesting?

Post It, Pardner! Handout

Suppose your group wants to generate ways to improve a bed. Group members place Post-it® Notes on the following objects and write the following associations for each:

- Door: wood, grain, alcohol
- Window: glass, clear, seeing
- Table: flat, smooth, slippery
- Coffeepot: hot, cold, icy
- Lamp: light, dark, black

The group then generates ideas using these associations:

- A built-in cereal dispenser (from "grain")
- An alcoholic beverage dispenser (from "alcohol")
- A bed with a children's slide on the bottom (from "slippery")
- A built-in heating and cooling apparatus (from "hot" and "cold")
- A built-in ice machine (from "icy")
- Variable lighting brightness and focus (from "light" and "dark")

100

PUZZLE PIECES

Background

In some respects, most problems are like jigsaw puzzles. We have to look over all the pieces, keep the big picture in mind, identify the boundaries, and plunge in and begin problem solving. If everything works out, we'll solve the puzzle and go on to other things. The Puzzle Pieces activity takes advantage of these similarities by using pieces of a jigsaw puzzle to put together ideas.

Objectives

- To help participants generate as many creative ideas as possible
- To help participants learn how to use the activities to generate ideas

Participants

Small groups of four to seven people each

Materials, Supplies, and Equipment

- For each group: markers, two flip charts, and masking tape for posting flip-chart sheets, one set of approximately fifteen blank jigsaw puzzle pieces available from school supply stores or online sources such as www.papergoods.com (If a blank puzzle isn't available, use the blank back of a standard puzzle)
- For each participant: pens or pencils, one sheet each of three different colors of sticking dots (½" diameter), and one pad of 4 x 6 Post-it® Notes.

Time

30 minutes

Related Activities

- Modular Brainstorming [62]
- Doodlin' Around the Block [95]

Brainwriting with Unrelated Stimuli

Procedure

1. Place a set of blank puzzle pieces on each table.

2. Tell the participants to mix up the puzzle pieces on their tables and divide them equally among the group members.

3. Have group members write one practical idea on the first piece, an unrelated word on the second piece, a practical idea on the third piece, an unrelated word on the fourth piece, and so on until all their pieces have been used.

4. Tell the group members to assemble the puzzle.

5. After they have finished, have them select two adjacent pieces and use the combination to spark ideas.

6. Tell them to write down their ideas on Post-it® Notes (one idea per note), select another two adjacent pieces, and continue this process until time is called (after about 20 or 30 minutes).

Debrief/Discussion

This is another activity that provides a game-like atmosphere during idea generation. It requires both analytical and creative thinking to put together the puzzles and generate ideas using unrelated words. The use of a hands-on activity provides a different experience than other activities. One downside is that it requires a fairly large number of puzzle pieces and group members might lose interest over time.

Also consider having participants debrief using the following questions:

- What was most helpful about this exercise?
- What was most challenging?
- What can we apply?
- How would you rate the value of this exercise to helping us with this issue?
- Will this exercise be helpful in the future for other sessions?
- What did you learn?
- What will we be able to use from this exercise?
- What ideas were generated, and which ones were most interesting?

101

The Shirt Off Your Back

Background

If you're in any type of competitive or stressful work environment, there are times when you would give the "shirt off your back" for a hot new idea. Well, this activity may help you get the idea you need, and you can keep your shirt on.

Objectives

- To help participants generate as many creative ideas as possible
- To help participants learn how to use the activities to generate ideas

Participants

Small groups of four to seven people each

Materials, Supplies, and Equipment

- For each group: markers, two flip charts, and masking tape for taping sheets of paper to participants' backs and for posting flip-chart sheets
- For each participant: pens or pencils, one sheet each of three different colors of sticking dots (½" diameter), and one pad of 4 x 6 Post-it® Notes
- For each participant: one sheet of 8.5 x 11 paper

Time

20 minutes

Related Activities

- Modular Brainstorming [62]
- Idea Pool [85]
- Museum Madness [86]

Procedure

1. Instruct all group members to take a sheet of 8.5" x 11" paper and tape two pieces of 4-inch-long masking tape—about 5 inches apart—on the top of the sheet, allowing at least two inches of tape to hang over the edge and two inches on the paper.

2. Tell them to write down one idea at the top of the sheet where the pieces of tape are located.

3. Have them ask another group member to tape the sheet high on their backs.

4. Instruct all participants from all groups to walk around the room reading the ideas on each other's backs and use these ideas as stimuli to generate new ideas.

5. Tell them that, when they think of an idea, they should write it on the paper attached to the other person's back. Caution them to be careful that ink does not bleed through to clothing!

6. After about 10 to 15 minutes of this activity, have the participants return to their groups, remove the papers from their backs, and record each idea on a Post-it® Note.

7. Tell them to place the notes on a flip chart, pick their favorite ideas, and then brainstorm any new ones, writing each one on a new Post-it® Note (one idea per note).

Debrief/Discussion

This can be a fun, energizing activity that will work well after lunch or at the end of a day. Just walking around and getting out of chairs can provide the energy required to spark additional ideas. The brainwriting involved helps ensure a fairly large number of ideas in relatively little time. And the brainstorming at the end allows group members to interact verbally and possibly generate more ideas. If the participants have experienced any other brainwriting activities, ask them to compare them with this one.

Also consider having participants debrief using the following questions:

- What was most helpful about this exercise?
- What was most challenging?
- What can we apply?
- How would you rate the value of this exercise to helping us with this issue?
- Will this exercise be helpful in the future for other sessions?
- What did you learn?
- What will we be able to use from this exercise?
- What ideas were generated, and which ones were most interesting?

References

Alexander, C., Ishikawa, S., & Silverstein, M., 1977. As cited in M. Michalko, *ThinkerToys*. Berkeley, CA: Ten Speed Press, 1991.

Andersen, H.R. *The Idea of the Diamond Idea Group.* Chicago: Mitsubishi Heavy Industries America, 1991.

Business Week, *The Web Smart 50 – Collaboration,* November 24, 2003.

Buzan, T. *Use Both Sides of Your Brain.* New York: Dutton, 1976.

Clark, C.H. *The Crawford Slip Writing Method.* Kent, OH: Charles H. Clark, 1978.

Crawford, C.C., & Demidovitch, J.W. *Crawford Slip Writing Method: How to Mobilize Brainpower by Think Tank Technology.* Los Angeles: University of Southern California, School of Public Administration, 1983.

Crovitz, H.F. *Galton's Walk.* New York: Harper & Row, 1970.

De Bono, E. *Lateral Thinking for Management.* New York: American Management Association, 1972.

Delbecq, A.L., & Van de Ven, A.H. "A Group Process Model for Problem Identification and Program Planning." *Journal of Applied Behavioral Science, 7,* 1971, 466–492.

Diehl, M., & Stroebe, W. "Productivity Loss in Idea-Generating Groups: Tracking Down the Blocking Effect." *Journal of Personality and Social Psychology, 61*(3), 1991, 392–403.

Dovidio, J.F., Gartner, S.L., Isen, A.M., & Lowrence, R. "Group representations and intergroup bias: Positive affect, similarity, and group size." *Personality and Social Psychology Bulletin, 21,* 1995, 856–865.

Faafeng, 0. Conversation with author. Oslo: Norwegian Management Institute, 1986.

Geschka, H. "Methods and Organization of Idea Management." Paper presented at Creativity Development Week II, Greensboro, NC: Center for Creative Leadership, 1978.

Geschka, H., Schaude, G.R., & Schlicksupp, H. "Modern Techniques for Solving Problems." *Chemical Engineering,* August 1973, 91–97.

Geschka, H., von Reibnitz, U., & Storvik, K. *Idea Generation Methods: Creative Solutions to Business and Technical Problems.* Columbus, OH: Battelle Memorial Institute, 1981.

Goodman, J., & Shields, J.T. *Brainwriting: Is There Life After Brainstorming?* St. Louis, MO: Maritz Performance Improvement Company, 1993.

Gordon, W.J.J. *Synectics.* New York: Harper & Row, 1961.

Griggs, R.E. "A Storm of Ideas." *Training, 22,* 1985, 66.

Grossman, S. "Releasing Problem Solving Energies." *Training & Development Journal, 38,* 1984, 94-98.

Grossman, S., & Catlin, K. "SuperHeroes." Paper presented at the 31st Annual Creative Problem Solving Institute. Buffalo, NY: The Creative Education Foundation, 1985.

Haefele, J. *Creativity and Innovation.* New York: Van Nostrand Reinhold, 1961.

Hall, D. *Jump Start Your Brain.* New York: Time Warner, 1994.

Kepner, C.H., & Tregoe, B.B. *The New Rational Manager.* Princeton, NJ: Kepner-Tregoe, 1981.

Koberg, D., & Bagnall, J. *The Universal Traveler.* Los Altos, CA: William Kaufmann, 1976.

MacCrimmon, K.R., & Taylor, R.N. "Decision Making and Problem Solving." In M.D. Dunnette (Ed.), *Handbook of Industrial and Organizational Psychology.* Chicago: Rand-McNally, 1976.

Michalko, M. *ThinkerToys*. Berkeley, CA: Ten Speed Press, 1991.

Morrison, D. Personal communication, 1997.

Olson, R.W. *The Art of Creative Thinking*. New York: Barnes & Noble, 1980.

Osborn, A.F. *Applied Imagination* (3d ed.). New York: Scribner and Sons, 1963.

Pearson, A.W. "Communication, Creativity, and Commitment: A Look at the Collective Notebook Approach." In S.S. Gruskiewicz (Ed.), *Proceedings of Creativity Week I*. Greensboro, NC: Center for Creative Leadership, 1978.

Phillips, D.J. "Report on Discussion 66." *Adult Education Journal, 7*, 1948, 181–182.

Pickens, J. *Brainsketching*. Norman, OK: University of Oklahoma, 1980.

Pickens, J. Conversation with author, 1985.

"Plugging in to Creativity." *U.S. News & World Report*, October 29, 1990.

Rickards, T. *Problem Solving Through Creative Analysis*. Essex, UK: Gower Press, 1974.

Russ, S.W. *Affect and Creativity: The Role of Affect and Play in the Creative Process*. Hillsdale, NJ: Lawrence Erlbaum, 1993.

Schaude, G.R. "Methods of Idea Generation." Paper presented at Creativity Development Week 1, Greensboro, NC: Center for Creative Leadership, 1978.

Simon, H.A. *The New Science of Management Decision* (rev. ed.). Englewood Cliffs, NJ: Prentice-Hall, 1977.

Souder, W.E., & Ziegler, R.W. "A Review of Creativity and Problem Solving Techniques." *Research Management*, July 1977, 34–42.

Tauber, E.M. "HIT: Heuristic Ideation Technique-A Systematic Procedure for New Product Search." *Journal of Marketing, 36*, 1972, 58–61.

Taylor, J.W. *How to Create Ideas*. Englewood Cliffs, NJ: Prentice-Hall, 1961.

VanGundy, A.B. *108 Ways to Get a Bright Idea*. Englewood Cliffs, NJ: Prentice-Hall, 1983.

VanGundy, A.B. *Managing Group Creativity: A Modular Approach to Problem Solving*. New York: AMACOM, 1984.

VanGundy, A.B. *Product Improvement CheckList (PICL)*. Norman, OK: VanGundy & Associates (avangundy@aol.com), 1985.

VanGundy, A.B. *Techniques of Structured Problem Solving* (2nd ed.). New York: Van Nostrand Reinhold, 1988.

VanGundy, A.B. *Idea Power: Techniques and Resources to Unleash the Creativity in Your Organization*. New York: AMACOM, 1992.

Wakin, E. "Component Detailing." Paper presented at the 31st Annual Creative Problem Solving Institute. Buffalo, NY: Creative Education Foundation, 1985.

Warfield, J.N., Geschka, H., & Hamilton, R. *Methods of Idea Management*. Columbus, OH: The Academy for Contemporary Problems, 1975.

Whiting, C.S. *Creative Thinking*. New York: Van Nostrand Reinhold, 1958.

Woods, M.F. "The Brainwriting Game." *Creativity Network, 5*, 1979, 7–12.

Wycoff, J. *Mindmapping: Your Personal Guide to Exploring Creativity and Problem Solving*. New York: Berkley Books, 1991.

Zwicky, F. *Discovery, Invention, Research Through the Morphological Approach*. New York: Macmillan, 1969.

About the Author

Arthur B. VanGundy, Ph.D., is considered a pioneer in his work on idea generation techniques and has written twelve books, including *Idea Power: How to Unleash the Creativity in Your Organization, 101 Great Games & Activities,* and *Orchestrating Collaboration at Work: Using Music, Improv, Storytelling, and Other Arts to Improve Teamwork.* He founded All Star Minds, a global Internet "e-storming" business and specializes in facilitating brainstorming retreats for new products, processes, and services, as well as providing training in creative problem solving. He has received leadership service awards from the Creative Education Foundation and the Singapore government.

Pfeiffer Publications Guide

This guide is designed to familiarize you with the various types of Pfeiffer publications. The formats section describes the various types of products that we publish; the methodologies section describes the many different ways that content might be provided within a product. We also provide a list of the topic areas in which we publish.

FORMATS

In addition to its extensive book-publishing program, Pfeiffer offers content in an array of formats, from fieldbooks for the practitioner to complete, ready-to-use training packages that support group learning.

FIELDBOOK Designed to provide information and guidance to practitioners in the midst of action. Most fieldbooks are companions to another, sometimes earlier, work, from which its ideas are derived; the fieldbook makes practical what was theoretical in the original text. Fieldbooks can certainly be read from cover to cover. More likely, though, you'll find yourself bouncing around following a particular theme, or dipping in as the mood, and the situation, dictate.

HANDBOOK A contributed volume of work on a single topic, comprising an eclectic mix of ideas, case studies, and best practices sourced by practitioners and experts in the field.

An editor or team of editors usually is appointed to seek out contributors and to evaluate content for relevance to the topic. Think of a handbook not as a ready-to-eat meal, but as a cookbook of ingredients that enables you to create the most fitting experience for the occasion.

RESOURCE Materials designed to support group learning. They come in many forms: a complete, ready-to-use exercise (such as a game); a comprehensive resource on one topic (such as conflict management) containing a variety of methods and approaches; or a collection of like-minded activities (such as icebreakers) on multiple subjects and situations.

TRAINING PACKAGE An entire, ready-to-use learning program that focuses on a particular topic or skill. All packages comprise a guide for the facilitator/trainer and a workbook for the participants. Some packages are supported with additional media—such as video—or learning aids, instruments, or other devices to help participants understand concepts or practice and develop skills.

- *Facilitator/trainer's guide* Contains an introduction to the program, advice on how to organize and facilitate the learning event, and step-by-step instructor notes. The guide also contains copies of presentation materials—handouts, presentations, and overhead designs, for example—used in the program.

- *Participant's workbook* Contains exercises and reading materials that support the learning goal and serves as a valuable reference and support guide for participants in the weeks and months that follow the learning event. Typically, each participant will require his or her own workbook.

ELECTRONIC CD-ROMs and web-based products transform static Pfeiffer content into dynamic, interactive experiences. Designed to take advantage of the searchability, automation, and ease-of-use that technology provides, our e-products bring convenience and immediate accessibility to your workspace.

Pfeiffer Publications Guide

This guide is designed to familiarize you with the various types of Pfeiffer publications. The formats s
tion describes the various types of products that we publish; the methodologies section describes the m:
different ways that content might be provided within a product. We also provide a list of the topic area:
which we publish.

FORMATS

In addition to its extensive book-publishing program, Pfeiffer offers content in an array of formats, fr
fieldbooks for the practitioner to complete, ready-to-use training packages that support group learning.

FIELDBOOK Designed to provide information and guidance to practitioners in the midst of action. M
fieldbooks are companions to another, sometimes earlier, work, from which its ideas are derived; the fieldb(
makes practical what was theoretical in the original text. Fieldbooks can certainly be read from cover to co
More likely, though, you'll find yourself bouncing around following a particular theme, or dipping in as
mood, and the situation, dictate.

HANDBOOK A contributed volume of work on a single topic, comprising an eclectic mix of ideas, c
studies, and best practices sourced by practitioners and experts in the field.

An editor or team of editors usually is appointed to seek out contributors and to evaluate content
relevance to the topic. Think of a handbook not as a ready-to-eat meal, but as a cookbook of ingredie
that enables you to create the most fitting experience for the occasion.

RESOURCE Materials designed to support group learning. They come in many forms: a complete, rea
to-use exercise (such as a game); a comprehensive resource on one topic (such as conflict management) c
taining a variety of methods and approaches; or a collection of like-minded activities (such as icebreak(
on multiple subjects and situations.

TRAINING PACKAGE An entire, ready-to-use learning program that focuses on a particular topic
skill. All packages comprise a guide for the facilitator/trainer and a workbook for the participants. So
packages are supported with additional media—such as video—or learning aids, instruments, or other devi
to help participants understand concepts or practice and develop skills.

- *Facilitator/trainer's guide* Contains an introduction to the program, advice on how to organize ;
  facilitate the learning event, and step-by-step instructor notes. The guide also contains copies of ţ
  sentation materials—handouts, presentations, and overhead designs, for example—used in the progr;

- *Participant's workbook* Contains exercises and reading materials that support the learning goal ;
  serves as a valuable reference and support guide for participants in the weeks and months that foll
  the learning event. Typically, each participant will require his or her own workbook.

ELECTRONIC CD-ROMs and web-based products transform static Pfeiffer content into dynamic, int
active experiences. Designed to take advantage of the searchability, automation, and ease-of-use t
technology provides, our e-products bring convenience and immediate accessibility to your workspace.

Pfeiffer Publications Guide

This guide is designed to familiarize you with the various types of Pfeiffer publications. The formats section describes the various types of products that we publish; the methodologies section describes the many different ways that content might be provided within a product. We also provide a list of the topic areas in which we publish.

FORMATS

In addition to its extensive book-publishing program, Pfeiffer offers content in an array of formats, from fieldbooks for the practitioner to complete, ready-to-use training packages that support group learning.

FIELDBOOK Designed to provide information and guidance to practitioners in the midst of action. Most fieldbooks are companions to another, sometimes earlier, work, from which its ideas are derived; the fieldbook makes practical what was theoretical in the original text. Fieldbooks can certainly be read from cover to cover. More likely, though, you'll find yourself bouncing around following a particular theme, or dipping in as the mood, and the situation, dictate.

HANDBOOK A contributed volume of work on a single topic, comprising an eclectic mix of ideas, case studies, and best practices sourced by practitioners and experts in the field.

An editor or team of editors usually is appointed to seek out contributors and to evaluate content for relevance to the topic. Think of a handbook not as a ready-to-eat meal, but as a cookbook of ingredients that enables you to create the most fitting experience for the occasion.

RESOURCE Materials designed to support group learning. They come in many forms: a complete, ready-to-use exercise (such as a game); a comprehensive resource on one topic (such as conflict management) containing a variety of methods and approaches; or a collection of like-minded activities (such as icebreakers) on multiple subjects and situations.

TRAINING PACKAGE An entire, ready-to-use learning program that focuses on a particular topic or skill. All packages comprise a guide for the facilitator/trainer and a workbook for the participants. Some packages are supported with additional media—such as video—or learning aids, instruments, or other devices to help participants understand concepts or practice and develop skills.

- *Facilitator/trainer's guide* Contains an introduction to the program, advice on how to organize and facilitate the learning event, and step-by-step instructor notes. The guide also contains copies of presentation materials—handouts, presentations, and overhead designs, for example—used in the program.

- *Participant's workbook* Contains exercises and reading materials that support the learning goal and serves as a valuable reference and support guide for participants in the weeks and months that follow the learning event. Typically, each participant will require his or her own workbook.

ELECTRONIC CD-ROMs and web-based products transform static Pfeiffer content into dynamic, interactive experiences. Designed to take advantage of the searchability, automation, and ease-of-use that technology provides, our e-products bring convenience and immediate accessibility to your workspace.

What will you find on pfeiffer.com?

• The best in workplace performance solutions for training and HR professionals

• Downloadable training tools, exercises, and content

• Web-exclusive offers

• Training tips, articles, and news

• Seamless on-line ordering

• Author guidelines, information on becoming a Pfeiffer Affiliate, and much more

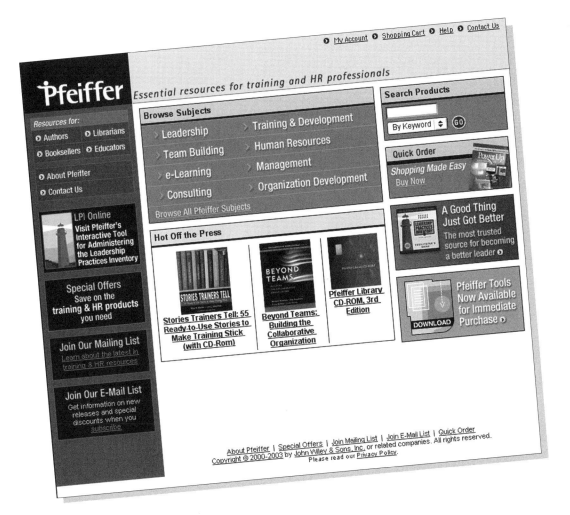

Discover more at www.pfeiffer.com

Customer Care

Have a question, comment, or suggestion? Contact us! We value your feedback and we want to hear from you.

For questions about this or other Pfeiffer products, you may contact us by:

E-mail: **customer@wiley.com**

Mail: **Customer Care Wiley/Pfeiffer**
10475 Crosspoint Blvd.
Indianapolis, IN 46256

Phone: **(US) 800-274-4434** (Outside the US: 317-572-3985)

Fax: **(US) 800-569-0443** (Outside the US: 317-572-4002)

To order additional copies of this title or to browse other Pfeiffer products, visit us online at **www.pfeiffer.com**.

For **Technical Support** questions call **(800) 274-4434.**

For authors guidelines, log on to www.pfeiffer.com and click on "Resources for Authors."

If you are . . .

A **college bookstore, a professor, an instructor, or work in higher education** and you'd like to place an order or request an exam copy, please contact jbreview@wiley.com.

A **general retail bookseller** and you'd like to establish an account or speak to a local sales representative, contact Melissa Grecco at 201-748-6267 or mgrecco@wiley.com.

An **exclusively on-line bookseller**, contact Amy Blanchard at 530-756-9456 or ablanchard @wiley.com or Jennifer Johnson at 206-568-3883 or jjohnson@wiley.com, both of our Online Sales department.

A **librarian or library representative**, contact John Chambers in our Library Sales department at 201-748-6291 or jchamber@wiley.com.

A **reseller, training company/consultant, or corporate trainer**, contact Charles Regan in our Special Sales department at 201-748-6553 or cregan@wiley.com.

A **specialty retail distributor** (includes specialty gift stores, museum shops, and corporate bulk sales), contact Kim Hendrickson in our Special Sales department at 201-748-6037 or khendric@wiley.com.

Purchasing for the **Federal government**, contact Ron Cunningham in our Special Sales department at 317-572-3053 or rcunning@wiley.com.

Purchasing for a **State or Local government**, contact Charles Regan in our Special Sales department at 201-748-6553 or cregan@wiley.com.